SHAKESPEARE AND POPULAR MUSIC

Also available from Continuum

Music in Shakespeare
Christopher R. Wilson and Michela Calore

Shakespeare and His Authors
Edited by William Leahy

Shakespeare on the Spanish Stage
Keith Gregor

Shakespeare's Politics
Robin Headlam Wells

Shakespeare in Japan
Tetsuo Kishi and Graham Bradshaw

SHAKESPEARE AND POPULAR MUSIC

ADAM HANSEN

continuum

Continuum International Publishing Group

The Tower Building	80 Maiden Lane
11 York Road	Suite 704
London SE1 7NX	New York, NY 10038

www.continuumbooks.com

British Library Cataloguing-in-Publication Data
A catalogue record for this book is available from the British Library.

ISBN: 9781441126986 (paperback)
ISBN: 9781441116499 (hardcover)

Library of Congress Cataloging-in-Publication Data
A catalog record for this book is available from the Library of Congress.

Typeset by Newgen Imaging Systems Pvt Ltd, Chennai, India
Printed and bound in Great Britain by CPI Antony Rowe,
Chippenham, Wiltshire

CONTENTS

PERMISSIONS

Lyrics from Akala's 'Shakespeare' (from Akala, *It's Not A Rumour*, Illa State, 2006) and 'Comedy Tragedy History' (from Akala, *Freedom Lasso*, Illa State, 2007) reproduced with kind permission from Illa State Records ©.

Lyrics from Chris Wall's 'Cowboy Nation' (from Chris Wall, *Cowboy Nation*, Cold Spring Records, 1994) reproduced with kind permission from Rhythm Wrangler Music/BMI ©.

Lyrics from 'Make 'Em Laugh' (Arthur Freed; from *Singin' in the Rain Original Motion Picture Soundtrack*, Turner Entertainment 1952/2002) reproduced with kind permission from CPP/Belwin Music and Alfred Publishing ©.

Lyrics from Joni Mitchell's 'A Case of You' (from Joni Mitchell, *Blue*, Reprise 1971) reproduced with kind permission from Joni Mitchell Music/BMI ©.

'I Predict a Riot' words and music by Nicholas Hodgson, Richard Wilson, Andrew White, James Rix and Nicholas Baines Copyright © 2004 RONDOR MUSIC LONDON LTD. All rights in the U.S. and Canada controlled and administered by ALMO MUSIC CORP. All rights reserved. Used by permission. From Kaiser Chiefs, *Employment*, B-Unique, 2005.

Lyrics from Pink Floyd's 'Astronomy Domine' (Syd Barrett; from Pink Floyd, *The Piper at the Gates of Dawn*, EMI, 1967) reproduced with kind permission from Westminster Music Ltd. ©.

Lyrics from Titus Andronicus' 'Fear and Loathing in Mahwah, NJ', 'Titus Andronicus', and 'Albert Camus' (Titus Andronicus; from Titus Andronicus, *The Airing of Grievances*, Merok Records, 2008) reproduced with kind permission from Merok Records and the band ©.

Lyrics from Kevin Hewick's 'Ophelia's Drinking Song' (Kevin Hewick, Factory, 1982) reproduced with kind permission from Kevin Hewick ©.

ACKNOWLEDGEMENTS

Many thanks to this book's generous and enthusiastic chorus of interviewees, correspondents, contributors and readers: Akala, Nicholas Alderton, Joyce Anderson, Rachel Baker and family, John Boden, Mark Deverill, Tom Ewing, Paul Frazer, Glynn Goodall, Graham Hall, Kevin Hewick, Ian Inglis, Marcus Kyd, Sinead Larkin, Cam Lindsay, Ben Lowes-Smith, Laurie McKee, Robert McKenzie, Zoe McKinnon, Chris O'Neill, David Polk, Mark Rowe, Brian Saxby, Julie Scanlon, Monika Smialkowska, David Stewart, Richard Thompson, Chris Wall, James Ward, Melanie Waters, Rosie White, and the online fan-site respondents. Thanks too to everyone who helped at Continuum, and the library staff at Northumbria University, especially Jane Shaw.

For stimulating discussions over the years about books and music and everything in between I'd like to thank Laura and Chris Bojke, Sandra Bruno, Mark Burnett, John Cann, David Clark, Pascal Clerotte, Megan Crane, Henry Dixon, Jonathan Dollimore, Sos Eltis, the Garratts, Tony Greenwood, Matt Hartman, Olga and Pete Ireson, the Kashiwagis, Cece Kiroska, John Love, Rurik Macrow, Alan Mankikar, Mark Moorhouse, Anna Osborne, Emma and Matt Pointon, Heather Roberson, Steve Roberts, Nina and Philip Shapiro, Emma Smith, Adrian Streete, Anne Todd, Steve Trick, David Walker, Ramona Wray, and all the students I have worked with and learned from in Poland, Macedonia, York, Oxford, Belfast and Northumbria. Any errors are mine.

This book is in memory of Siobhan Kilfeather, who was kind when it counted, and Michael Wagner, with whom I learned about life, music and Shakespeare. It is dedicated to the people whose love and support made it possible: Gary and Helen Bate; Lars and Mila, my mum and dad; my partner, Angela; and our beautiful boy, Joe.

A WHOLE LOTTA SHAKESPEARE GOIN' ON?

The music doesn't wear. *It cannot be repeated, whereas good music lasts, mellows and gains fresh beauties at every hearing. It stands, like Shakespeare, through the centuries. No passing craze can shake it.*

C. A. Lewis, cited in Frith, 1988, 30

You can study Shakespeare and be quite elite . . .

Freed, 1952

As soon as one starts to discuss music, one enters the realm of thought, and no power on earth has the right to silence this.

Adorno, 2002, 85

Popular music is nothing if not dialogic, the product of an ongoing historical conversation in which no one has the first or last word. The traces of the past that pervade the popular music of the present amount to more than mere chance: they are not simply the juxtapositions of incompatible realities. They reflect a dialogic process, one embedded in collective history and nurtured by the ingenuity of artists interested in fashioning icons of opposition.

Lipsitz, 1990, 99

. . . what is pop music if not an argument anyone can join?

Marcus, 1992, 742

This book brings together loves I've had since I could read and listen (and love): Shakespeare and popular music. Why? Because fascinating things happen when we learn how Shakespeare exists in and becomes popular music, in all its diverse and wonderful forms. Hopefully, when we think about this, we can hear popular music differently, and see how to make Shakespeare not just relevant but different too, because we realize the different ways his work is read and heard.

This means we can challenge a few myths and misconceptions about Shakespeare, popular music, and how they may relate. One of the enduring myths about how Shakespeare and popular music relate is that they *don't*. Like any myth, this one is still worth thinking about, even before we pop it. The myth is encapsulated by the first epigraph above. Here, C. A. Lewis, the BBC's inaugural programme organizer in the 1930s, implies that popular music is inferior to classical music because it is ephemeral and insubstantial. To reinforce his point, Lewis calls on Shakespeare, as an example of elite or high culture's apparently lasting power, to contrast with low or mass-cultural products, like popular music: whatever the Bard is, he isn't *that*. As we will see, many others have reinforced this division. But as we will also see, Shakespeare was, and is, a popular phenomenon. So, reworking the second epigraph above, this book demonstrates that we can and should study (and enjoy) Shakespeare and *not* be 'quite elite'. The fact that these lines from *Singin' in the Rain* can refer to Shakespeare tells us his relationship to popular music is not completely unthinkable, and demands a closer listen.

To do this, *Shakespeare and Popular Music* addresses several questions. How have Shakespearean characters, words, texts and images been represented in popular music? Do all types of popular music represent Shakespeare in the same ways? If not, why not? And how do the links between Shakespeare and popular music alter what we think we know about Shakespeare, and what we think we know about popular music?

HOW THIS BOOK WORKS

Shakespeare and Popular Music tries to base its answers to these questions on certain principles. Because this book brings together debates, periods, subjects and perhaps readers that haven't always been brought together before, I have tried to make it as clear and lively as possible in style and content. Reading it should make you feel smart, not stupid. So you can expect to see excerpts of interviews with musicians alongside discussions of particular pieces of music, case studies and comments from fans. And to fully explore what happens when things are brought together in new ways, and to think about the challenges this creates, I have also tried to refer to writers from different disciplines whose ideas might be useful. This means musicologists like Richard

Middleton and Simon Frith work alongside Shakespeare scholars like Julie Sanders, Wes Folkerth, David Lindley, Douglas Lanier and Stephen M. Buhler. This also means that cultural theorists like Raymond Williams and Theodor Adorno figure prominently. Williams's ideas about how history and culture relate, and about the forms and functions of culture, feature in this introduction and guide the arguments in the rest of the book. In his way, Adorno is important because his writings on music, popular and otherwise, were cantankerously polemical and wittily brilliant: he was constantly 'thinking with his ears' (Adorno, 1997, 19). *Shakespeare and Popular Music* may not always agree with his ideas or do justice to them. But it does contend that his brilliance is increased not diminished *because* he was polemical, *and* because he was committed to the notion that music has a 'serious function' (Witkin, 2000, 3). Just as music does amazing things to and for us, we can do amazing things with ourselves and our world, however hard this may seem. The third epigraph above, from Adorno, hints at this.

In turn, *Shakespeare and Popular Music* also tries to pick up the challenge laid down by other consciously committed commentators like Alan Sinfield. In 1989 he noted that many progressive political movements and cultural theory in the post-war period failed to explore the 'possibility of working with – politicizing – actual popular cultures'; for Sinfield, this was a 'historic missed opportunity' (250). The opportunity to do what? Sinfield provides part of the answer:

> Societies have to reproduce themselves culturally as well as materially, and this is done in great part by putting into circulation stories of how the world goes. . . . It is through such stories that ideologies are reinforced – and contested, for subordinate groups struggle to make space for themselves, and attempts to legitimate the prevailing order have to negotiate resistant experience and traditions. (2)

Shakespeare and Popular Music upholds this view, and tries to shows how it works. Here's what I mean: in their own ways, Shakespeare and popular music tell us a dazzling range of stories about themselves, about each other, about human experience, about the worlds we and others live in, and about the worlds we and others have aspired to live in. How we respond to these stories creates a no less diverse set of stories. What we say about Shakespeare and popular music, together and apart, can tell us about how we understand ourselves and the world we inhabit, or would like to. In part, suggest philosophers, anthropologists, and neuroscientists, this is because of the social significance we invest in music:

> Why does music matter at all to anyone? Music's attraction and power over us . . . stems from its elemental social character. . . . Music's social character is evident in the role it plays in every culture, past and present, in creating and reinforcing social bonds . . . Any so-called 'private' experiences of music . . . carry a social meaning. . . . There is no such thing as 'music itself' that can be experienced without reference to a context or shared social understandings. (Bicknell, 2009, viii–ix)

Popular music, more particularly, deals in and with people's fantasies, realities, dreams and nightmares. It stimulates incredible creativity and pleasure. If music has this social significance, so too does Shakespeare. This is because Shakespeare's stories, and the stories we build around them, have a particular power in many cultures. As Sinfield suggests:

> Shakespeare's plays constitute an influential medium through which certain ways of thinking about the world may be promoted and others impeded, they are a site of cultural struggle and change. . . . Shakespeare is one of the places where ideology is made. (1994, 155–56)

But because not all people have the same power, neither do all stories (or ideologies). In other words, just as some people are more privileged or seen as more valuable than others, so are some stories (usually those told *by* such people). Because of this, at different times, some people have been able or allowed to act on the stories and ideologies they tell about themselves and others, and some people have not. And so some of the worlds and ways of living evoked by all these stories, and the people creating them, remain only potential.

We can relate these issues to Shakespeare and popular music. If we think there is no space in Shakespeare for expressions of the popular voice, and that he has nothing to do with popular culture past or present, including music, we construct a story about him that says he is elite, and suitable only for a few (and we also tell a story that says popular culture has nothing to do with him). This means we silence the different and sometimes conflicting experiences in and of his work, and put Shakespeare in the service of the biased interests of a limited range of people. But what happens when we begin to create stories about Shakespeare that remind us of his intense relations to, and existence as, popular culture – culture made by and for a *wide* range of people, not an elite? By doing this, we become entitled to argue *with* Shakespeare – both against and using him – in the ongoing cultural and therefore political conflicts that make up the stories we tell about ourselves, and the worlds these stories make possible or impossible. Concentrating on Shakespeare, even in relation to popular music, might seem to reaffirm the authority of an old-fashioned, exclusive cultural system. But as Sinfield asserts: 'Shakespeare is, simply, the most provocative point at which to break in to (or is it "out of"?) the system' (2006, 21). With this in mind, *Shakespeare and Popular Music* doesn't try to make Shakespeare our contemporary, or ignore the huge differences between the world he wrote in and sub-sequent worlds, or thereby reduce the reality or possibility of change in societies. On the contrary, this book tries to give meaning and context to how and why popular musicians in different times and places have made Shakespeare *their* contemporary.

This is not an ideologically neutral approach. As Raymond Williams and others would describe it elsewhere, it involves 'a recognition of the social reality of man in all his activities, and of the consequent struggle for the direction of this reality by and for ordinary men and women' (1968, 16). This perspective has been defined by Williams as cultural materialism, 'a theory of culture as a (social and material) productive process' (2005, 243). It is opposed to the idea that culture somehow tran-scends or is separate from the contexts where it is made and consumed, because this idea can be used to depoliticize and limit culture's sources and effects. Sinfield notes that cultural materialism has been criticized, for being politically predictable or naive, for relying on dodgy construc-tions of historical reality, and for raising more 'problems' than it can solve. But if cultural materialism now 'appears less new' than it once did, 'that does not make it less true' (2006, 6, 2).

GENRES AND PERIODS

As that last paragraph implies, to understand how Shakespeare and popular music relate, we need to locate both in specific social and historical contexts. This is vital if we intend to think about how both work as 'real practices, elements of a whole material social process', as

Williams put it (1977, 94). In other words, we have to see and hear Shakespeare's works and popular music in relation to particular times and places to realize how they make and are made by the experiences, aspirations, desires, needs, pains, pleasures, values and meanings (and the contradictions in and between all these) embodied by real people and the communities, cultures and ideologies they build.

But these times, places and realities – the material contexts of cultural production and reproduction – don't just include the contexts where Shakespeare's *Hamlet* was first written, published or performed, or where The Birthday Party's 'Hamlet (Pow Pow Pow)' was first recorded, sung or sold. These works and others like them also make, acquire and have meaning in the times and places where people *consume* them. These times and places can be a long way from either Elizabethan or post-punk London. And so sometimes when people consume old works they can also make them have new meanings. As Williams argued: '[T]he making of art is never itself in the past tense. It is always a formative process, within a specific present' (1977, 129).[1] When it comes to works by Shakespeare or in popular music, this point is even more important. Yet while we're carefully trying to understand specific times and places, we also find that both Shakespeare and popular music have an amazing capacity to echo themselves and each other, disrupting our sense of the distinct contexts in which they work. How can we begin to solve this dilemma? To Williams, any culture often contains 'residual' elements, surviving from 'some previous social and cultural institution or formation': for example, the royal family is a leftover of feudalism in the United Kingdom (1977, 122). We can adapt Williams's ideas to appreciate what is special about Shakespeare and popular music in specific periods when they are produced or consumed. But we can also use Williams's thinking to describe Shakespeare as a residual element in modern culture, and more specifically in popular music.

The place of any residual elements in the 'contemporary cultural process', is, says Williams, 'profoundly variable'. Williams suggests these older residual elements are 'at some distance' from contemporary culture. This can mean they have the authority of tradition on their side, and can serve modern authorities. Dominant sections of a culture could incorporate the past to support present arrangements of power and resources. So a rock song sung by a male singer might use *Romeo and Juliet* to reinforce the idea that women are weak and men are strong, or a critic might refer to Shakespeare to suggest popular culture is rubbish in comparison. But any residual elements are still slightly removed from the ideas and institutions that dominate a culture, its power and its resources. And *this* means they can sometimes offer 'alternative or even oppositional versions' of aspects of that dominant culture, expressions of 'human experience, aspiration and achievement which the dominant culture neglects, undervalues, opposes or even cannot recognize' (1977, 123–24). So a female rapper might refer to *Romeo and Juliet* to make an ironic comment on the failings of a male lover, or a critic might locate Shakespeare in popular music to show the vital power, ingenuity and creativity in both. For just as early modern popular music from previous periods and other contexts was in part a 'residual' element in Shakespeare's works, so Shakespeare is a 'residual' element in *modern* popular music – a peculiarly resonant, echoic medium – and his presence in it pushes such music in new directions. At the same time, popular music puts Shakespeare in new contexts. When we think about matters in this way, we can see and hear Shakespeare and popular music as the products and producers of particular, distinct locations. But we can also recognize that distinctions might be broken down, between periods and between different cultural products and producers. *Shakespeare and Popular Music* shows how (and why) modern musicians attempt to create continuities or connections between what they do and what Shakespeare did; it also shows that the power of these continuities between popular music and Shakespeare can disrupt understandings of cultural chronology or historical precedence. In simple terms, and in the words of the title of a film covered in more detail later, in the weird world of pop, it becomes possible to realize that 'Shakespeare was a Big George Jones Fan'.

We might attempt a similar kind of solution with regard to genre. According to Richard Middleton, *all* music works by 'manipulating difference': 'structurally' in terms of how a piece contains 'repetition, variation and change' within itself (overture–first movement, or intro–verse–chorus–verse, and so on), and also 'semiotically', in relation to the meanings of other musical 'practice and repertory' (2000, 60). Within *popular* musics, genre serves as a powerful differentiating force. This is significant. Williams argued that in terms of literature, genre isn't neutral, 'neither an ideal type nor a traditional order nor a set of technical rules' (1977, 185). Because literature, like all culture, is the 'process and result' of productive work within specific socio-historical conditions, genres combine 'different levels of the social material process' (46, 185). If this seems abstract, we can again adapt Williams's ideas for the purposes of this book, and to understand popular music. To use genre as a way to interpret popular music (and Shakespeare's relation to it) means we have to acknowledge the diverse and complex conditions, identities, positions, locations and contexts in and by which that music is produced and consumed; these include but aren't limited to period, nation, 'race', ethnicity, subculture, sexuality and musical features. When we do this, we recognize both the aesthetic and ethical power of such conditions and identities: genre matters in terms of how we hear music and how we think about those hearing or making it (including ourselves). To put this another way, performers, the music industry and audiences invest a lot in genres – they are a key context in which music is made and consumed. We cannot hear what happens to Shakespeare in popular music without recognizing this.

Not much has changed perhaps since the early modern period. Genre in Shakespeare's time was significant, and significantly political – the way writers told stories was meant to affect how audiences responded to those stories, in the theatre and beyond.[2] But now more than ever, using genre to analyse a cultural product like popular music also reproduces commercial, commodified and very often *racialized* discriminations: we end up speaking of, listening to or buying a homogenous 'black' music (however it is packaged otherwise – as 'urban', for example), implying there is such a thing as a homogeneous 'white' music. This, despite the fact that popular musics are produced and consumed on an international scale *and* in local settings, through technologies that allow the sampling, incorporation and 'transfer of sounds from one recording to another', and where 'contemporary musicians' can 'access the global memory banks of recorded sound' (Hesmondhalgh, 2000, 280). This process may be exploitative or reverential, but in this context, such musics (and the subjects and communities that make them) are not stable or discrete forms: 'If nothing else, popular music study rests on the assumption that there is no such thing as a culturally 'pure' sound' (Frith, 1989, 3). Mash-ups and mix-downs rule. We will see this played out in what popular music does with Shakespeare, and vice versa. In this regard, we can compare popular music again to early modern drama. The lack of definition affecting genres was self-evident in the theatrical world Shakespeare occupied. *Hamlet* reflects and mocks this through the description of dramatic genres Polonius offers, which moves from seemingly discrete to hybrid types: 'tragedy, comedy, history, pastoral, pastorical-comical, historical-pastoral, tragical-historical, tragical-comical-historical-pastoral' (2.2.398–401). Any attempt to define genres caused permutations to proliferate, but this *enabled* writers. As Lawrence Danson has argued, the 'nominal instability' of genres (they were hard to define) suggested 'a healthy ability to live comfortably with the unruliness of a theatre where genre was not static but moving and mixing, always producing new possibilities' (2000, 10–11). Significantly, Polonius ends his list with the phrase 'poem unlimited' (2.2.401): in this drama, the potentials were vast. By comparison, however, we are sold popular music, in stores or online, and however we consume it, singly or as part of an audience clued up about the genres we love, we might want to think of it in the same way: *unlimited.*

This means genres are arbitrary in the fullest and most ambivalent senses of the word: as constructs derived from socially and historically specific contexts, they convey both discrimination and randomness. For the purposes of this book, then, characterizing music by genre is and is not useful. As we will see, sometimes genre serves as a frame for discussions, sometimes it does not. This should not obscure the fact that some genres – and the cultures and audiences they represent – are more resistant to or accepting of Shakespeare than others. In turn, some genres use Shakespeare in significant ways because of the cultural politics and identities both he and they represent. *Shakespeare and Popular Music* tries to negotiate these issues by using generic labels where it seems important to do so, but also by considering the phenomena of Shakespeare and popular music *between* and *beyond* genres, on a global scale.

WHY NOW?

Until recently, commentary on both Shakespeare and popular music did not look like it would grasp these issues, and so get to grips with the missed 'opportunity' Sinfield describes above. Initial research for this book involved vainly scouring the indexes of works on popular musicology, to find a significant lack of Shakespeare between The Shadows (or Shakatak) and The Shangri-Las (or Sham 69). *The Oxford Companion to Popular Music*, for example, contains only five references to Shakespeare: three relate to musicals based on his plays, two to popular early modern ballads in his work (Gammond, 1991). Moreover, until recently the little scholarship that *had* looked at Shakespeare and popular music did not reinforce their relationship, but resorted to lists of artists whose works and lyrics alluded to Shakespeare (or other literary figures and texts), and offered suggestive but brief explanations for these allusions – they rely on Shakespeare's 'familiarity' to give 'respectability' to popular songs (Duxbury, 1988, 19–23).

In the past five to ten years though, critical debate and opinion have decisively shifted, to listen more closely to the 'dialogic' possibilities of Shakespeare's communication with popular music and vice versa, in the terms of the fourth epigraph above, or to consider how Shakespeare has been shaken, or at least remixed a little, by the passing crazes and crazy passions of popular music, in a manner declared impossible (and undesirable) by Lewis in the first. Some of this criticism has emphasized the contention and tension between Shakespeare and popular music; some has revealed the connections between the two. Whatever forms such recent scholarly attention has taken, it has considered Shakespeare's complex relationships with popular music in ever more sophisticated ways.

This increasing critical sophistication might be seen as a necessary reaction to changes in the ways people produce and consume culture, 'popular' and otherwise, and to changes in Shakespeare's place in these processes. This increasing sophistication is also due to changes in the character of Shakespeare scholarship in general, notably a now rampant interest in appropriations of his words and work. As scholars have studied Shakespeare on film, for example, so the use of music in such films has become relevant, not least in terms of what Richard Burt terms 'cinem(edi)a': 'the circulation of all kinds of mass media in film . . . how film circulates from one big screen to another, how it is dispersed across media ranging from shooting scripts and screenplays to CD-ROMs and DVDs, and how sound (noise, music and so on), is deployed in those exchanges' (Burt, 2002, 201–2). By discussing music in the work of film makers like Baz Luhrmann, Derek Jarman, Julie Taymor and Julien Temple, *Shakespeare and Popular Music* tries to contribute to this area.

The shift in scholarly attentions may also be in part due to changes in the community of Shakespeare scholars, some of whom seem more attuned to or sensitized by popular cultures than ever before. Now academics confess they are compelled to connect: 'Many moments in Shakespearean drama play themselves out in my mind to the accompaniment of popular music' (Marshall, 2000, 98). As we will see, this kind of open and newly energized approach has yielded a wealth of insightful and inspired critical interventions on Shakespeare and popular music from the United States, notably regarding constructions of gender and 'race'. And as many of these studies have explored the ways popular music engages with particular canonical plays or characters, so something of a canon of concerns, songs and artists has developed. But while mindful of this canon and what has already been said and done, *Shakespeare and Popular Music* also attempts to suggest new areas of debate and study in a field of material that is ever expanding and diverse. So this book acknowledges the importance of the United States for popular music (it could do little else), yet also considers what happens to Shakespeare in popular music produced on the other side of the Atlantic. And to compensate for any Anglocentric, UK-based bias, it *also* tries to think about Shakespeare's place in a world of global popular music production and consumption, listening to popular music in an international context, and to fans of popular music.

Chapter 1 explores the continuities between Shakespeare and *early modern* popular music, as recorded in his appropriations and uses of such music in his plays. This might cast Shakespeare as the original 'sampler'. Since discussing early modern popular music means we have to detail the very different soundscapes enveloping people in the past, this section also considers the problems of over-emphasising these continuities. Chapter 2 moves forward to look at the various and sometimes opposed ways in which Shakespeare's relationship with modern popular music, and popular culture more generally, have been expressed in such musics, in existing Shakespearean criticism, and in contemporary critical and cultural theory. Chapter 3 develops these concerns with historically specific soundscapes to suggest that the technologies of modern popular music – phonography, video, digital media – necessarily distinguish modern from early modern experiences of popular music. Yet we'll see that Shakespeare has had a role to play in unsettling as well as consolidating such distinctions.

After these critical overviews, subsequent chapters establish some specific cultural and socio-political contexts in which Shakespeare and modern popular music might be located. Chapter 4 surveys musical and critical responses to Shakespeare's relations with African-American musics such as jazz and rap. This section also involves interviews with musicians, exploring the effects of such musics' global dissemination, not least in the work of artists like Akala in the United Kingdom. From there, Chapter 5 offers a view of the cultural politics of invoking Shakespeare in a self-consciously 'blue-collar' musical form such as country, with a detailed case study of the role of Shakespeare in the work of Cowboy Jack Clement. Chapter 6 shifts from the United States to the United Kingdom and charts the relationship between two icons of nations changing under two different Elizabeths: The Beatles and Shakespeare.

Moving beyond existing discussions of references to Shakespeare in Beatles' songs, this chapter explores the diverse ways in which the band and their contemporaries engaged with the Bard. Progressing chronologically, and culturally, Chapter 7 develops the idea of Shakes-punk: what happens to Shakespeare in the work of artists related to the late-1970s' music scene like the Sex Pistols, Derek Jarman and Elvis Costello. Chapter 8 discusses the ways in which the politics of early modern drama might compare and contrast with the politics of modern popular music. In order to do this, this section considers how one contemporary group, the Kaiser Chiefs, has engaged with what Steven Mullaney has termed the 'symbolic topography' of early modern London's suburban theatres (2007, 26). Do their performances of songs such as 'I Predict a Riot' at the Globe construct Shakespeare as a subversive Britpop icon, signal a nostalgia for seemingly authentically subversive early modern popular culture, or reveal the limited political horizons of modern popular music? After this tightened focus, Chapter 9 takes a wider scope to ask the question: if Shakespeare is a global icon, what happens when 'world music' (however that difficult term is defined) engages with Shakespeare? Finally, Chapter 10 draws upon the developing area of fan studies in cultural theory to discuss the diverse and often contentious responses of devotees of popular musicians who reference or evoke Shakespeare.

Given all these concerns, and to invite reactions, *Shakespeare and Popular Music* can only be selective, not definitive; provocative, not conclusive.[3] However you sample it – as discrete chapters (like downloaded songs), as a developing and incremental sequence of themes, preludes and echoes (like a more traditional album) – you will sense that in and beyond these pages, there *is* a whole lotta Shakespeare goin' on. As the rock critic Greil Marcus implies in the final epigraph above: join in. Where better to start thinking about what popular music does to Shakespeare than by thinking about what Shakespeare himself did with popular music in his own time, the early modern period?

NOTES

1 Williams' ideas here have been updated, if not augmented, by the development of 'presentism' in Shakespeare studies. See Hawkes, 2002; and Grady and Hawkes, 2007.
2 See, for example, Tennenhouse, 1986; Bamber, 1982; and Howard and Rackin, 1997.

3 For a comprehensive list of Shakespeare in music, see Gooch and Thatcher, 1991. On Shakespeare and popular music more generally, see Sanders, 2007, 182–93; Folkerth, 2006; Buhler, 2002 and 2007. On Shakespeare in classical music, including scores for ballet and films, see Sanders, 29–72; Wilson, 1922; and Hartnoll, 1966. For Shakespeare in musicals, see Sanders, 73–95; and Everett and Laird, 2002. In opera, see Sanders, 112–34; and Clark, 2001.

CHAPTER I

SHAKESPEARE AND EARLY MODERN POPULAR MUSIC

Early modern music, popular and otherwise, was consumed and produced in very different ways compared to modern popular music. We need to be aware of this to understand what Shakespeare did with the popular music of his own time, and how what he did still has relevance for contemporary musicians. So this chapter looks at what made early modern popular music of the kind Shakespeare heard and reproduced distinctly early modern, but also considers the ways modern popular music confuses this distinction between past and present. In turn, this *in*distinction will underscore the continuities this book discusses between Shakespeare and popular music.

MUSIC IN THE EARLY MODERN PERIOD

Richard Middleton reminds us we cannot assume that the 'resonances' or meanings attached to modern popular music existed in 'pre-industrial societies', and points out the fundamental 'impact of "modernization"' (1990, vi). Bruce R. Smith confirms this to suggest that there are significant differences between modern and early modern soundscapes, the acoustic worlds people inhabited and made:

> Two inventions – electricity and the internal cumbustion [sic] engine – make it difficult for us even to imagine what life in early modern England would have sounded like. (1999, 49)

Thinking about Shakespeare's relationship to the popular music of his own time means we have to recognize the special ideological and social conditions in which people consumed or created such music. The ability to produce and suppress sounds like music in the early modern period was intrinsically linked to authority: 'Whoever controlled sound commanded a vital medium of communication and power' (Garrioch, 2003, 18). This is encapsulated by the famous *Rainbow Portrait* of Elizabeth I, from the turn of the 1600s, showing the Queen's dress embroidered not only with eyes but also ears: representing her authority involved sound and sight, audition as well as omniscience. Sometimes this power to hear or create hearing was beyond mere mortal apprehension. To early modern theorists, how we experienced sound physically embodied our subjection to and direction by a higher intelligence:

> Mark and observe also the art and curious workmanship appearing in the inward part of the ear, how exquisitely it is made and trimmed with little labyrinths, windings, little windows, a sounding tympan or timbrel; three small bones, a stirrup, an anvil and a hammer; the small muscles, the nerve or sinew of hearing, and the cartilaginous or gristle passage, prepared for conveying all sounds unto the sense . . . the infinite goodness and bounty of God shineth in this excellent workmanship. (Crooke, 1615, 386–87)

In early modern Europe, Richard Leppert asserts, specific types of sounds, regulated by spiritual or secular authorities, 'could help stabilize and authorize hierarchical social position and the various means by which it was gained and held'. This applied to church music before and during the Reformation, and to the notated secular music enjoyed by the aristocracy, theorized on the basis of Plato's 'continuum of order-disorder': vicious sounds enraged and bestialized, virtuous ones pacified and elevated, and some 'set you apart' (Leppert, 1995, 43–44). For Plato, since 'good or vicious musical representations' aroused strong 'emotions' in impressionable young people, it was best to defer to authority in matters musical: 'we shall interpret the wishes of the lawgiver and arrange to *his* liking our dancing and singing' (1970, 303, 290).

But this meant music could also cause chaos. So while Plato preluded the connection of 'aurality and obedience' in early modern thought, the tensions in this connection were also amplified by music at certain points (Folkerth, 2002b, 18). To English Puritan reformers such as William Prynne, writing in 1633, overwrought music was 'impudent' and 'whorish', immodest and emasculating (cited in Lindley, 2006, 46). For Stephen Gosson, in 1587, the only 'right musicke' to which people should attend was that divine harmony underscoring orthodox political, gender, social and religious hierarchies and values (cited in Lindley,

2006, 49). We can hear hymns to this harmony in many moments in Shakespeare's plays, not least *Henry V*:

EXETER   For government, though high and low and lower,
          Put into parts, doth keep in one consent,
          Congreeing in a full and natural close,
          Like music. (1.2.180–83)

Yet still the fragility of such resolutions resonated, as in *Troilus and Cressida*, where social disharmony sounds a bum note:

ULYSSES   Take but degree away, untune that string,
           And hark what discord follows. (1.3.109–110)

Hence, in 1604, though informed by these discourses linking sound and authority, Thomas Wright described the profoundly various effects of music on listeners:

So in musicke, divers consorts stirre up in the heart, divers sorts of joyes, and divers sorts of sadness or paine: the which as men are affected, may be diversely applyed: Let a good and a godly man heare musicke, and he will lift up his heart to heaven: let a bad man heare the same, and hee will convert it to lust . . . these sounds diversificate passions . . . (cited in Lindley, 2006, 29)

Like language or rhetoric, early moderns' music generated 'radical uncertainty' about its influence and effects on diverse consumers, and their *diversificated* passions (Lindley, 2006, 44). This uncertainty only increased when the music was *popular*, and Shakespeare's plays realize this.

POPULAR MUSIC IN SHAKESPEARE

It is important not to overestimate the frequency of pre-existing popular songs in Shakespeare's plays:

The songs performed in something like complete form within Shakespeare's plays are much more often art songs – freshly written pieces by a professional author, that author usually being

> Shakespeare himself – than popular or traditional ones. (Gillespie, 2006, 175)

It is also hard to tell if existing allusions to popular songs were meant to be spoken or sung, or if centuries of readers and performers have missed an allusion. But this should not mean we ignore the fact that the plays ring with 'scraps of the actual words of old songs' (Naylor, 1931, 68).[1] To employ terms from modern music, Shakespeare was a canny sampler, a pirate and a plunderer. Equally, early modern popular music wasn't simply represented by the well-known words or tunes of such songs. It also included bell ringing, street sellers' calls and harvest rhymes. Leppert has even suggested that 'among the lower social orders in Europe', music was not a 'separate sonoric entity' or 'art', but 'life' itself: 'musical sound was as important to peasants as the sounds their animals made, a reassurance of . . . both individual and communal identity' (1995, 44). Even a recognizable popular song form like the ballad was an inclusive genre, with huge publication rates and printed and oral circulation: this meant ballads had diverse functions and meanings in the culture at large. This suggests that we need to expand what we think of as 'popular music' in Shakespeare's plays: they throb with processions, dances, jigs, 'trumpets, sackbuts, psalteries, and fifes, / Tabors and cymbals and . . . shouting' (*Coriolanus*, 5.3.50–51). Whatever forms early modern popular music took in Shakespeare's drama, its incorporation within the soundscape of the early modern theatre proved to be 'so popular' that the King's Men 'retrofitted the Globe to include a curtained music room in the balcony above the stage' in the early 1600s (Smith, 1999, 221). And by later plays like *The Winter's Tale*, music has the power to bring people, if not *the* people, to life:

> PAULINA   Music; awake her; strike! (5.3.98)

Shakespeare invested some types of early modern popular music with particular power. Smith notes that characters seize on 'popular ballads in moments that require lyrical intensity' (1999, 169). Ballads in Shakespeare's plays also signify 'pastness and passion' (Smith, 2006, 196). All such states converge around Desdemona's 'willow song' in *Othello,* 4.3, with its melancholy memories of mothers and maids, and intimations of death. And precisely because of their evocative qualities *and* popular consumption, for Smith, ballads 'establish a commonality of memory that unifies the audience and imbricates its members in the fictional world of the play'; this is a 'common culture' operating 'across the platform's edge' (2006, 196, 200). Ballads expressed the spatial and semiotic relationship of the 'street to the stage'; in other words, to sing a ballad onstage was to perform a performance of a ballad offstage, bringing players and people closer together (Smith, 1999, 168–69). Such relations would fulfil commentators' worst fears about the power of music to stimulate diverse and potentially unorthodox effects.

However, David Lindley notes that figures in the late romances complicate this sort of analysis. When Caliban sings his song of 'Freedom, high-day!' (*The Tempest*, 2.2.186), he heralds a development in his downcast status that resonates through the play:

At this point popular music becomes oppositional rather than merely antithetical. This is continued in 3.2, where rebellious energy again finds expression in musical form. (2006, 221–22)

Because Caliban's songs can be 'firmly associated with the world of the tavern and "low life"', like ballads they have a 'strong potential' to reach beyond the stage and implicate the audience in 'conspiratorial combination'. Yet even as Stephano and Trinculo's carousing catch ends with 'And scout 'em and flout 'em, / Thought is free', Caliban responds 'That's not the tune' (3.2.124–26): something isn't ringing true for him. And as Caliban's words are followed by watching Ariel taking up the melody, the violently emancipatory ambitions of the 'rebellious' song are co-opted and overcome (Lindley, 2006, 221–22). Furthermore, since popular songs could also be blatantly commercial artefacts, this commodification again complicates their purpose. At the Bohemian sheep-shearing feast in *The Winter's Tale*, 4.4, Autolycus sings and sells tunes that simultaneously mock – mimic and *ridicule* – the form of and market for outlandish matter both on and off the stage.

Nonetheless, to Lindley, the popular songs sung by lowly or socially marginal figures, like the Fool in *King Lear* for example, can still act as a complex 'subversive critique' of the 'court-world', a critique both 'expressed and mitigated' by being in popular song (2006, 162–63). Comparably, as Stephen M. Buhler has shown, the 'riotous snatches' of ballads sung by errant knights like Toby Belch in *Twelfth Night* and Falstaff in the *Henry IV* plays powerfully signify those 'carnivalesque' moments when the everyday world was turned upside down for a while. Ballads likewise 'destabilize gender roles', as male actor-singers take female parts to lament patriarchal injustice and betrayal: 'In *Hamlet*,

Ophelia uses ballads not only to express grief but also to assert a prophetic judgement against male authority' (2007, 158–60). Her songs are simultaneously angry and mournful; they are also 'indecorous' for the way they cause these destabilizations, and confuse 'public and private worlds', the 'popular' and the political (Lindley, 2006, 157).

Such indecorousness echoes both the theatre's appeal and the development of ballads as a popular musical form into the 1600s. As Lindley argues, many popular songs 'clearly derive' from the commissioned and professionalized music of earlier royal courts, in a process of cultural downshifting; conversely, many were stylistically or lyrically cleaned up for publication (2006, 73). Lindley affirms: 'The lines of demarcation between "popular" and "high-brow" music were always permeable' (89). When actors and musicians found themselves dislocated in this turbulent period's social and legal re-arrangements, then ballads could be as out of place as their subjects and singers.

BEYOND THE EARLY MODERN STAGE

Popular musical forms like ballads performed multiple functions on the Shakespearean stage. Most importantly perhaps, popular music persisted in the plays, because it consolidated the plays' own success. Put differently, it could be argued that in some cases Shakespeare survived *because* of popular music. This has been true in the present and the past. A far-from-popular play such as *Timon of Athens* was given a new lease of life, thanks to its association with Duke Ellington's 1963 score (revived in the 1990s in stagings, and recordings such as Stanley Silverman's adaptation). Looking further back, Julie Sanders reminds us that during the Restoration, London's stages were 'anything but precious' about songs in Shakespearean texts, and 'the theatres of William Davenant and Thomas Killigrew were more than willing to add songs by contemporary musicians' (2007, 31). In this way, Shakespeare was adapted anew for new audiences. And as Smith points out, Thomas Percy's *Reliques of Ancient English Poetry* (1765) includes 'Ballads that illustrate Shakespeare'. Smith argues that this makes us aware of the presence and survival in popular music of modified Shakespearean texts and responses to specific stagings: 'Ballads did not *record* performances; they *perpetuated* them'. In some senses, they *were* the performance: ballads 'circulated in early modern culture as widely as – and even more widely than – the printed script' of the plays. As such, ballads become 'neglected documents in the history of the cultural institution known as "Shakespeare"' (2006, 194–95, 207, 205). Smith discusses one ballad titled 'The Lamentable and Tragical History of Titus Andronicus' (c. 1625, but reprinted many times after). Here, Titus sings 'all the events of the story – even his own death'. Only the 'tongueless Lavinia' also speaks. Whether 'singing the ballad alone' or 'performing it for others', notes Smith, 'the singer . . . becomes the titular hero' of this play: 'in possessing the ballad as a physical object, and in getting it by heart, one can perform the play in one's own voice' (1999, 203–5). When Shakespeare becomes a ballad, he becomes early modern popular music, offering the potential to *anyone* who could read, hear or simply learn a tune to reproduce his work, far beyond the metropolitan and theatrical context of a play's inception.

This sense of a shared bond between Shakespeare and early modern popular music, and the popular cultures they both give voice to, continues to attract attention. Sometimes this is audible in modern film adaptations or dramatic productions. In the 2009 staging of *Romeo and Juliet* at London's Globe Theatre, directed by Dominic Dromgoole, the composer Nigel Hess sought to 'create music which is part of Verona's world, albeit heard through the ears of English Elizabethans'. Hess took 'inspiration' from the 'vibrant, bawdy' tenor of the definitively popular 'street music of Italy in the sixteenth and seventeenth centuries', especially forms like the villanelle, 'the street equivalent of the more upmarket madrigal'. The show began with a rendition of Filippo Azzaiolo's 'Chi passa per sta strada' ('He who passes this way') from the 1500s, and was interspersed with songs that combined early modern lyrics (translated from Renaissance Italian, and by English Renaissance poets) with 'new tunes'. This kind of project is untroubled by issues of ahistoricism – it imagines we can hear 'through the ears' of those long dead without too many problems. Indeed, Hess's description of his composition process ends with a fantasy whose informal address, use of mixed tenses, and final ellipses, offer the possibility of connection with the Bard and seek to prove how 'timeless' both he and popular music can be:

Will Shakespeare loved music . . . so I hope he would approve of the musical bed on which we've laid our version of this timeless story, and that somewhere up in the Gallery he'll be singing along . . . (2009, 14)

We might easily criticize this kind of fantasy and the image of a still present, genial, toe-tapping Shakespeare it promotes. Sure enough, other Shakespearean reproducers have used early modern music in ways that partly emphasize the ironic distance between past and present. Gus Van Sant's film *My Own Private Idaho* (1991) re-imagines *Henry IV 1* and *2*, and those scenes where the appropriations from Shakespeare are most obvious are scored by 'cod-Elizabethan music', which, notes Sanders, serves to signify the 'hyperreality and intertextuality of these moments' (2007, 157). In other words, the film draws attention to its own debts and heralds the artifice of its own construction, toying with ideas of musical and textual authenticity. This both sustains and diminishes the difference between a film about gay hustlers, and plays about a prince's and a nation's coming-of-age.

But Hess's work for the Globe continues to raise some vital questions about Shakespeare's relations with early modern popular music in the modern era. Is the music in his production *popular* music or not? It certainly was once, but does its place in a prestigious Shakespearean heritage site now reduce or revive this? And are these songs combining new tunes with old words early modern or just modern? Given the very different contexts of their production and consumption, does a staging like this deliberately blur distinctions between early modern and modern popular musics? Ultimately, perhaps this kind of staging only capitalizes on perceived continuities between early modern and modern popular music.

EARLY MODERN AND AFTER

Despite the evident cultural and experiential differences between early modern and modern popular musics, and the different material conditions they evoke, many commentators have suggested modern musical forms have early modern roots, and have implicated Shakespeare in connecting the two. In other words, even when commentators give accounts of popular music that suggest a combination of technological and social factors conditioned its modern forms, Shakespeare comes to appear as a kind of Zelig figure, discovered at various points in these accounts.

Middleton dates the beginnings of popular, commercial music as it is now experienced to the technological and cultural conditions of the eighteenth century, but admits an 'organized music business' began to exist alongside the 'great popular agitation' and 'democratic political theory' of the half-century before. He pushes the point, though, to note that dating the birth of popular music 'could go even further back, say, to Shakespeare's "All the world's a stage"', as 'mercantile capitalism' coincided with 'consciousness-shifting encounters with foreign "others"'', and the development of opera (2006, 252). Though hedged by his characteristically perceptive concerns, Middleton's repeated urge to listen 'further back', and invoke Shakespeare when doing so, implies connections exist between the world of the early modern stage and modern musics. These 'innumerable links' exist 'at the level of musical materials and conventions', scored into the 'subterranean stratum' of twentieth-century songs: 'some blues and rock bass patterns can be traced back to sixteenth-century dance music' (1990, 117–19). Shakespeare emerges as an arranger and producer of such sounds and the world that listened to them: for Folkerth, Shakespearean 'playtexts' evoke 'past acoustic events' as potently as any modern phonographic technology (2002b, 7). If Shakespeare records and reuses sounds past, then popular music booms with comparable reactions, irruptions, repetitions, remixes, 'weird cultural survivals, time walkers, loop tracers' (Marcus, 2001, 434). In popular music, nothing escapes and everything is up for grabs. As one tongue-in-cheek handbook for chart success affirmed, written by The Timelords (musicians whose pseudonym suggested their power to exploit such survivals, and cause chronological disturbances): 'Every Number One song ever written is only made up from bits of other songs. There is no lost chord' (1988, 674).

With these tones ringing in our ears, we can conclude this exploration of early modern popular music with two examples of the ways in which Shakespeare has been scored into some of the formative moments of modern popular music. First, Greil Marcus's account of Robert Johnson, the seminal early twentieth-century blues musician, attempts to make a 'good musical case' for Johnson's status as 'the first rock 'n' roller of all'. Yet Marcus also makes a *literary* case that involves Shakespeare, when discussing one of Johnson's lyrics in the song 'Preaching Blues':

'Studying rain' is symbolism, carried forward into many Bob Dylan songs, echoing back to Shakespeare: it means to contemplate dread, to absorb fear into the soul. (2000, 22)

This insight might seem like another use of Shakespeare to legitimate a popular music artist: Johnson is good because he uses Shakespearean imagery. But Marcus offers more than this. He establishes a continuity between Shakespeare, Johnson and Dylan that not only legitimates Johnson but also encourages us to re-hear or rethink Shakespeare. Marcus goes on to cite a letter from his friend Langdon Winner, who makes this move more boldly: 'How can you understand Aeschylus, Augustine, Shakespeare and Nietzsche if you can't listen to Robert Johnson in your own time?' (2000, 212) Marcus responds by observing that this suggests 'if Robert Johnson is an ancestor, or even a ghost, he is really a contemporary' (2000, 36). Yet in the temporal and cultural disruptions or echoes popular music creates, Shakespeare too becomes a 'contemporary' once more, located in the early modern past while also audible in the inaugural moments of modern rock 'n' roll.

Second, in his entertaining history of popular music, Ian Whitcomb records a meeting with the English pop impresario, Jack Good, who recalled his initial encounter with the American rocker Gene Vincent, in the early days of British rock 'n' roll:

> He was wearing a red felt ice hockey jacket which didn't go well with my image of him . . . So I thought 'This won't do at all! This is not what my people want.' What was I going to do with him? Then I noticed that he walked with something of a limp and studying his footwear saw that one of his shoes was reinforced by some sort of iron bar.
>
> The limp fascinated me and I thought, 'This is surely something we can build up on.' It struck me that what we wanted to achieve here was the evil Richard III malformed image. My mind raced ahead with the idea of Shakespearean types of costume. Richard III – YES! The limp, that's right! But also a touch of Hamlet – the misunderstood young man alone in the world. But also he *is* a motor cyclist, or should be, so he *must* have black leather. . . . The whole exercise achieved an evil effect which went over very well with the public. (1972, 252)

Good was a salesman. In this reflection he is, in part, selling us on his own cultural assurance and entrepreneurial flair. Yet he is also making the point that *Shakespeare* sells, not just or even *as* Shakespeare, but when mixed up with other, later cultural forms. As we shall see, the mixture of leather, limp, Shakespeare and rock 'n' roll would reverberate, not least in the Teddy-boy and then the punk eras, in which the angry-looking, alienated, *different* Vincent was a talismanic figure.

These examples noted, we can now ask: how *does* Shakespeare relate to *modern* popular music?

NOTE

1 An exhaustive list of such scraps occurs in Naylor, 1931, 68–93. For a more recent survey of survivals and allusions, see also Duffin, 2004.

CHAPTER 2

'WHERE SHOULD THIS MUSIC BE?'[1]: LOCATING SHAKESPEARE AND MODERN POPULAR MUSIC

Discussing modern popular music and Shakespeare raises challenging questions, focused largely on definitions. This chapter explores what we mean by 'popular music', the issues generated by this form, and how musicians, scholars and teachers have thought about the ways Shakespeare relates to them.

WHAT AND WHEN

Is modern popular music defined by its musical qualities (or lack of them)? Theodor Adorno opined that such music is 'usually characterized by its difference from serious music' (1941a, 437). But as Evan Eisenberg notes, this meant popular music included 'everything from polkas to Charlie Parker', and Adorno himself was painfully conscious of the ways in which commercial songs quoted high art, as we will see (Eisenberg, 1987, 23). If popular music is hard to define in terms of distinct style or content, it is no easier to locate in time, and given the continuities identified at the end of the previous chapter, any difficulties around locating popular music in time influence how we think about the ways Shakespeare relates to it. Dave Russell commences his study of modern popular music in the 1840s because of specific cultural and technological shifts: 'the emergence of the singing-class movement; [Alfred] Novello's first cheap music publications; the appearance of the railway as a factor in musical life' (1987, xiii). But *The Cambridge Companion to Pop and Rock* picks a later date to start its 'brief chronology': '1877 Thomas Edison demonstrates the first phonograph' (Frith et al., 2004, xi). Then again, *The Faber Book of Pop* begins its survey in the 1940s, as vinyl replaced shellac, and pop charts began in the United States, consolidating the triumph of recorded over printed music (Kureishi and Savage, 1995, 5).

Matters don't get any clearer when we start to think about who produces or consumes popular music. Is modern popular music made by or made for 'the people', generated from mass populations or sold to them? Russell accepts but reduces the 'troublesome' nature of the term to suggest popular music is 'the music that was offered to, listened to and performed by the majority of the population', and this combination of popular production and reception, context specific as it is, prevails here (1987, x–xi). There are ideological implications to this. Richard Middleton affirms that as a far from 'pure' product of and response to the subjections generated by the economic and cultural 'machinery' of modernity, popular music is 'the voice of the people' and therefore 'always plural, hybrid, compromised' (2006, 23). As such, popular music past and present has been seen in terms of how it 'supports or disrupts the dominant ideology', and it is impossible to think about Shakespeare and popular music without recognizing this (Robinson et al., 1991, 27). Yet when we do so, the ideological concerns only increase as we try to define the premodifier 'popular':

> Although 'the popular' can be made to carry a range of different meanings, what all these have in common is the idea of L *popularis*, belonging to the people. In particular, the idea of the popular is often a way of constructing, categorizing and dismissing the cultural and social practices of 'ordinary' people. In other words, definitions of the popular are never neutral; they are always entangled with questions of culture and power. (Storey, 2005, 264)

These issues of dominance, culture and power have often centred on Shakespeare too. At certain times, certain critics have thought it best to portray Shakespeare as a mouthpiece for an elite cultural and ideological authority. Yet discourses in his own time and after suggesting Shakespeare was antagonistic to the popular and popular culture have been historicized, deconstructed and dismantled.[2] One recent overview of how Shakespeare has been positioned as the 'Bard of high culture' suggests he has 'never been exclusively or stably held aloft' (Henderson, 2007, 6). For this reason: Shakespeare's writing 'was itself created from materials that might genuinely be described as being "of the people"' (Gillespie and Rhodes, 2006, 1). As we have heard, such materials included popular music of the broadest range.

Many commentators note that with Shakespeare's 'transmission and appropriation' through profit-seeking, mass-market popular culture, including popular music, the issues of dominance, culture and power noted above intensify. And in some genres, where issues of power or power-lessness are particularly pressing, these issues are particularly potent:

> Is Shakespeare being brought into dialogue through rap with urban street subculture? Or is Shakespeare simply a vehicle for main-streaming rap, for blunting its capacity for critique and resistance, making it nothing more than a trademark for rebranding products as hip? (Lanier, 2006, 75)

This is an important point about the commercial imperatives now linking Shakespeare and specific genres. But this commercialism is nothing new. We would do well to bear in mind David Lindley's comments on the sale and singing of ballads in *The Winter's Tale*: 'Autolycus's songs are specifically calculated to drum up business' (2006, 166). But because under Western capitalism the production and consumption of what is seen as high art like Shakespeare has now assumed the commercialism of popular culture, an urge to discriminate the two comes into play, from guardians of the perceived special qualities of that high art, *and* from critics of capitalism.

THE PRICE OF POP

In a series of bracing essays on the pulse of the twentieth century's dark heart, Adorno set the tone for this debate about popular music and capitalism. To him, in modern culture, music existed 'exclusively' as a 'commodity', with all aesthetic value subordinated 'to the process of exchange'. The technologies and transmission of music are controlled by 'powerful monopolies', whose power extends into the 'innermost cell of musical practices', how we make and listen to music (1932, 391). As part of mass society, popular music promoted cultural and ideological 'standardization', and 'musical automatism' in its internal structures, as also in its modes of production and reception: songs sounded the same, turned the same tricks, and had the same effects (1941a, 438–39). This suited conformist, industrialized, capitalist social systems, founded on 'conditioned' responses (1941a, 442). Here, musical parts within pop-ular songs, consumers of such songs and the songs themselves functioned 'as a cog in a machine': 'Listeners become so accustomed to the recur-rence of the same things that they react automatically' (1941a, 440, 447).

Because songs are so relentlessly plugged, consumers think they are making a 'free choice' on an 'open market', but they aren't (1941a, 445). They are in fact like 'children', in terms of the simplicity of the music they are sold, and in terms of their passivity and irresponsibility as they respond to it (1941a, 450). Popular music seems to express authentic and spontaneous emotions and seems to let us express individual freedom about what and how we hear. But all this only confirms our subjection:

> Those who ask for a song of social significance ask for it through a medium which deprives it of social significance. The use of inexorable popular musical media is repressive *per se*. (1941a, 460)

In this way, music becomes a 'recreational' activity, helping the 'tired masses to gain new strength and . . . get away from the drudgery of their practical existence' (1945, 385). In short, it becomes a tool for totalitarianism. Some uses of popular music in relation to Shakespeare would illuminate this assessment. At the end of Julie Taymor's 1999 film *Titus*, Titus Andronicus serves his pies of human flesh to the sound of very melodic, jolly music: 'Vivere', written by Cesare Bixio. The jolliness is deeply ironic of course, and the song rightly leaves a bad taste in the mouth. But Taymor's taste is acute, since the song featured in Guido Brignone's 1930s' movie *Vivere!*, one of Fascist Italy's most popular films. With this, Taymor uses popular music to suggest the menace of autocracy and also of mass culture's role in its rise. Shakespeare offers a prelude to this. In *The Merchant of Venice*, Shylock rails against the 'drum / And the vile squealing of the wry-necked fife' that soundtracks the 'shallow fopp'ry' of the Venetian masque, to which he closes his 'house's ears', in an act of 'sober' control (2.4.29–36). This may cast him as a shadow of 'Puritan attitudes', as a patriarch concerned about cultural, domestic and sexual continence, or as an anti-comic character with 'no music in his soul' (Lindley, 2006, 214). But however compromised Shylock may appear, and whatever motivates his concerns about the masque, he is right to be concerned. Under cover of these festivities, Christian Venetians expropriate his possessions, demean his identity and provoke his 'own flesh and blood to rebel!' (3.1.32). As part of these festivities, then, popular music soundtracks Jessica's rebellion against her father and identity, but also divides and coerces non-Christian 'others'.

Let us be under no illusions: popular doesn't necessarily mean progressive. Following Adorno, popular music has been seen to commodify creativity and desire, alienating producers and consumers from themselves and each other. Yet while this reproduces the connections between sound and power in the early modern period, it also reproduces the tensions those connections generated. So, on one hand, rock music, to take a genre, remains one of (too) many 'bastions of laissez-faire capitalism' (Buxton, 1983, 438). Yet, on the other hand, modern music's materialistic and commercial imperatives might themselves disturb those imperatives:

> Rock music is consumer capitalism writ too large, and some performers, especially since punk, cultivate artificiality rather than authenticity. . . . [T]he scandal of rock music, which may give it paradoxical political force, is the way it overstates key market motifs. (Sinfield, 1989, 177, 302)

As one example of popular music, then, rock can sometimes exaggerate the way desires are stimulated and marketed when people are told to want to buy (or to be or to do) something new. This exaggeration can throw those desires, and the way they are marketed, into stark relief, exposing the conditions that cause exploitation. Adorno himself was not prepared to discount the idea that music might challenge repressive, inhumane social structures:

> The question regarding the possible dialectic contribution which music can make toward [social] change remains open. . . . It is not for music to stare in helpless horror at society: it fulfills *[sic]* its social function more precisely when it presents social problems through its own material. (1932, 392–93)

In places, Adorno was even prepared to admit this of *popular* music. Though servile and subjugating in its modern state, popular music could sometimes have dissident powers, as when, for example, 'the vulgar song type' performed by the 'youthful bourgeoisie of the seventeenth and eighteenth centuries', once 'unmasked feudal hierarchy and made fun of it' (1932, 426). And despite his fairly unambiguous pronouncements about the music of his own time, Adorno also recognized the limitations of his own prejudices, and of others: 'the obscure realm of light music remains unexamined; there is, therefore, nothing to be gained from pre-judging its topography' (1932, 427). As a thinker committed to social progress, however dogmatic, he could do little else. When consumers could redirect the will they displayed as they forced themselves to like something they knew was tat and trash, they might actively reject their mutilated lives, passionately recover their humanity and hear again music's power to express it. This is how Adorno describes just such a reversal, and the metamorphoses it would involve:

> They [consumers of popular music] need their will, if only in order to down the all too conscious premonition that something is 'phony' with their pleasure. This transformation of their will indicates that will is still alive and that under certain circumstances it may be strong enough to get rid of the superimposed influences which dog its every step. . . . In order to become a jitterbug or simply to 'like' popular music, it does not by any means suffice to give oneself up and to fall in line passively. To become transformed into an insect, man needs that energy which might possibly achieve his transformation into a man. (1941a, 468)

From another perspective, and again to echo the early moderns' concerns about music, the 'scandal' of modern popular music is that it brings together and stimulates diverse desires and people cut off from mainstream markets and politics. So, according to Richard Leppert, though Adorno 'heard right' with the limited material he referenced, he also 'heard wrong', being deaf to the 'hybrid nature' and 'notable musical experimentation' of popular music in his own period and after. These qualities have allowed some forms of popular music and the subcultures they celebrate or evoke to act 'against the tendency towards sameness' dominant in most cultural structures (2002, 348). Given the ways markets penetrate and co-opt all socio-cultural contexts, such subcultures may be inherently conditioned by or 'tangled up with' the very normative conditions against which they rebel or resist: 'There is nowhere else to be, no miraculously free space' (Sinfield, 1989, 178). To cite Jacques Attali, 'today, wherever there is music, there is money' (2003, 3). This applies to musical subcultures, which are so often commodified by mainstream culture 'into mass-produced objects', sanitized via media labelling, and so lose their explosive charge through 'diffusion and defusion' (Hebdige, 1996, 93–94).

But subcultures can also cause or effect a 'strategic reordering of what is to hand', appropriating from normative or dominant cultures, and from elsewhere when possible (Sinfield, 1989, 178). When this happens, the 'contradictions' or fault lines experienced in such cultures can be 'obliquely represented' (Hebdige, 1996, 133). This is especially true with subcultures centred on, or expressed in, popular music, which have the capacity to integrate, animate and elevate audiences, and even be radicalized by the very factions who despise their disruptive potential. Thus Jon Savage describes the process of subcultural identification in the development of UK punk, but with relevance beyond:

> England is a highly static society, with a strongly defined ruling class and a narrow definition of the acceptable. If you fall outside it for any reason, you're marginal. As with any cluster of minorities, if you put them together, you make a majority: pop – a marginal industry in itself – is a place where many of them meet, as dreamers and misfits from all classes, to transform if not *the* world, then their world. (1992, 12)

Likewise, Richard Dyer observes the ways in which disco empowered ethnic and sexual minorities in the 1970s: 'The anarchy of capitalism throws up commodities that an oppressed group can take up and use to cobble together its own culture' (1979, 413). How disco and punk 'take up and use' a cultural commodity like Shakespeare, then, will emerge as key case studies in this book.

The popular music industry undoubtedly exploits artists and audiences – the politics of its production and consumption all too often conserve and reproduce social inequalities. But not always: as Ray Pratt observes, 'The political meaning of any music depends on its use' (1990, 1). The same is true *of* Shakespeare, and *in* Shakespeare, as the end of *The Tempest* reminds us. There, harmonies simultaneously enchant and demystify, enslave and enliven, as Prospero uses sonorous magic to awaken his subjects from a stupor he has induced:

> PROSPERO   And when I have required
> Some heavenly music – which even now I do –
> To work mine end upon their senses . . .
> A solemn air, and the best comforter
> To an unsettled fancy . . . (5.1.51–59)

LEGITIMACY, AWE AND CONFLICT

So how might Shakespeare relate to the diverse forms and potentials of modern popular music? Regarding Shakespeare's relations with contemporary mass media, Lanier notes: 'The "and" in "Shakespeare and popular culture" marks not just a link but a distinction' (2006, 3). The same is true of Shakespeare and popular music. When Shakespeare's 'face' acts as 'the sign of pop's desire' for the 'cultural authority, quality, legitimacy and upward mobility' that he continues to 'symbolize', then his power also 'remains the sign of that culture which pop proclaims it isn't' (Lanier, 2007, 99). This means that 'though Romeo and Juliet are quite often named' in popular songs, 'they are almost never quoted, for their youthful rebellion is directed against precisely what Shakespeare's language represents: authority, age, propriety, respect for tradition'. This also means, conversely, that using Shakespeare as a 'source or analogue for popular culture' consolidates its 'worthiness' (Lanier, 2006, 72, 95). By this, as we will see, Shakespeare adds legitimacy to genres derogated for their class or 'racial' associations.

Yet such processes might be seen to consolidate the lowness of popular musical cultures by privileging Shakespeare's elevation. In other words, because popular music needs Shakespeare, it reminds us how inferior it is in relation to him. Some popular songs express this. The hook and title of the second single offered by One True Voice, an act generated by a 2002 UK TV talent show, lamented the group's emotional illiteracy, while also bemoaning their lack of linguistic skill: they wanted 'Shakespeare's (Way With) Words'. This was particularly poignant coming from a group whose first single lost out on the number-one slot in the chart to a rival act, and who were blighted with (hardly unfounded) claims that they were manufactured, inauthentic and disposable (claims levelled at many popular musicians). This group's elevation of Shakespeare is thus symptomatic of one aspect of pop's awed relation to his work.

The biggest artists are not immune to this awe, and the frustration it provokes, as we can hear in Elvis Presley's versions of the song now known as 'Are You Lonesome Tonight?'. Elvis's original recorded interpretation copied Al Jolson's 1950 performance to contain a spoken word section that echoed Jaques' speech about the ages of man from *As You Like It*, 2.7: 'All the world's a stage'. But this section in the track erased Shakespeare (and Jaques): the words are only attributed to an unnamed someone. In one way, this could suggest how easily Shakespeare disappears when enveloped in the powerful embrace of popular song. Yet this moment also indicates how Shakespearean quotations can now be seen as having the power of popular, proverbial meaning, confirming his status as some universally appealing and understood figure who barely needs naming. In turn, perhaps this overly casual displacement occurs precisely because of the extent of Shakespeare's range and appeal: though popular, would The King singing someone else's words ever be bigger than The Bard, who 'never blotted out a line', to the disdain of his contemporary, Ben Jonson (1640, 394)? In his later Vegas years, Elvis diminished the words' and wordsmith's import further, saying the lines in a hammy mock sob, and ad-libbing for comic effect. Again though, as he used such moments to comment on the state of his own career, this may have been to cover his insecurities about the stages *he* was now playing in a sheen, if not a sequinned jumpsuit, of irony. Even artists who enjoy critical acclaim for the quality of their work confess their inability to express in comparison with Shakespeare. A song on a 2005 Burt Bacharach album ponders the big issues of life and love, but has a title and hook that can only confess unknowing: 'Go Ask Shakespeare'. This situates Shakespeare as an existential as well as a cultural authority, to whom popular musicians should defer.

Yet though Shakespeare emerges as someone or something to revere or respect, he and his texts also generate a compulsion to resist or reject. On the single 'Let's Hear It for the Boy', Deniece Williams seems unconcerned that her lover can't sing, dresses badly and isn't rich: the fact that he's no Romeo won't stop her indulging in expressive 'whoas' to show how deeply he moves her. And when musicians are still respectful, not all interactions between Shakespeare and popular music are hierarchical or deferential. The 2002 album *When Love Speaks* made this point in several ways. In addition to recitals of specific sonnets by notable British actors, the album features various artists' musical versions of Shakespearean verse. The album's title suggests that the musical and the spoken sonnets all speak the same, on the same theme, and emanate from the same source, diverse as their modern forms may seem. In other words, expressive emotion becomes synonymous with Shakespeare himself: when love speaks, so does *he*, and his words are endlessly updatable, endlessly translatable, in infinite genres and styles. But is the love Shakespeare articulated made to speak only via his technological and musical updating? Several performances on the album invite this question. Keb' Mo' set Sonnet 35 ('No more be grieved') to a slow R 'n' B groove, complete with slide guitar (comparable to a human cry), and synthesizer swashes sounding like a choir. Do these voice-like textures, circling the sung lines, compete with or complement the seemingly personal mode of the sonnet? Does the presence of such sounds compensate for or emphasize Shakespeare's absence (or the lover's)? Who, to appropriate the poem's lexicon, is the 'accessory' to whom here? These questions are not easy to answer, and are made more difficult because the track and the poem are themselves so unsettled. The song has a regular 4/4 time but this groove is disrupted by an irregular snare beat. This may cause a disjunction between the generally iambic rhythm of the poem and the stilted tempo of the song, or that stilted tempo might amplify those moments in the poem when the iambic rhythm is strained (lines 6 and 13, for example). Put differently, maybe this disjunction is itself expressive, because it suits this sonnet, obsessed as it is with internal tensions ('civil war'). In the poem, these tensions derive from the speaker's diverse needs: to reconcile themselves to some misdemeanour by the object of their affection, the 'sweet thief' that 'sourly robs'; to then reconcile themselves to that object; and then to reconcile 'sense' and 'sensual fault', 'love' and 'hate'. Yet when updated as a song, the tensions are as much between Shakespeare's poem and its modern reproducer as they are between Shakespeare's persona and their false beloved.

Another track on the album voices comparable issues. Backed by a gossamer-light string section, Bryan Ferry's version of Sonnet 18 ('Shall I compare thee') is almost self-parodic in its characteristically intimate, close-miked, breathy delivery. This breathiness is entirely appropriate for the poem, as its closing couplet suggests:

So long as men can breathe or eyes can see,
So long lives this, and this gives life to thee.

Ferry's performance merely validates Shakespeare's predictions about the longevity of his verse. Yet seen or heard another way, Ferry's breathy take ambiguously breathes life into Shakespeare. The ambiguity centres on 'this', in the final line. When *read*, this line encapsulates how the *sonnet* evokes the speaker's sense of powerlessness in the face of mutability, and the reality that the addressee will also die and decay, with the only means of survival coming through biological or textual reproduction (the 'this' is the life-giving but self-privileging poem). When *sung* by Ferry, this interpretation remains, but is joined by another: 'this' *performance* gives life to what these words express. The poem privileges its own ability to give 'life'; so does the song, but the addressee alters. The figure surviving in song is not a young man, but Shakespeare himself, who has 'life' only through such modern reproductions.

Evidently, the tensions between (and within) Shakespeare's words and his modern musical adaptations can produce new interpretations. Sometimes these tensions with transposing Shakespeare begin as simply technical, but become more profound, as Christopher Wilson noted in the 1920s:

> Personally, I think that no sonnet ought to be set to music, but I know that quite good musical authorities differ from me, and I am content to say that either the whole sonnet or none of it must be set. It is impossible to cut a word or a sentence out of a sonnet without spoiling its form and balance; and, if these essentials are gone, how can it make a perfect song? (1922, 166)

This is not an argument against merging Shakespearean verse and music, but against doing so in ways that compromise the apparent integrity of both. More recent composers have been less concerned with this integrity, for very good reasons. When John Boden, a musician working in the English folk tradition, embarked on providing a score for a production of *As You Like It*, he found the rhyme scheme of the songs 'frustrating', and as a result 'changed the words quite a lot'. In later adaptations, Boden learned to 'work ways around the awkwardness', and 'edit out an additional syllable'. The result, though, meant this was not a more or less pure Shakespeare (since the texts themselves show the hands of so many compositors or editors), but a *new* Shakespeare: the 'melody you write is always different to the one in Shakespeare's head'. As a consequence, Boden moved from frustration with some model of an authentic but unattainable Shakespeare to an engagement with potential Shakespeares, and he observes that the 'clashes' between his music and Shakespeare's words, are 'genuinely more interesting' as a result (2009).

These examples – and others to follow in this book – suggest that a range of popular music artists and works, and commentators on these, display perceived continuities and discontinuities with a diverse and contradictory range of figurings of Shakespeare: as popular or commercial artist, as source of decontextualized or universal proverbs, or as '"proper" art promoted by official educational and cultural institutions' (Lanier, 2007, 99).

STUDYING SHAKESPEARE WITH POPULAR MUSIC

But such institutions change and have changed. As a result, scholars have begun to develop different ways of thinking about how Shakespeare has been located in popular music (and vice versa). Some have described the 'interactive reception of a work by Shakespeare' as a form of jazz (Bristol, 1996, 23). Terence Hawkes has offered the most sustained and suggestive exploration of this idea. In *That Shakespeherian Rag*, Hawkes notes that 'blues and jazz' reach out to and invade a 'listener's being', as 'the player, music and audience' become 'simultaneously part of the same momentary whole' in which 'the boundaries of meanings' loosen. For Hawkes, many moments in Shakespeare do something similar, as the 'play-text reaches out and draws us irresistibly towards itself and the *jouissance* or *jazz* . . . which it promises', meaning we experience a blissful, almost orgasmic pleasure in what he and we get up to with words (1986, 88–89). Developing this notion, Hawkes makes jazz his 'abstract model' for potentially subversive interpretations and appropriations, whereby 'interpretation *constitutes* the art' not only of the 'jazz musician', or the critic, reader or performer, but also of Shakespeare (1986, 117–18). In *Shakespeare in the Present*, Hawkes returns to this model of critical play straying from textual certainty. He explores how any 'creative "departure"' from a Shakespearean play text in performance or interpretation is a 'deformation' comparable to the way jazz musicians '"deform" written-down musical notes . . . or even play their instruments 'wrongly' in order to produce unexpected, literally unheard-of, effects'. Hawkes suggests this 'rhapsodic, jazzy' way of reworking music and texts offers an agenda for future non-traditional approaches to Shakespeare, including those perhaps which relate him to popular music (2002, 112, 126).

Following Hawkes's lead, other critics have approached Shakespeare's relations with popular music by focusing on constructions of gender and 'race'. For example, Stephen M. Buhler has traced the contexts and developments of what popular music has done with *Romeo and Juliet*. Peggy Lee's 1958 version of 'Fever' synthesized new lyrics, 1950s slang and an 'entertaining approximation of Elizabethan language' to evoke Romeo and Juliet's passions, revivifying the dynamic of the pair's relations: 'While the focus remains on Romeo, his ardor is reciprocated by Juliet'. The song's 'sparse' arrangement only intensifies the lyrics and the emotions they describe (2002, 248–49). As Buhler notes, however, though this revivification might have cast Shakespeare in contemporary terms, it was culturally and musically specific: inspired by the success of *West Side Story* (which opened in 1957) and conscious of racially and generationally segregated consumers, Lee had adapted, marketed and subsequently 'crossed over' a pre-existing rhythm-and-blues song for white audiences, teenage and adult (2002, 248–49).

Buhler goes on to suggest that musicals such as *West Side Story* and other youth-oriented adaptations of *Romeo and Juliet* like Franco Zeffirelli's 1968 film version have also had an impact on later artists' engagements with Shakespeare. This is evident in Bruce Springsteen's 'Incident on 57th Street' and 'Point Blank', Tom Waits's 'Romeo is Bleeding', Lou Reed's 'Romeo had Juliette', and Dire Straits' 'Romeo and Juliet'. As Buhler explains, all these tracks offer spirited and nuanced engagements with Shakespeare, with the commodification of modern popular music and media, and with constructs of romantic love, gender and the 'individual' (2002, 252–62). Some artists, like Bob Dylan, have returned to Romeo and Juliet throughout their careers, imagining and giving voice to the hero in 'Desolation Row', but only according Juliet comparable significance and expressiveness in later work such as 'Floater (Too Much to Ask)'.

Dylan's shift in emphasis from Romeo to Juliet reflects other changes. As women have found a more prominent place in the developing cultures of rock and pop, female performers and singer-songwriters (rather than the men listed above) have covered or created Shakespearean songs to realize different connotations. For Buhler, one notable example of female rewriting of male rockers' and Shakespearean identities comes with The Indigo Girls' version of Dire Straits' song on their album *Rites of Passage*, which presents 'feminist and same-sex recodings of one of the defining narratives of heterosexual romance' (2007, 157–58). The Indigo Girls have also notably re-presented Ophelia: on 'Touch Me Fall', a track on their album *Swamp Ophelia*, the band relocate Ophelia geographically to America's turbid and alluvial Deep South, and reinforce this relocation musically. As the lead vocal 'swims amid rich layerings of electric guitars', any passivity ascribed to the play's Ophelia, or 'vulnerability' in the lyrics, is 'offset by . . . sonic aggression' (Buhler, 2007, 167–68). Again, these re-presentations, like those of Natalie Merchant in her song 'Ophelia', might in part be considered a response to the figure reconstructed by a male singer-songwriter, in whose songs the drowned female appears all too often as a 'frustrated songstress . . . unable to give voice to her desires' (Buhler, 2007, 166).[3] In contrast, all *these* songs feature strong female voices, and, in the case of Merchant's 'Ophelia', voices in languages other than English: though still constrained and conditioned by marketing, women's expression in popular music is now irrepressible.

We might modify Buhler's catalogue to hear this elsewhere. In 'A Case of You', Joni Mitchell's narrator echoes Caesar's words from 3.1.60 of *Julius Caesar*:

Just before our love got lost you said,
'I am as constant as a Northern star',
And I said, 'Constantly in the darkness, where's that at?'

In the lines this passage evokes, Caesar arrogantly explains (and justifies) his isolation, permanence and power. Yet as the words slip from a Shakespearean register to a 1960s hipster tone, they prick this masculine arrogance, as they also point out the pain caused by it. To be powerfully remote and removed is to be in the dark about emotions and the effect one has on others. And just as Caesar is felled so this love, and this lover, are rejected, though not without conflict.

If gender doesn't figure in *Shakespeare and Popular Music* as prominently as it has in other recent studies, it is not because that issue isn't important (it is), or because this book ignores it (it doesn't), but because work like Buhler's treats the topic so well. This much is hopefully conveyed by this book's cover, which shows Kathy Kiera Clarke as Ophelia in Conall Morrison's 2005 production of *Hamlet* for the Peacock/Abbey Theatre (Dublin) and the Lyric Theatre (Belfast). In her despair at her father's murder and Hamlet's contempt, Ophelia did not act like a wistful Celtic or indeed Elizabethan maiden. Instead she wheeled on stage and sat bow-legged at a DIY souped-up synthesizer, from which she conjured dissonant soundscapes. This was an anti-lyrical Ophelia, a distraught young woman attuned to the white noise of the computer age, not lilting madrigals. Clarke held this sexualized, traumatized pose for long enough to induce palpable and comparable unease in the audience, all the while making a sound that both reproduced and shattered the conventions of popular music and Shakespeare on stage. In ways different to the model of female expression Buhler identifies, such stagings, and the use of music in them, evoke the strains of technological and existential decay, giving Ophelia's and women's pains new voices and locations, though no words are spoken.

By developing Buhler's insights though, we can see that as mainstream rock has become more accepting of different genders (if not completely), so it has become more open about the different sexualities of performers and audiences. Sometimes this has informed the way musicians approach Shakespeare. Rufus Wainwright's version of Sonnet 29 ('When, in disgrace'), on *When Love Speaks* begins in a low vocal tone, with the singer-persona bemoaning his isolation from men, and confessing his unrequited desires to be as empowered as other men are. Yet with each four lines Wainwright's voice ascends in pitch, 'like to the lark', consummating the song and the sonnet with acoustic and verbal 'wealth', as a lament for 'him' becomes the 'hymns at heaven's gate' of love. Wainwright is aptly cast here. Redoubtable vocal talents notwithstanding, as a prominent gay performer he possesses the authority to make his rendition of this sonnet credible. Likewise, Wainwright expressed his musical fluency, and his perception of the fluidity of gendered, sexual and Shakespearean roles, by casting Jeff Buckley as an Ophelia figure in his song 'Memphis Skyline'. Unsurprisingly, Wainwright's suitability as a combiner of Shakespeare and popular music found other outlets that allowed him to challenge perceptions of gender, sexuality and popular song. In 2009, he collaborated with the director Robert Wilson and Bertholt Brecht's Berliner Ensemble, providing musical accompaniment to a cross-dressing staging of the Sonnets. This incorporated *minnesang* in the style of medieval German courtly lovers, arrangements inspired by Brecht and Kurt Weill, and modern textures on electric guitar. As the example of Buhler suggests, Shakespearean scholarship has a role to play in identifying such syntheses, and in contextualizing what motivates or informs them.

STUDYING POPULAR MUSIC WITH SHAKESPEARE

Since Shakespeare scholars now explore the cultural politics of their subject and the contexts of his ongoing appropriation through popular music, this has worked both ways, as academic and non-academic commentators on popular music resort to Shakespearean allusion to describe their subjects. Sometimes this means giving lyrics a Shakespearean gloss, even when no allusion is evident, and even when the boldness of the claim is muted by a writer admitting the incongruity of the connection:

[I]n my discussion of [Elvis Costello's] 'No Dancing', from *My Aim is True*, I come close to claiming that the narrator . . . means something not very far removed from King Lear's 'when we are born, we cry, that we are come to this great stage of fools'. No one in their right mind would claim that Costello comes within a million miles of matching the significance of Shakespeare's lines *on paper*, but listen to the way he sings his line and it's a completely different matter. (Gouldstone, 1989, ix)

Such insights only partly re-enshrine Shakespeare as incomparable poet. Other commentators on popular music are less diffident about elevating popular musicians through Shakespearean analogy. Alongside substantial citations of William Blake, Robert Browning, John Keats and Alfred Lord Tennyson, the index to Christopher Ricks's 2003 study of Bob Dylan contains around 42 direct references to Shakespeare, more or less equal with T. S. Eliot, and bested only by the Bible (around 50 references). Ricks records many instances of semantic and acoustic continuities between Shakespeare and Dylan. In 'Country Pie' (112), he hears echoes of Hamlet's ribald riffing on 'country matters' (3.2.111). He detects 'overlaps' between 'On a Night Like This' and its possible 'source or analogue', the exchanges between Lorenzo and Jessica in *The Merchant of Venice*, 5.1. (164–66). He relocates the 'exacerbated sexuality' in the opening of *Richard III* to 'Seven Curses' (236). He listens for echoes of Polonius's maxims from *Hamlet* in 'the ammunition of the Maxim gun that is *Subterranean Homesick Blues*' (253). He perceives how the refrain from Feste's closing song from *Twelfth Night*, 'the rain it raineth every day', mutates 'to rain, to *A Hard Rain's A-Gonna Fall*' (329). And he suggests that '*Give me*, the swell of the Duke [in the opening lines of *Twelfth Night*], gets informally urgent as *gimme* [in *Planet Waves*' 'You Angel You']' (401). Other (literary) critics do something similar (Corcoran, 2002).

Ricks consolidates the intensity of the interplay he proposes by suggesting that Dylan's and Shakespeare's works share comparable means of production and consumption: '[Dylan's] life is *his* business; his art is something else, not being business but a vocation, even while – like Shakespeare's – it earns his living' (149). All this emphasizes Dylan's position in a literary tradition, affirming his status as a poet (and the critic as critic) despite or because of his popularity as a musician:

> *Not Dark Yet* stands to Keats's *Ode* [to a Nightingale] very much as Keats's *Ode*, in its turn, stood to Shakespeare's Sonnet 73. . . . The continuity and community of the poets constitute a success that is a succession. (367)

But Ricks' use of Shakespeare in relation to Dylan operates in more complex ways. The tone for this complexity is set from the start, as Ricks compares interpreting Dylan's work with William Empson's 'spirited dealings' with a Shakespeare sonnet (1). Ricks consistently uses emotive, sensual verbs to describe the experience of comprehending Dylan. He tells us how an image 'feels to me'; what a lyric 'might be felt to figure'; he admits his speculation on a Shakespearean link might be far-fetched, but it 'sure feels right'; and he reveals how he has been able 'to see and hear' meanings (371, 88, 166, 304). It is as though Ricks is trying to recuperate a special form of subjectivity for the modern critical process, an *association* of 'sensibility' counteracting the 'dissociation' so infamously identified by T. S. Eliot, whereby poetic appreciation is redeemed to become not just cerebral but visceral, not just 'thought' but emotion, spirit and 'experience' (1921, 64). Shakespeare, as much as Eliot or even Dylan, is central to this project. So intense and immediate are the literary, experiential and emotional continuities in Ricks's readings that it becomes difficult to work out who signifies what to whom when:

> The *meaning* of Dylan's music of joy and sorrow? 'I would suggest', T.S. Eliot said, 'that none of the plays of Shakespeare has a "meaning", though it would be equally false to say that a play of Shakespeare is meaningless.' (336)

Is this Ricks on Dylan, or Eliot on Shakespeare, or Ricks on Eliot on Shakespeare, or Ricks on Eliot on Shakespeare on Dylan? Who has chronological or cultural priority here, and who or what is privileged? Poet, playwright, critic, editor, singer, fan, past or present, thought or emotion? Semantic and acoustic relations cause temporal disruption as much as a sense of literary 'continuity and community': Shakespeare becomes 'Dylanesque', *not* vice versa (60). These continuities envelop the reader of Shakespeare as well as the listener to Dylan, and by attending to Dylan, Ricks implies how we might hear Shakespeare anew.

Some Shakespearean pedagogy has ventured to contrive comparable continuities, with numerous projects seeking to integrate Shakespeare and popular music, 'breathe life' into the Bard, as some musicians have, and thereby insist on the vitality of his work (Ko, 2006, 3). Yet in contrast to critics like Ricks, some pedagogy has also employed popular music to more discontinuous and unsettling ends. Cynthia Marshall reasoned her students required an 'expanded sense of context' to comprehend the ideological constructs of romance, gender and sexuality in *Romeo and Juliet*. To attain this she 'turned to the conscious artifice of early rock and roll'. Rock of the 1950s and 60s 'mystifies heterosexual coupling' in the same way as, and offers 'striking congruencies' with, the play. But rather than using such music to establish a strained connection between past and present, Shakespeare and pop, or insist upon the timeless 'relevance' of the play texts, Marshall sought to defamiliarize students' experience of a very familiar play, by encouraging them to deconstruct such 'stylized', and now old-fashioned, music: 'an earlier era's songs are revealed by time to be conventional period pieces that are anything but simple expressions of truth'. In other words, students became able to detect the culturally specific ideological and rhetorical values evident in the play, by hearing them in now old-fashioned popular music. In actuality, then, through this 'radical form of intertextuality', pop music is not used to make Shakespeare our contemporary, but to help historicize him, emphasizing the distance of his world from ours (2000, 98–107).

All these examples suggest that scholarship and education have begun to locate Shakespeare in popular music, and have historicized and helped define both in the process. Yet sometimes this locating can disrupt our sense of historical and cultural chronology. As the next chapter will consider, other historically specific institutions and formations exhibit similar effects and ambiguities, especially technology: what role has *this* played in the relationship between Shakespeare and popular music?

NOTES

1 *The Tempest*, 1.2.390.
2 See the seminal discussions in Patterson, 1989; and Levine, 1988.
3 As Folkerth observes (2006, 372), other examples of Ophelia-referencing male songwriters include The Grateful Dead with 'Althea', and Peter Hammill with 'Ophelia'.

CHAPTER 3

SHAKESPEARE AND THE TECHNOLOGIES OF POP

This chapter argues that modern experiences of Shakespeare have been profoundly affected by the technological developments that make the present so different from the past. We have heard a prelude of this argument in the idea that early modern soundscapes were unlike our own, and in the discussions of artists like Keb' Mo', whose processed vocal textures both sustain and supplant Shakespeare's words. And just as previous chapters have begun to show how Shakespeare has been written into the history of popular music, and has been rewritten by such music, so this chapter suggests he has also been implicated – for better or worse – in technological developments. Technological developments *also* made modern popular music possible: technology is a '"mode" of music production and consumption . . . a precondition for music-making' (Théberge, 2004, 3). Understanding Shakespeare's relations with popular music therefore involves considering his relations with its technologies. As Alan Galey and Ray Siemens note: 'New media frequently stage encounters with old media, and with surprising frequency Shakespeare supplies the script' (2008, 201). This chapter considers these relations, and then pays close attention to Baz Luhrmann's 1996 film *William Shakespeare's Romeo + Juliet*, as a way to see their effects in action.

TECHNOLOGY, IDEOLOGY AND MASS CULTURE

To some theorists, any interaction between Shakespeare and the techno-logies of popular culture could only obscure and damage his significance. For Adorno, as we've heard, mass culture turned high cultural forms into commodities, and so debased those forms, depleting their seriousness. In turn, popular music's allusions to and quotations from high cultural forms were only ever infantile mimicry, repackaging art for child-like minds. Quotations, ranging from 'ambiguous and half accidental allu-sions' to 'completely latent similarities', were part of the 'regressive

musical language' of music popularized by the technologies of commercial media (1938, 308). In this regard, a lyric in a popular song that
cited Shakespeare, who was to Adorno one of the 'greatest artists of the
beginning of the [bourgeois] epoch', would have been beneath contempt
(1955/1967, 627). Adorno himself connects the forms and technologies
of popular music that debased 'serious' music, and popular culture that
debased high art like Shakespeare:

> There is the revealing joke about elderly ladies who express delight
> in *Hamlet* with the single reservation that it consists of quotations.
> In the realm of music radio has realized a similar tendency and has
> transformed Beethoven's Fifth Symphony into a set of quotations
> from theme songs. (1941b, 263)

What Adorno would elsewhere term ' "*light*" music', meaning 'commercial art and song', greedily absorbed 'as much from above as is accessible
to it', subjecting higher forms to diabolic degeneration into 'the bottom-
less underworld far beyond the bourgeois "hit song" ' (1932, 425). Art
disintegrates in these conditions. The commoditized, fragmentary quote
is the music. But other theorists, such as Walter Benjamin, would suggest
that this technological reproduction of high art might empower – and
change – audiences, transforming us from being consumers to being
re-creators. Such re-creators might engage with art cheaply, on a large
scale, democratically, progressively and actively, rather than in the passive
service of some stultifying respect for the past and its authorities:

> One might generalize by saying: the technique of reproduction
> detaches the reproduced object from the domain of tradition. By
> making many reproductions it substitutes a plurality of copies for a
> unique existence. And in permitting the reproduction to meet the
> beholder or listener in his own particular situation, it reactivates
> the object produced. These two processes lead to a tremendous
> shattering of tradition. (1936, 215)

Adorno could not agree.[1] Popular consumers weren't sufficiently critical,
and popular culture wouldn't make them so. Quoting and reproducing a
high artist in popular, commercial mass media, was 'at once authoritarian and a parody' (1938, 308). Parody might diminish masterpieces, but,
ultimately, parody preserves deference: 'It is thus that a child imitates
the teacher' (1938, 308). We are supposed to respect the master and their

work, even as that work and its maker are brought low. So for Adorno, the technological quotation of a figure like Shakespeare is part of the way commercial music caused social control, and this control is total. Because we endure 'the absolute predominance of the economy' we only experience life in damaged or mutilated forms (1951, 58). There is no escape: we can't think, do or be beyond this mental and material space already occupied by exploitation, technology, commerce and capital:

> What the philosophers once knew as life has become the sphere of private existence and now of mere consumption, dragged along as an appendage of the process of material production, without autonomy or substance of its own. (1951, 15)

Rather than offering release from these conditions, popular music brings the coercive technologies and practices of capitalism ever closer. When we consume such music, we are given the illusion of power in choosing, and of choosing something worthwhile, personally significant or culturally valuable. But this is a (self-)deception: 'The consumer is really worshipping the money that he himself has paid for the ticket to the Toscanini concert' (1938, 296). If we were to listen and look more closely, we'd see and hear this, says Adorno. And if we did so, we'd understand how far what is echoed or reflected back to us is from *un*damaged life. Technology confirmed this. The sound of a disc is an ersatz echo, and the sheen of the vinyl or shellac is a beguiling mirror: 'people cling to what mocks them in confirming their mutilation of their essence by the smoothness of its own appearance' (1951, 147). The cultural, intellectual and ethical void that is popular music is 'only filled by the hearer' (1927/1965, 275). This does not mean, as Benjamin suggested, that we have the will and authority to generate our own meanings. On the contrary, like the dog on the record label, Adorno recognizes we are attuned only to our '*master's voice*', which, in our bestial ignorance and technological subjection, we mistake for our own: 'What the gramophone listener actually wants to hear is himself . . . Most of the time records are virtual photographs of their owners, flattering photographs – ideologies' (1927/1965, 274).

'THE GHOST IN THE MACHINE'

Adorno is characteristically strident on these matters. Yet there are other suggestive ways to attend to what the technology of pop does to someone like Shakespeare, and what someone like Shakespeare does to such technology. As Folkerth relates, one of the earliest known sound recordings of Shakespeare occurred in London, in 1888, only 11 years after Thomas Edison had first demonstrated his phonographic device for writing sound onto wax cylinders, to be played back as and when listeners chose: this was still unsettlingly new technology.[2] The recording occurred when George E. Gourard – 'Thomas Edison's representative in London' – visited his friend, the renowned Shakespearean actor, Henry Irving. Gourard recorded Irving delivering the opening of *Richard III*, parts of *Henry VIII*, 'and other roles he was famous for playing'. The recording captured Irving's 'idiosyncratic vocal mannerisms', his 'nasal' tone, and his '"naturalistic" style of speaking the verse'. This mechanical reproduction would consolidate how Irving's delivery 'altered the way Shakespeare's verse was spoken in the theatre' and 'changed the way we hear the plays today'. But, as Irving realized, as Gourard learned and as Folkerth reveals, on playback these were not the immediate effects: 'Is that my voice? My God!', said Irving, with 'horrified fascination'. As with the wider population, Irving would become accustomed to recording and recordings; yet Folkerth explicates Irving's initial unease: 'The talking machine immediately alienates him from his own voice, a personal attribute and artistic tool very closely tied to his sense of professional identity' (2002b, 1–3). Folkerth records an interaction between Shakespeare's words and the technology that would revolutionize how popular music was made and consumed. But why did Gourard ask Irving to read *Shakespeare* into the new technology, and what are the implications for Shakespeare's relationship with the popular music communicated through such technologies? Of course, speaking Shakespeare was what Irving was famous for, and his inimitable delivery would consolidate the technology's uncanny power – Gourard wouldn't want or have to miss a trick. But the conjunction of phonography and dramaturgy served another purpose, that of reducing the potential alienation Irving himself experienced and confessed. Just as the very name for the new technology – phonography – made reassuring connections between newer and older systems of expression, oral and written modes, and Ancient Greek and modern English, so in this instance, and after, Shakespeare is used as something recognisable in an alien context. Thus Shakespeare sometimes serves as a way to accommodate other listeners to the potentially alienating sources and effects of popular music, not least its technologies.

Sometimes, but not always. Shakespearean allusions haunt Evan Eisenberg's idiosyncratic and ingenious account of the powerful effects and experiences of power transmitted through recordings of popular music. At times, Eisenberg employs these allusions to suggest these powers are greater than anything Shakespeare could have staged. For example, Eisenberg casts Othello as the original bluesman, yet somewhat idealistically notes that phonographic technology gave voice to identities in ways and contexts Shakespeare could not:

> On records the black musician was no longer a minstrel with shining eyeballs, but simply a musician. . . . And that is just how the black sensibility did – to a degree – conquer America. (1987, 89–90)

However, Eisenberg's allusions more typically locate Shakespeare in mass experiences of the technologies of popular music:

> We have all become like Prospero, able to conjure up invisible musicians who sing and play at our pleasure. . . . Prospero's magic makes Ariel make music, which in turn (like an incantation) works magic on Caliban and the Mantuan castaways. We make magic when we work the phonograph, causing spirits to make music. (55, 59–60)

That said, and remembering Eisenberg's comments on Othello, the continuities between Shakespearean motifs and modern modes are imperfect: 'Unlike Prospero, we cannot see the spirits we summon, and that makes things a little spooky' (56).

So do these allusions make new technologies and the new experiences they create more familiar, or ever stranger? Describing T. S. Eliot's echoes of *The Tempest* in *The Wasteland* as a gramophone is played, Eisenberg warns: 'The phonograph reassures, but spuriously' (95–96). And so the echoes continue their equivocal effects. Caught up in Shakespearean and recorded sounds, Eisenberg's allusions proliferate, the stranger the experience he describes:

> The record listener and the musician – . . . like a man and his familiar ghost – do not inhabit the same world. This is the premise of their intimacy. And their intimacy is only closer when the ghost is heard but not seen. . . . But then the ghost has power over the man – as Hamlet's ghost has when, having gone underground, he cries 'Swear!' As Ariel has when, singing 'full fathoms [sic] five thy father lies,' he leads Ferdinand by the nose. 'This is no mortal

business, nor no sound/That the earth owes. I hear it now above me,'
says Ferdinand. Above, beneath, somewhere, but not in this world.
. . . 'Is it not strange,' asks Benedick on hearing the fiddler, 'that
sheeps' guts should hale souls out of men's bodies?' (57–58, 227)

If Shakespeare prefigured the strangeness of experiencing modern
popular music, he also helps us make sense of that experience. But if
this makes a connection between Shakespeare and popular music, it
is one in which Shakespeare's words are as eerie and uncanny as the
experiences those words describe. To Galey and Siemens, 'recording
technology and the Shakespeare text serve . . . to invest each other
with authority'. But in their mutual 'intimacy' and alienation from each
other, their simultaneous continuity and discontinuity, Shakespeare
proves the strangeness of pop's technologies, as pop makes Shakespeare
strange too, a 'ghost in the machine' (2008, 202).

WILLIAM SHAKESPEARE'S ROMEO + JULIET

As this discussion of phonography suggests, some technologies have
manifested these ambiguities more obviously than others. And the development of other, newer technologies means this process is progressing in
new ways. Through the twentieth century, as audiovisual technologies
evolved alongside, determined and were driven by changes in popular
music production and consumption, these continuities and discontinuities between Shakespeare and popular music have been amplified.

As Ian Inglis has argued, film and popular music have 'separate
historical trajectories' but also 'substantial and significant similarities',
based on their development of nineteenth-century 'technological innova-
tions', their dependence on 'a new kind of mass audience', their transition
from 'novelty beginnings' to 'major international industries', and their
'artistic affinities'. Music videos have only increased these affinities and
the 'complications' for separating film and music (2003, 1, 3). Mindful
of these developments, Luhrmann's *William Shakespeare's Romeo +
Juliet* offers a particularly intense and reflexive take on the audiovisual
technologies of Shakespearean allusion, citation and remediatization,
and on the interactions between 'high' and 'popular' cultural forms.[3]
This reflexivity also includes the film's use of music: it presents synergies between Shakespeare and popular music, and film and other visual
and musical formats. As Burt has noted, MTV screened a 1996 special

on Luhrmann's film, and the film's editing is 'MTV-inflected' (1998, 5). So was its marketing: the film spawned two albums of related and featured music (released in 1996 and 1997), and a special 2002 edition of the DVD includes two music videos. Sanders suggests that the content of these albums reinforced the idea that 'classical' modes (of music, or drama) could coexist with modern, popular forms. The first album featured commercial popular songs compiled, produced or commissioned by Nellee Hooper; the second contained Wagner, and Craig Armstrong's classical pieces for the film:

> Sometimes these orchestral arrangements were of the same 'pop' songs that featured in the first volume, thereby creating an effect of developmental refrain even within the CD format. (2007, 168)

Armstrong's orchestral score runs almost throughout, abating most notably in the protagonists' death scene (even there, after a moment's silence, a deep cello drone intrudes). If this mixture of modes was pervasive, the conjunction of Shakespeare and popular music Luhrmann orchestrated proved contagious. Ash's song 'Starcrossed' not only included lyrical references to the play, but was marketed with a video that reproduced visual motifs from the film, including the band performing inside a church.

However, these audiovisual synergies, and the connections between Shakespeare and popular music, are at once tested and confirmed in the film. Popular music performs a disjunctive role for Luhrmann that punctuates the orchestral backdrop, by providing the only non-Shakespearean language, and by intensifying and ironizing events. In the film's opening scenes, popular music evokes the soundscape of Verona Beach, as a multicultural, postmodern, media-saturated, urban environment. The Montague youth cruise on to booming hip-hop, boisterous, brash, and full of front (these are skinny white boys appropriating African-American modes), while the Capulets swagger to Tex-Mex flourishes, suiting their Latino sartorial and cultural inflections. Popular music is crudely mimetic here then, consolidating the divisions of the city-space and characters' identities. This mimetic function is sustained when we encounter Romeo for the first time, alone at Sycamore Grove. The wiry, spare and sparse guitar lines, the distorted percussion, and the angular juxtaposition of electronic and 'traditional' instruments in Radiohead's song 'Talk Show Host' soundtrack the hero's emotional alienation and restlessness. This is anguished music of the most juvenile kind, befitting the hero's introspective attempts at articulation, as he writes in his journal.

But the connections between Shakespeare and music, and character, space and song, both climax and come undone at the Capulets' party, not least with the remixed and updated version of Candi Staton's 1976 disco classic 'Young Hearts Run Free' sung on the soundtrack by Kym Mazelle and exuberantly performed by Mercutio (played by Harold Perinneau) in the film. On one level, Mercutio's performance of the song, in drag, on stairs, flanked by dancers, reaffirms the music video aesthetic 'in quickly paced zooms, zips and pans' (Burt, 1998, 159). In turn, this aligns Shakespeare, film and popular music in powerful ways. But why should Mercutio perform in drag an updated disco song remixed as a house track, and in what ways does the performance problematize the synergies Luhrmann elsewhere seeks to create? To answer this question, and explore Shakespeare's relation to the technological reproduction of popular music in more detail, it is necessary to offer some context for the song and its performance.

'THE LIFE AND DEATH OF THE DISCO' (JARMAN, 1992, 217): TRAGEDY, ECSTASY, REPETITION

Disco began in the early 1970s in US clubs as a 'meeting between gay and black cultures around the erotic centrality of the dancing body' (Chambers, 1985, 188–89). As such its connections represented a hedonistic and utopian response to racist and sexist repression. The club cultures generated by disco had – and *have* – the capacity to unsettle normative social and personal identities. Mercutio's performance makes these capacities and connections clear, not least *because* this disco hit has been remixed. Later remixing didn't just revive the musical forms of disco, but also revivified some of the aspirations of those forms' contexts, 'notions of community, love and hope' (Rietveld, 1998, 6). As Simon Reynolds suggests, disco returned as house, (re)born in depressed post-industrial cities like Chicago 'of a double exclusion . . . not just black, but gay and black'. By resurrecting and then technologically mutating disco, house celebrated its 'cultural dissidence', by 'embracing a music that the majority culture deemed dead and buried' (1998, 15).

Some of this sexual and social dissidence is captured in Mercutio's 'transvestitism', which has in part been interpreted as 'a consequence of Romeo's diminished capacity, his drug-induced hallucination' (Burt,

1998, 160). True enough, the editing of the scene creates a woozy sensation, and prior to the party Romeo takes a pill provided by Mercutio during the Queen Mab speech in 1.4, a pill whose form and effects approximate the 1990s' clubber's drug of choice, Ecstasy or MDMA. But Ecstasy offers only a 'mildly trippy, pre-hallucinogenic feel' (Reynolds, 1998, xxv). So though its hallucinogenic properties are limited, it has other effects as an empathogen and an entactogen, letting people *feel* more, physically and emotionally. When these effects are intensified by repetitive, trance-inducing and joyful music, it encourages blissful communality, though that bliss may be ephemeral, spurious or fatal. In this context, MDMA becomes a 'remedy for the alienation caused by an atomized society . . . a *social* drug' (Reynolds, 1998, xxii, xxvi). As the 'unmatched form and feature of blown youth', Leonardo DiCaprio's Romeo may be 'blasted with ecstasy', with his 'noble and most sovereign reason' being woefully 'jangled out of tune and harsh', as Ophelia describes Hamlet (3.1.160–64), but this trip is shared, and more than mere fantasy. Fittingly, the repeated grooves of disco and then house, evoked and replayed in the scene, facilitate a 'collective "loss of the subject", in a state . . . of *jouissance*', as unconscious or repressed drives are exuberantly and communally satisfied (Middleton, 1983, 262). As the refrain from Fingers Inc.'s classic 1988 Chicago house tune put it, in a phrase that affirms as much as it wonders (because it is missing a question mark): 'Can You Feel It'.

Because Mercutio's performance is compelling, it distracts the party goers, the camera and the audience from the play's protagonists: in this sense, it is necessary for Romeo and Juliet's union. Yet this distraction is also a displacement. Romeo and Juliet may go on to talk about escaping the identities they have been ascribed ('What's in a name?' muses Juliet, in 2.1), but in his performance Mercutio comes to embody the errant potentials dance music offers seemingly fixed subjects:

> Can Mercutio be read as wholly African-American when, seen from the perspective of Romeo on ecstasy, he lip-synchs a female vocalist's disco hit and crossdresses in white, calling up Ru Paul or possibly even Marilyn Monroe? (Burt, 2002, 207)

This might seem like Mercutio's – and house music's – triumph: he embodies a freedom Romeo and Juliet crave, as his performance dissolves isolated subjectivity: 'It is not clear at all points who is singing or lipsynching' (Burt, 1998, 162). And as one becomes many, the intra- and

interdomestic violence of 'households' in Shakespeare's play also momentarily dissipates into the loved-up empathies of *house* music. This fulfils
Mercutio's promise to remedy the hero's morbid lovesickness earlier
in the play:

ROMEO	Give me a torch. I am not for this ambling;
	Being but heavy, I will bear the light.
MERCUTIO	Nay, gentle Romeo, we must have you dance.
ROMEO	Not I, believe me. You have dancing shoes
	With nimble soles; I have a soul of lead
	So stakes me to the ground I cannot move.
MERCUTIO	You are a lover; borrow Cupid's wings,
	And soar with them above a common bound.
	(1.4.11–18)

If this song and dance are hardly 'peace', of the kind someone convulsed
by rage like Tybalt professes they 'hate', they are more harmonious than
mere 'noise' (1.1.67–72). And this remedy accords with the liberation
house music offers:

> As every clubber knows, to dance is not just to experience music as
> time, it is also to experience time as music, as something marked off
> as more intense, more interesting, more pleasurable than 'real' time.
> (Frith, 1998, 156)

This staging of dance culture evokes those 'oceanic states . . . which the
music is supposed to induce' (Middleton, 2006, 183). Mercutio's tran-
scendent performance therefore preludes Romeo and Juliet's suspension
from *their* time (their repressive context) and space, as they kiss between
floors in a lift, or are repeatedly shown through or floating in liquid.
Carol Chillingham Rutter suggests Juliet's 'element is water (against the
conflagration on the streets)' but this fluid, beatific state saturates all
(2007, 262). This scene in the film also prefigures Romeo and Juliet's
'timeless end' (5.3.162) as signifiers of doomed love in suspended
animation, living on and not, deified and divine, as powerfully as the
still at the film's close, freezing their underwater kiss. That night a DJ
saved their lives, truly.

This reminds us of and prefigures the divine, transcendental, ecstasy-
inducing qualities of music that people in the early modern period feared
and wondered at, and that Shakespeare himself identifies in another
play, signalling a sense of the power and immediacy in music that can

transport an ecstatic soul to heavenly, immortal realms.[4] This much is conveyed by those lines in *Much Ado About Nothing* that so exercised Eisenberg:

BENEDICK   Now, divine air! Now is his soul ravished. Is it not strange that sheep's guts should hale souls out of men's bodies? (2.3.57–59)

And yet the upbeat potentials and states evoked in this scene are haunted by shadows, as Romeo admits:

I fear too early, for my mind misgives
Some consequence yet hanging in the stars
Shall bitterly begin his fearful date
With this night's revels (1.4.106–9)

For all its glitter and dazzle, Luhrmann's reproduction of this scene is similarly fretful, in part because the technologies and cultures of popular music Luhrmann gestures at have often been seen as evoking or enduring loss. Disco and its remixed musical progeny are conscious of mortality, not least because the communities creating and enjoying these musics have been persecuted and have suffered through racism, homophobia and AIDS: 'during its early formative years in the gay clubs, disco encompassed everything from joy to pain' (Walters, 1988, 652). In the dance, ecstasy meets tragedy. The vexations of this increase as 'Young Hearts' plays out. The song's lyrics themselves offer the perspective of someone whose love is long since lost. They are world-weary, even as they celebrate youth. The scene's dramatic ironies are such that what is sung and heard isn't necessarily understood by the characters in the way an audience only too conscious of the characters' fates, or the song's drives, might interpret events. A moment that appears to offer the lovers protection from their times and endorse their desire for each other actually presents a 'nonsynchronization of sound and narrative': what we hear *isn't* what we know we will see in this story (Burt, 1998, 160). Given Mercutio's ultimate demise, and the lovers', the song records a tragic *in*ability to escape: 'Mercutio may opt for divadom but he really has nowhere to go, just as Romeo and Juliet are already bound to their roles and their families from the start' (Burt, 1998, 160). Identity may be negotiable: what *is* in a name, or a gender, or a sexuality? Remixing may revive and recycle, whether the subject is Shakespeare or disco. Yet 'the transvestite voice is at best a DJ, a *poseur* whose claim to authorship is limited to remixing and sampling codes already enunciated by others' (Burt, 1998, 165). And if remixing involves repetition, then repetition is equally problematic. For Freud, something's double, its repetition, was its 'preservation against extinction'; but a double could displace and fragment the original, and so become an 'uncanny harbinger of death' (1919, 356–57). Comparably, as Middleton observes, in music, while the cessation of repetition 'is to die', repetition itself – as the persistent 4/4 beat of disco and house, or as a remix – is 'also a kind of death'; it allows 'renewal' of the source, yet obscures it (2006, 137). As we've heard, Benjamin believed technological reproduction could sustain alternative expressions; but Adorno countered that repetition was no answer to repression. So though disco's doublings and repetitions might fulfil desire, they also betray wants, the deferral of fulfilment: 'house is the beat that can never satisfy or be satisfied . . . the music's a repetition-complex, a symptom of some unstaunchable vacancy of being' (Reynolds, 1990, 178). The ambiguity of this state was famously evoked by the opening lines of *Twelfth Night*, where Duke Orsino both does and does not want to hear a melody, whose haunting repetition both does and does not assuage his ache:

> If music be the food of love, play on,
> Give me excess of it that, surfeiting,
> The appetite may sicken and so die.
> That strain again, it had a dying fall. . . .
> Enough, no more, . . . (1.1.1–7)

In turn, because it is on-screen, this scene from Luhrmann's film itself is only a shadow or echo of an already compromised alternative club culture, whose fulfilments and freedoms are therefore further deferred. Mercutio's performance generates a 'dream world', as immersive and enveloping as a disco or house club, but this world 'does not exist' outside of the club or this scene; community here is 'intense yet ephemeral', as diverse people and desires are accommodated, but the 'house' is limited in ways the characters are barely aware of (Rietveld, 1998, 192, 204). Whatever the future for house's sexual and aesthetic subcultures, the film's music, what it echoes (in Shakespeare, and in disco), and its resonance in the world tragically evoke this:

> Desire is always desire for something which is not yet; in that sense
> it is forward-looking, addressed to the future. But desire is also

about the past and memory, and in that sense it is about going back. Ecstasy pressured by loss. (Dollimore, 2001, 36)

Following this scene, juxtapositions between past and future, story and song, and Shakespeare and popular music, increase the tragically dramatic ironies the characters endure. Just prior to the marriage scene the audience hears the chorus from The Cardigans' 'Love Fool', a song whose lyrics record love at its most obsessive, desperate and uncertain. They might therefore be taken to suggest the protagonists' delusions: Romeo loved and then displaced Rosaline – will he do the same with Juliet? Their love may be intense, but can their families be fooled? After the ceremony, some sweet-voiced and soulful choirboys reinterpret another clubland floor filler, Rozalla's 'Everybody's Free (To Feel Good)'. This may seem to joyously confirm the protagonists' (and 'Everybody's') license to love, realizing redemptive harmonies between vocal house and its roots in gospel. But again this is highly ironic, not least because the rendition's religiosity mutes the original track's energy, and because the performance reinvokes a memory of Mercutio: there is no universal, oceanic manumission here, just limited pleasures. This use of popular music to create dramatic irony is perhaps most intensely realized in the scene where Juliet waits for Romeo, in ignorance of his killing Tybalt, and listens to (or we hear) Stina Nordenstam's 'Little Star'. Our difficulty in establishing whether the song is diegetic or non-diegetic (in the character's ears, or audible to us alone) works to separate Juliet from the audience. The song's whispered, clean and simple vocal line and uncluttered production suggests and demands seclusion, and its gentle melodic lilt perfectly encapsulates and complements Juliet's sense of security in her relationship with Romeo. As a model of dramatic irony, however, it is utterly at odds with what the audience knows of the reality of what has gone on beyond the confines of her bedroom, in the dark, bloody city. The track's title works only to remind us of the fate the 'star-crossed lovers' do not know awaits them, but that is heralded from the play's prefatory chorus. What seems a song of innocence is one of ignorance.

Have we come a long way – too far? – from Shakespeare's text here? Not really. Repetition is built into the structure of the play itself, and our sense of it. Who now doesn't have some feel for what *Romeo and Juliet* is about? Even if you haven't read the play, you'll know the story, or have seen the film, or heard a song that cites it – the story is transmitted through innumerable cultural iterations. Luhrmann makes this blatant: in the film, the prologue is 'already retrospective', reported and reflexively framed on the TV news at the start (Rutter, 2007, 261). Even in Shakespeare's period, this retrospection and repetition was explicit and self-evident. He appropriated from other sources, that themselves appropriated from others: working along with Ovid's *Metamorphoses* (with its story of Pyramus and Thisbe), and William Painter's prose version of the Romeo and Juliet story in *The Palace of Pleasure* (1567), Shakespeare cribbed from Arthur Brooke's *The Tragicall Historye of Romeus and Juliet* (1562), which itself translated Pierre Boaistuau's *Histoires Tragiques* (1559), which remixed Matteo Bandello's 'Romeo e Giulietta' (1554). This process of creative reproduction is internalized within the play in various ways. The Chorus, for example, repeatedly tells us about the painful tragedy we know will happen or has happened. But repetition also accompanies pleasure, most audibly when the lovers converse in kisses and harmonize in the rhyme and lines of a sonnet, completing each other, and each other's words:

> ROMEO Thus from my lips, by thine my sin is purged.
> JULIET Then have my lips the sin that they have took.
> ROMEO Sin from my lips? O trespass sweetly urged!
> Give me my sin again.
> *[He kisses her]*
> JULIET You kiss by th' book. (1.5.106–109)

Freud contended that the 'compulsion to repeat' was evidence of our urge for 'instinctual satisfaction which is immediately pleasurable' and for the mastery of pain; but this compulsion also caused 'unpleasure' because 'it brings to light' past traumas, and 'activities of repressed instinctual impulses' (1920, 290–93). You don't need to agree with him to see and hear comparable compulsions, and the contradictions they evoke, in *Romeo and Juliet* and *Romeo + Juliet*. The uncanny, haunting repetitions sounded in popular music, and by its technological reproductions, can help us experience anew the pleasures and pains, the tragedies and ecstasies, of the intercoursings of words, books, sounds, acts, bodies and desires in Shakespeare's works.

NOTES

1 For one attempt to synthesize Benjamin and Adorno, while maintaining their differences, see Mowitt, 1987.

2 Recent evidence has suggested that a Parisian inventor, Édouard-Léon Scott de Martinville, developed a device called a phonautogram which was used to record, among other things, an excerpt of *Othello* in French. This has been speculatively dated as being made as early as 1857. See Cowen, 2009.

3 See Donaldson, 2002; and Tatspaugh, 2007.

4 See Bicknell, 2009, 5–9; and Finney, 1947.

CHAPTER 4

'SHAKESPEARE WITH A TWIST':
THE BARD, 'RACE', AND POPULAR MUSIC

So far, it will have become clear that we can identify continuities or connections between Shakespeare and popular music. The next two chapters will discuss how some types of popular music seem even more insistent than others on celebrating these continuities, or recognizing *dis*continuities, especially where the production or consumption of those types are inflected by discriminations based on constructions of 'race' or class. Doing this, and thereby doing justice to the work already done in the United States on this area, might give this chapter the feel of a survey of existing scholarship. But some survey of this scholarship is vital, because it confirms that no type of popular music is detached from the first of these inflections: 'Race relations lie at the centre of the history of twentieth-century popular music' (Frith et al., 2004, 205).

This chapter will show how popular musics grounded in the African-American experience such as jazz and rap embody the tensions surrounding relations with a dead white male like Shakespeare. Yet, as we will see at the end of this chapter, artists *outside* the United States who have inherited and developed the musics of African-American cultures, like the British rapper Akala, have a take on Shakespeare that might offer a way to acknowledge (but not forget) such tensions, for progressive social and cultural ends. Because, of course, these tensions *cannot* be forgotten, nor can common trends in musics that share roots, while not being essentially the same. To survive, African-American musics have appropriated elements of hostile environments in complex ways, subverting and parodying musical norms, as much as legitimating them through borrowing.

The cultural theorist Henry Louis Gates Jr. offers a useful model for contextualizing these processes of appropriation: Signifyin(g). Signifyin(g) is 'a metaphor for textual revision', a form of 'refiguration' that also '*extends* . . . figures present in the original' (1988, 88, xxvii, 63). A multifaceted phenomenon, involving diverse performances, identities, motivations, voices and registers, irony and implicit suggestion, Signi-fyin(g) reveals that explicit articulation is difficult, and hints at why. Discussing African-American narrative practices and rhetorical tradi-tions, Gates offers various definitions of the term, and cites numerous sources for its meaning. Significantly, he finds several examples of this process in how jazz musicians reinterpret each other's work: this can be both parodic and a sign of 'admiration and respect' (63). We hear these characteristics updated in rap and hip-hop too. Hip-hop's samples reproduce earlier cultural forms, sometimes reviving and sustaining a musical legacy, sometimes ironically juxtaposing sources to unsettle assumptions about the relationships between different sounds, periods and people. The lyrical flow and metrical attack of rap, complemented by the visual flow or angular poises of graffiti or dance, evoke rhythmic connections, often soundtracked by skittering breakbeats sliced and sequenced from longer pieces. The vibe is continuous and discontinuous, new and old, distancing and inclusive. As a medium where this 'flow and juxtaposition' are 'everything', hip-hop 'may rewrite tradition, but it never rejects it' (Shapiro, 2009, 107–8).

The ambivalences sustained by Signifyin(g) in jazz and hip-hop are intensified by what jazz and other musics derived from African-American experiences do to Shakespeare:

> What gives the conjunction of Shakespeare and African-American music its special frisson is that throughout much of the last century the two have been emblematic of what have been perceived as distinct cultural realms. (Lanier, 2005, 2)

In early moments of this conjunction's history, it might have seemed as though any distinction was reduced. Lawrence W. Levine influentially revealed that 'Shakespeare actually *was* popular entertainment in nine-teenth-century America' (1988, 4). Levine's research of playbills, performances and programmes showed Shakespeare in the 1800s 'pre-sented as part of the same milieu inhabited by magicians, dancers, singers, acrobats, minstrels, and comics' (23). Burlesques and parodies of the plays and characters only made sense if Shakespeare was 'integ-ral' to American popular culture of various kinds (15). This culture doubtless manifested divisions according to 'race', and Shakespeare's eventual cultural elevation in the United States was in part a kind of whitening. Nonetheless, Ian Whitcomb reports a nineteenth-century scene where African-American culture, religion, Shakespeare and popular musics from diverse traditions combined:

> In 1823 a genteel observer ventured into . . . a black Brimstone Church to witness a black Methodist preacher chanting a musical Hamlet: 'To be or not to be – dat is him question. Whether him nobler in de mind to suffer or lift up him arms against one sea of hubble-bubble and by oppossum endem.' Upon the word 'oppossum' the congregation cried out for 'Possum up a Gum Tree', a current slave hit. Was this an African tune? To the genteel observer it sounded British. (1974, 22)

Yet this moment is skewed by its provenance and reporting. For one thing, in his survey of nineteenth-century American Shakespeares, Levine suggests another source for the story (and offers slightly different inflections to the words). *He* attributes it to the visit made by Charles Mathews, a British comedian, to the '"Nigger's (or Negroe's) theatre" in New York' (14). However murky this story's history, its intent is murkier. The discursive, intertextual and cultural hybridity on show here is represented as monstrous: this story suggests these worshippers perform a misinterpretation and misrepresentation, of Shakespeare and of orthodox religion, using their popular music to do so. Only discrimination could enforce sanctity.

And while Shakespeare may once have been integrated into a broad stream of US popular culture, Lanier suggests hybridizations of Shakespeare and African-American musics were confined to demonized or 'marginal appearances' in that culture (and maybe still are). Moreover, Lanier asserts, these appearances first took their modern, mass-marketed and mass-consumed forms in racist nineteenth-century blackface minstrel shows that used crude racial stereotypes to parody Shakespearean characters. Even as these shows registered fears about black social mobility and political agency, they sought to diminish this mobility and agency by mocking characters like Othello. Shakespeare thus becomes a 'symbolically powerful means for denying African-Americans the mantle of cultural authority', part of a discriminatory, exclusionist and disenfranchising culture industry. By this logic, African-Americans are shown to relate to Shakespeare only in terms of how they corrupt his genius. Yet Lanier also notes that however 'marginal' such appearances of hybridity were, when they occur, they have a 'particular symbolic resonance'

(2005, 2). These issues of marginality and resonance can be heard in the relations between Shakespeare, jazz and hip-hop.

SHAKESPEARE AND JAZZ

Evading the minstrel shows, as African-American musics and cultures rose to global popularity in the first half of the twentieth century, the terms of the engagement with Shakespeare shifted. One of the most notable examples of this shift was the 1912 song 'Shakespearean Rag'. In addition to listing 'various characters', the lyrics by Gene Buck and Herman Ruby asserted 'that although "Bill Shakespeare never knew" ragtime, "his syncopated lines" "surely fit," the ragtime hits' (Folkerth, 2006, 402). Shakespeare had become a figure artists could use to legitimate and popularize jazz and its sources and offshoots, often in sophisticated and subtly politicized ways. Such artists included Louis Armstrong, Benny Goodman and others, with their 1939 collaborations on a musical comedy version of *A Midsummer Night's Dream*, titled *Swingin' the Dream*, and Duke Ellington with *Such Sweet Thunder* and *Incidental Music for Timon of Athens*. These kinds of engagements 'respond to selected Shakespeare characters in dramatic, formalistic, or thematic contexts':

[Ellington's] "Sonnet to Hank Cinq" [on *Such Sweet Thunder*] is a portrait of King Henry V expressed in fourteen melodic lines, a musical analogue to the sonnet form. (Buhler, 2007, 151)

As Buhler notes elsewhere, this piece's mutability offers 'aural reflections' of Henry V's 'capacity for chameleon-like change'. Another song on the same album, 'Circle of Fourths', 'progresses through all twelve major keys in fourths . . . adding a flat to the scale, or subtracting a sharp'. This is not merely noodling, but explores the 'interconnections among the four genres in which Shakespeare composed' (2005, 4, 6).

These are also politically charged syntheses. Ellington's suite of Shakespearean characters 'begins and ends with blacks', emphasising their significance in the canon. Such portraits are literally and metaphorically brassy, musically textured and tender, even as they celebrate 'black erotic power' (Lanier, 2005, 13). And as Julie Sanders suggests, not only are these renderings influenced by recent theatrical performances of Othello by Paul Robeson and James Earl Jones, but these textures are powerfully vocal, with the sounds achieved through the use of plungers in the brass instruments manifesting the presence of articulate black bodies, though no words are sung (2007, 20–21).

As US racial politics altered, so did the sounds. Ellington's choice to score *Timon* when he did 'hints' at 'parallels' between his status as beneficent entertainer and the tragic protagonist's abused generosity, and between Timon's violent 'bitter impulses' and the increasing militancy of the civil rights movement, 'responses' Ellington 'consistently rejected':

> Thus the musical theme that Ellington assigns to revolutionary Alcibiades and his men, instruments of that violence: a pompous march in which momentary appearances of a major key quickly lead back to a minor tonic. (Lanier, 2005, 15)

Not all appropriations of Shakespeare were as self-consciously politicized. In the United Kingdom, Cleo Laine and John Dankworth's long-standing effort to engage with the canon has produced many albums of light, and light-hearted, jazz. Yet given the music's global reach, the politicized alignment of Shakespeare and jazz was not confined to the United States, or to records. The year 1962 saw the release of the film *All Night Long*, directed by Basil Dearden. Set in London, and centred around a night-time party to celebrate the anniversary of the (white) singer Delia Lane to the (black) jazz bandleader Aurelius Rex, the film features appearances from jazz musicians such as Dankworth, Dave Brubeck and Charlie Mingus. Significantly, the couple at the film's core is subjected to deceits echoing Iago's in *Othello*. Barbara Hodgdon (1991) has argued that *All Night Long* mutes or avoids issues of conflict between 'races', in the play and in its own setting. Yet for Paul Skrebels, the film not only points to race relations in the period, with references to Apartheid-era Johannesburg, but also emphasizes that 'the play, like jazz, is shot through with the tragic history of black/white relations' (2008, 153). Because the film foregrounds the jazz scene, with its 'intimacy, rivalry, ambition, success, and failure', it also evokes jazz's past, as an art form generated by members of one community and appropriated, exploited and demonized by those of another (148). But because this is Shakespeare in the jazz age, new resolutions are possible: Rex and Delia live on, and it is the hybridizing, multicultural potential of jazz culture that provides the context, however utopian, for this to happen.

Some recent films have repoliticized Shakespeare and jazz in very different ways. In Richard Loncraine's 1995 *Richard III*, Richard's authoritarian schemes are set to the tune of swing and big bands. And in Taymor's *Titus*, the disputing brothers enter the screen accompanied by the sound of 1930s' jazz, and during Saturninus' debaucheries jazz also plays out. The sonic worlds evoked by Loncraine's film, and by Taymor's collaborator, Elliot Goldenthal, suggest competing ideologies and the decadence of Weimar Berlin. Yet *Titus* is careful to dissociate these conditions from ethnicity – the music appreciably quietens when the camera closes in on Aaron (Harry Lennix), and he isn't its source or audience. It is as if Taymor and Loncraine have provided a visual complement to Adorno's controversial suggestions that the jazz he heard had nothing 'at all to do with genuine black music', and that in certain contexts, like pre-war Germany, jazz could be 'easily adapted for use by fascism' because it featured martial sounds and repetitive beats (1936, 477, 485).

Whatever their political motivations, for some jazz artists and their listeners, productive syntheses between Shakespeare and the music are possible because of the perceived continuities between jazz's concerns and modes of creation, production and reception, and Shakespeare's. Ellington himself consistently emphasized the proximity of Shakespeare and jazz, in terms of how art is made and how it is received:

In the final analysis, whether it be Shakespeare or jazz, the only thing that counts is the emotional effect on the listener. Somehow, I suspect that if Shakespeare were alive today, he might be a jazz fan himself – he'd appreciate the combination of team spirit and informality, of academic knowledge and humor. (cited in Lanier, 2005, 12)

More recent productions have sought to reproduce jazz's energies, to re-energize Shakespeare. For a 2001 staging of *Macbeth* at London's Globe, directed by Tim Carroll, Claire van Kampen, the Director of Theatre Music, deliberately generated a jazz score, released in 2001 as *Sleep No More*. In her sleevenotes van Kampen explains she chose jazz for specific reasons:

In support of the play's modernity, and its constant emphasis upon night-time imagery with which it weaves its hypnotic web, I decided to focus on a style of music that is closely associated with both

magic and the 'Dark Side of the Moon' – Jazz – and with a particular
performer/composer in mind – Miles Davis. (2001)

For van Kampen, Davis's omnivorous, double-drummer-rocking, genre-
and-mind-expanding 1970 *Bitches Brew* channelled a 'coursing underground stream of African Voodoo connections'. True enough, Davis's
album boils up 'th'ingredience' (*Macbeth*, 4.1.34) of ('white') rock
dynamics, and funk rhythms and jazz instrumentation from the African-
American tradition, almost fulfilling Hecate's injunction to the witches
in the play as they make their 'hell-broth boil and bubble' (4.1.19):

Black spirits and white, red spirits and grey,
Mingle, mingle, mingle, you that mingle may. (4.1.44–45)

For van Kampen, precisely because it conjured 'an esoteric hinterland
of exotica', the 'mingle' of *Bitches Brew* made it more, not less, valuable
for the project of scoring *Macbeth*: 'Hecate-like, its form and power
remain essentially out-of-reach'. Arguably, there are a few problems
with van Kampens' approach. When she casts the play as 'an archetypal
chronicle of our own age', she collapses historical differences between
the modern and early modern period (2001). And even if we relate
Davis's project to the imagery of the play, van Kampen's descriptions
might be seen partly to unintentionally perpetuate positive fetishes and
negative stereotypes about jazz, and about African-American music as
irrational, diabolical and dangerously seductive. In typically polemical
form, Adorno observed – but ridiculed – the perception that jazz subjected 'the over-stimulated Western nerves to the vitality of blacks',
and embodied some 'elementary force' that could regenerate 'ostensibly
decadent European music' (1936, 471, 477). He deplored such perceptions because they were racist, and, to his ears, misheard jazz and the
social contexts that produced it. To Adorno, whatever the reality of jazz's
'African origins', 'all the formal elements of jazz', its instruments, tonal
and rhythmic structures, and means of technological transmission via
print or radio, 'have been completely . . . pre-formed by the capitalist
requirement that they be exchangeable as commodities' (1936, 477).
This commoditisation affected performers too, reducing them to mere
instruments to be sold, and so continuing, but not overcoming, the
'bondage' of black experience: 'the skin of the black man functions as
much as a coloristic effect as does the silver of the saxophone' (1936,
477–78). However improvisational its forms, however 'primordial' its

perceived 'instincts', because jazz came into being in repressive and mutilating 'modernity' it did not – *could not* – sound like 'longed-for freedom': 'The archaic stance of jazz is as modern as the "primitives" who fabricate it' (1936, 478).[1]

But these points cannot account completely for the way Davis audibly functions as a source of power for the music in this production. Van Kampen's use of a specific type of Afrocentric post–Second-World-War jazz also builds on concepts of female (and black) power in Davis's work, and signals music's power to augment Shakespeare's staging of violence, sexuality and the chaos afflicting nation-states; as van Kampen notes: 'The music we play replaces lights, becomes Gods, Goddesses, Hecate. It breathes its way around the main heartbeat, Shakespeare's five-beat verse' (2001). What resulted was a beguiling synthesis. On its own terms, as Davis-influenced jazz, the music worked. When imbued with regular rhythm, it was *profoundly* rhythmic, and intoxicatingly repetitive; even when the tempo slowed, notes elongated languidly; this was captivating but never *easy* listening. When combined with that Shakespearean 'heart-beat', the music came to exert its own authority over the play: the witches 'danced and spoke over the more rhythmic tracks'. To van Kampen, however 'progressive' the 'style' of her jazz and what it did to the play, the play invited this kind of synthesis:

> There was also a satisfying sense of tradition here; in Act III Sc IV of the Folio text of 1623, the Witches and Hecate engage in what in 17th century terms was clearly a song and dance spectacular! (2001)

Despite their persistence and variety, such syntheses, and the perceptions that underpin them, have not always been endorsed or well-received by aficionados of Shakespeare *or* jazz: 'For the most part, only jazz artists dedicated to reaching general audiences have continued to borrow from Shakespeare' (Buhler, 2007, 151).[2] It could also be argued even the assimilation celebrated by Ellington was consciously incomplete: 'the music is entirely instrumental, bypassing the issue of setting Shakespeare in an African-American idiom' (Lanier, 2005, 13). Evidently, the shifts in African-American musics' engagements with Shakespeare were not and could not be finalized, given historical and ongoing disenfranchise-ments. Mid-century US bebop was heard as 'an expression of a dissident spirit within the younger black community', a community willing to improvise its way beyond conforming to musical or social expectations

(Townsend, 2000, 127). As such, bebop rejected Shakespeare, in accordance with its 'new racial politics' (Lanier, 2005, 10). But even this rejection signalled a relationship, with the titles of many bebop songs playing upon Hamlet's notoriously vacillating question (Lanier, 2005, 23). This play had a serious purpose: would African-American cultures 'be', autonomous and sustainable within or from other cultural domains, including those that sustained Shakespeare as cultural authority; or would they 'not be' through repression by and assimilation to such authorities and domains?

This ambivalence is echoed in other, later, African-American genres. The first track on *School's In*, a recent album by funk legend James Brown's erstwhile saxophone maestro, Maceo Parker, is also named 'To Be Or Not To Be'. With call and response chants of the title punctuating a characteristically fluid melodic line and crisp backing, Parker explicitly mentions Shakespeare, and cites Hamlet's line, to wonder whether the track will or will not be funky. Given these hints – the album's title, and its cover image of Maceo dressed in a suit, glasses in hand, in front of a blackboard with musical notation – his questioning is significant. Reminding listeners of the roots of contemporary hip-hop in jazz and funk, the question, song and album pose a pedagogic challenge to the musical and political consciousness of black American youth: what will contemporary African-American music's relationship with its heritage, with Shakespeare, and the cultural power he once signified or still signifies, 'be' or 'not be' in the future?

SHAKESPEARE, RAP AND HIP-HOP

Parker's track intimates how these questions continue in genres such as the 'evolving phenomenon' of 'rap Shakespeare' (Lanier, 2006, 80). Certainly the (in)compatibility of rap, hip-hop and Shakespeare has occasioned much debate. In the 1990 trial of the notorious rap group 2 Live Crew, Henry Louis Gates Jr. was called as an expert witness to determine the worth of the act's lyrics, which featured the extensive use of obscene and sexual language. Gates observed that many of the Western canon's esteemed authors employed such language. Yet when quoted some of the group's lyrics, Gates responded: 'I never said it was Shakespeare' (cited in Burt, 2002, 205). In critical response to this perspective, some rappers would later assert their obscenity *as* Shakespearean. Guesting on Kelis's 2003 track 'In Public', Nas explicitly re-jigs Hamlet's famous internal debate about 'the question' (3.1.58), but echoes his filthy play with 'country matters'(3.2.111), to wonder whether he should put his erect penis – manifestly, an all 'too too solid' piece of 'flesh' (1.2.129) – in his paramour's mouth or vagina, as a modern form of 'consummation / Devoutly to be wished': there's the 'rub', indeed (3.1.65–67).

Beyond reminding us that Shakespeare's *dramatis personae* could express enough sexual objectification to warrant a 'Parental Advisory' sticker and make the toughest gangsta blush, what *are* the terms of the relationship between Shakespeare and modern African-American musics like rap? As Lanier has described, rap adaptations of Shakespeare can sometimes parody Shakespeare and 'reverence' for him, even as they make rap itself 'an object of parody' (2006, 74). Rap and Shakespeare can seem like no easy fit. But connections do take place: their engagement is facilitated as comedy, commerce or pedagogy, while complicated by the marginal status of rap performers in relation to popular music in general, and in relation to the genre itself.

In terms of comedy mediating the relationship between Shakespeare and rap, Lanier discusses William Shatner rapping Shakespeare in *Free Enterprise*, a homage to Star Trek fandom. Lanier suggests that this is a 'camp travesty' of Shakespeare and Shatner as Star Trek icon; but, we might argue, it also travesties rap (2006, 14–15).[3] Despite or perhaps because of comedy, the distance between Shakespeare and rap is maintained. Nevertheless, some artists seem conscious of these parodic representations (of Shakespeare and rap), and work beyond them. We can hear this in Biz Markie's 2003 track 'Tear Shit Up'. Here, Biz says his rapping isn't an encounter between phaser-wielding humanoids and threatening aliens (as in *Star Trek*). He isn't about to rationalize (like Dr. Spock) or colonize and seduce (like Captain Kirk), nor is he trying to travesty *Star Trek* or rap (as in *Free Enterprise*). In fact, as he suggests when he raps, he is like Shakespeare, who shares his lyrical flow. This not only bigs up Biz Markie, but also Shakespeare: both electrify audiences when they perform, we are told. Of course, Shakespeare's acting came second to his writing, but Biz's lyrics on this track suggest the Bard is embodied on stage through his texts, a presence evoked as others act his words.

Biz Markie has had a long and illustrious career in hip-hop since its early days. Other artists invested in the heritage and conscious of the history of rap have also made efforts to get to grips with Shakespeare. Beyond his play with 'country matters' discussed above, Nas has called on Shakespeare's bleaker, tragic textures to inspire the angry, elegiac tones of his work. On 1994's 'N.Y. State of Mind', he seems to repeatedly echo Hamlet's repeated words on mortality and somnolence (themselves repeating an old connection): 'To die, to sleep' (3.1.62); 'that sleep of death' (3.1.68). Substituting M-16s for bodkins, Nas connects with this passage from the play to evoke to mainstream America the hard-knocked, nightmarish 'weary life' (3.1.79) of urban ghettoes, an 'undiscovered country' (3.1.81) of seemingly morbid netherworlds. Concentrating on the prince's own fascination with edgy states of existence, and relaying his lyrics in the gaps between the track's hollow beats, Nas portrays the strung-out, wired, drug-induced, gun-toting paranoia of hellish states, where lives are lived on the margins of legality and society, where stray weapons kill, and where the 'many confines, wards, and dungeons' of a labyrinthine city are a 'prison' (2.2.246–49). In other work, such as his guest feature on Jay-Z's 'Success', Nas reads Shakespeare differently to identify with a black character and cast himself as an Othello from the ghetto. In this role he accepts he may appear like a villain, but contends he has sacred blood in his veins, and it won't be spilt as he betters his adversaries. This usage counsels against prejudging surfaces (while acknowledging prejudice's power), and evokes Othello's dignity and grandeur (while trying to avoid his fate).

Since these references feature in short verses, marginal guest slots or lyrical echoes, perhaps we have to listen elsewhere to hear how the apparent distance between rap and Shakespeare has been overcome more comprehensively. This may mean we attend to musicians who operate on the margins of rap, but their very marginality means they can find power in Shakespearean appropriation. Outkast is a phenomenally popular and innovative hip-hop outfit who nonetheless uses costume and role play to deconstruct the stereotypes of nihilistic, materialist masculinity blighting recent rap. For Folkerth, the Shakespearean reference in the final verse of Outkast's song 'ATLiens', which echoes 'All the world's a stage' (2.7.138) from *As You Like It*, assists this deconstruction: 'With Shakespeare's help, "ATLiens" sends the message that everyone . . . can live their lives in a way that celebrates personal freedom and individuality' (2006, 369). These marginal appropriations can be particularly 'striking': Buhler explores just such an example in a track by a female rapper, Sylk-E. Fyne's 'Romeo and Juliet' (2002, 260). As the Capulets' ball becomes a club, this track relocates the play's gender dynamics and factional strife to the contemporary hip-hop scene. According to Tricia

Rose, female rappers tend to concentrate on themes of 'heterosexual courtship', 'the importance of the female voice', and 'public displays of physical and sexual freedom' (1994, 147). Consolidating Fyne's status as female artist in a male-dominated genre then, Buhler suggests she articulates as 'a very assertive Juliet', who is 'confident of her ability to answer and even to overmatch her Romeo's verbal skill, sexuality, and emotional ardour' (2002, 260).

If rappers marginal to hip-hop's masculine norms can use Shakespeare to good effect, what about rappers who are not African-American? Given hip-hop's global dissemination and its self-conscious, in-built modes of appropriation, it would be a mistake to ignore the ways in which a 'black idiom . . . that articulates the problems of black urban life' also involves the 'pleasure and participation of others' (Rose, 1994, 4). In other words, rap has grown to involve a wide range of non-black artists. This is particularly apparent with rap and Shakespeare: some of the earliest examples of their synthesis were produced by non-black figures, including 'II Be or Not II Be', featured on Malcolm McLaren's 1990 album *Round the Outside! Round the Outside!* This tradition was maintained with MC Honky's album featuring Shakespearean raps, *I am the Messiah*, whose play on a derogatory term for 'white' signalled a reflexive awareness of the problems of appropriating a predominantly African-American genre. But because one of the most notorious of these non-black others, Eminem (aka Marshall Mathers, aka Slim Shady), is notably a *white* rapper has led commentators to ascribe Shakespearean associations to him in a way that might be less likely if he was African-American:

> In a hip-hop edition of Shakespeare's *A Midsummer Night's Dream* in which rappers or their personas were the players, Puck, the comedy's fairy instigator, could be no one but Slim Shady. . . . Slim Shady is like Shakespeare's Fool: the character who darts across the plot to tip the audience to truths unseen . . . He may annoy or illuminate, but he won't be ignored. (Bozza, 2004, 67)

Eminem has cultivated and extended such associations himself, and in his raps as a guest on Jay-Z's track 'Renegade', observes that many call him a modern Shakespeare. Significantly, 'Renegade' features on the work of a pre-eminent *black* rapper, who does not make the same claims, and while Jay-Z's African-American guests (such as Nas) compare themselves to black Shakespearean characters, only Eminem compares himself to the Bard. This self-designation reveals more than a desire to legitimate rap in general. It also indicates a white rapper's need or ability to call on a figure of cultural authority like Shakespeare, without African-Americans' history of justified cultural anxiety. But as Eminem suggests, this is not just self-aggrandizement, and rap commentators have made the connection for him. Sometimes this connection has been less than flattering, though. Analysing the performance of and responses to Toby Stephens's portrayal of Hamlet for the Royal Shakespeare Company, Gary Taylor termed him 'a Hamlet for the Eminem generation', whose 'narcissistic misogyny' mirrors 'innumerable hip-hop videos' (2004). Taylor's reading of young women's desire for Toby Stephens/Hamlet is coloured by his reading of the messages of rap:

> That's why so many women love Eminem, or Stephens's Hamlet. They take their misogyny as an entirely justifiable contempt for all those other women who really are whores and bitches. (2004)

It would seem that through their collocation with Shakespeare, rappers (or just white rappers?) are paradoxically normalized and demonized, as are those who enjoy their music.

In other contexts, Shakespeare and rap have been paired to more progressive ends, notably in terms of pedagogy. And while rap Shakespeares sometimes maintain an air and tradition of travestying African-American *and* Shakespearean idioms, they can still stimulate:

> Rap offers the performer a new form of blackface that, first, trades on and thus attempts to legitimize the alternative discourse of urban youth, and second, makes the claim that an interactive cultural exchange across time with the classics can fend off the danger of their growing inert. . . . In the context of a performance for youth, "blackface" provides a revisionary idiom that acknowledges a student's resistance to Shakespeare while enabling engagement. (Ko, 2006, 4)

Stagings like the Honolulu Theatre for Youth's *Othello* (in 2002 and 2006) signal how globalized Shakespeares now interact with internationally significant popular musics such as rap, far from such music's original sites of production, in the conurbations of the East and West

US coasts. These interactions both revivify the drama and extend the music's cultural penetration:

> HTY staged this show, not for any young audience, but a specifically Hawaiian young audience. This meant, for one, that they expected a multiethnic cast and an audience that would understand the racial tensions in the play in Hawaiian terms. More specifically, the actor cast as Othello (Charles Kupahu Timtim) . . . was Native Hawaiian, whose ethnicity was very visibly highlighted . . . by Polynesian tattoo markings on his face. . . . The raps, quite simply, offered the most direct access for the audience into the adapted play. (Ko, 2006, 4–5, 8)

Despite these laudable pedagogic aims, the commercial imperatives in rap Shakespeare are undeniable. Whether these imperatives attest to Shakespeare's power, or to rap's, is debatable, at least in the United States where divisions based on 'race', class and culture remain powerful. As Lanier notes, the musical *The Bomb-itty of Errors* (2000) did bring together Shakespeare and hip-hop, but had 'the unmistakable flavor of an updated minstrel show' (2005, 22). Will such stereotypes still sell in Obama's America?

SHAKESPEARE AND UK HIP-HOP

From the example of Honolulu, we can see that in locations beyond mainland America, where cultural conflicts are no less acute but have perhaps proved more surmountable, other visions of how Shakespeare and hip-hop might relate have been conceived. Shifting focus again to a UK context shows how hip-hop culture has come to have a special relationship with Shakespeare. The Brotherhood, a trio of British rappers, comprised, in their own words, 'one mixed race, one Black, one Yid', and proclaimed themselves 'international, outernational, never rational, oh I can't forget the indiginal'. One of the personae of the group displayed his ethnic and religious identity by using the name 'Shylock', and so revealed how conflicts about ascribed or assumed difference, but also frank debates about them, have been inherent to UK culture past and present. More recently, Akala, a British rapper and educator, has run workshops combining Shakespeare and rap to empower young people in multicultural and deprived urban environments. His 'Hip Hop Shakespeare' project develops a conception of Shakespeare *and* of rap that is political because it brings about change, however small:

> Hip Hop Shakespeare is basically an entity . . . that explores the cultural, linguistic, and social parallels between the work of the Bard and of modern day rap as well – I say modern day, but really it's rappers from 10, 15 years ago that we mainly reference, the period in which hip-hop was most socially conscious, and most poetic. And we use these two art forms to engage and inspire young people, and try and challenge the way they look at both hip-hop, both Shakespeare, and, of course, themselves. (2009)

In this context, Shakespeare not only speaks in new voices and ways, but performs in new attire, reanimated for new spectators, as Akala puts it on the 2006 track 'Shakespeare':

> It's Shakespeare, reincarnated, . . .
> Except I spit flows and strip hoes naked . . .
> Plus I don't write, I recite my shit now . . .
> No more tights, now jeans saggin'
> If I say so myself, I'm much more handsome . . .
> I'm similar to William, but a little different
> I do it for kids that's illiterate, not Elizabeth . . .
> It's a matrix, I try and explain it . . .
> Thou shalt not fuck with dis.

Akala affirms that Shakespeare may have had an elite audience, but he also has the capacity to engage the disenfranchised, and it only takes a 'little' difference in how he is made to work now to realize this. In turn, his lyrics and interviews suggest that it is a mistake to elevate Shakespeare as an 'aloof entity' separate from the world around him and us. When we do this we perpetuate a 'narrow version of history', ignore the 'matrix' of cultures past and present, and depoliticize Shakespeare. On the contrary, unimpressed by Eurocentric interpretations of Shakespeare, and inspired by the Afrocentric connections in his work, Akala argues that Shakespeare's texts display as 'many influences of the globe' as contemporary culture, including hip-hop, which he contends is 'as good, as poetic, as powerful, as any other cultural form'.

By this logic Shakespeare's words are only 'seemingly opposite' to hip-hop (2008). In reality, their concerns concord:

Hip hop writes about and deals with human society, the trials and tribulations of what's going on, and some of that is ugly, and some of that is wondrous, and it's the same with Shakespeare. So, you'll get the same scenes and themes of violence, of the state of the nation, or war, of greed, of poverty. (2009)

In some lyrics, Akala seems to nod towards one of Eminem's rap personae, Slim Shady (as seen, often conceived in Shakespearean terms), the diction of US hip-hop, *and* Shakespearean drama, to evoke how any opposition can be overcome:

Spit poetry so shady
For Lords on road and my hood Ladies (2006).

Yet to Akala US hip-hop has been too maligned and 'degraded' by commentators, and is 'so violent, so negative', it has 'lost its way in the public domain' (2008). Its ability to engage with a cultural icon like Shakespeare, and with audiences who might benefit from its consciousness-raising powers, is spent. So Akala has had to rethink the form and function of hip-hop in the United Kingdom, as well as Shakespeare, to make this connection. This has involved revising his own version of rap. Akala does this sonically as well as lyrically: 'Shakespeare' features a sloweddown, beefed-up riff from Tomcraft's 2003 techno stormer 'Loneliness', meaning the new track literally counters any isolation between musical genres – and cultural forms – by being eclectic and inclusive. Moreover, as recorded, 'Shakespeare' originally featured the recurring lyric 'It's like Shakespeare with a nigga twist'. Yet in Akala's 'constantly evolving' performances subsequent to the track's release, he has 'abandoned' the word 'nigga' because he realizes rap audiences have been 'desensitized' to it, in a way contrary to rap pioneers' intended appropriations of the term (2008).

Akala's ability to move things to another level is exemplified by the 2007 track 'Comedy Tragedy History', a piece saturated with allusions to Shakespearean lyrics, and that references the title of every play (improving on Cleo Laine and John Dankworth's 1978 jazz track 'The Compleat Works'). This track emphasizes how Akala's hip-hop has the capacity to absorb Shakespeare (and Shakespearean popular music), while also redefining – and *reincarnating* – rap and the UK rapper as a desirable performer:

Call it urban, call it street
A rose by any other name, smell just as sweet,
Spit so hard, but I'm smart as the Bard . . .
Akala, Akala, where for art thou
I'm the black Shakespearian.

In this sense, only Shakespeare and hip-hop in their global – including Black British – forms can interact to redeem each other, and perhaps their audiences:

It makes you feel a sense of entitlement. If you're entitled to Shakespeare, then you're entitled to anything, 'cos Shakespeare is presented as the most high-brow, unattainable thing in the world . . . so I do think it is important to engage young people in so-called 'high-culture'. (2009)

From this perspective and position, Akala offers us a way to think about Shakespeare and rap that doesn't marginalize either, but acknowledges both have something to say about contemporary social and cultural concerns (and to each other). By calling upon traditions in hip-hop now seemingly silenced, Akala reclaims Shakespeare *for* politicized rap, and *from* the guest slots, role plays, one-offs, side projects, comedies and burlesques to which he is often relegated. But UK hip-hop has had historical difficulties in achieving mainstream – let alone US – success. As such, it remains to be seen whether Akala's sense of Shakespeare and rap sharing a beat will be at the heart of new versions of both, in the United Kingdom and beyond, or will remain on the edge of the musical culture that he, for one, justly invests with great power.

NOTES

1 For evaluations and critiques of Adorno's controversial views on jazz, see Witkin, 2000, 160–80, 193–94; Gracyk, 1992; and Schonherr, 1991.
2 See also Buhler, 2005; Teague, 2005; and Corrigan, 2005.
3 For example, Lanier discusses rap and Shakespeare meeting in comic formats such as MTV's claymation *Celebrity Deathmatch*, featuring Busta Rhymes, and *The Cosby Show* (2006, 74–75).

CHAPTER 5

'HIGH-CLASS DREAMS': SHAKESPEARE, STATUS AND COUNTRY MUSIC

The previous chapter explored how issues of 'race' have been a significant factor in popular music, and in such music's engagement with Shakespeare. This chapter focuses on another genre – country – to develop these concerns and bring in another related factor: class. As Nicholas Dawidoff has observed, in its early days country music 'satisfied many needs': 'it enabled poor Southern white people to hear the strains of the black working-man's music while keeping their distance from poor working-class blacks' (1997, 10). Dawidoff suggests that as the genre developed through the 1900s, it continued to be important to 'farm people', but became no less significant to those experiencing 'dislocation and rural nostalgia' with urban industrialisation (18). Throughout its history then, country offered 'a way to express frustration at . . . social exclusion . . . and . . . solidarity for people who felt marginalized by American society' (19). In other words, country was and remains a genre sensitized to class, ascribed and self-identified as a popular and low cultural form. How might Shakespeare relate to it?

SHAKESPEARE GOES COUNTRY

For the singer–songwriter Chris Wall, Shakespeare stands as a powerful figure of expressive and emotional authority. On 'Cowboy Nation', from the 1994 album of the same name, Wall poignantly notes the way life teaches you lessons, some of which have been taught to or by others before. As we progress on our journey, counsels Wall on the song, we'll start 'to see what it is the old man means'. Who might 'the old man' be?

> Shakespeare says our doubts are traitors,
> think about this whole thing later,
> there's an answer waiting for me somewhere down the road.

Here Wall cites Lucio's words to Isabella, petitioning her to appeal to Angelo's mercy for her brother's sake, in *Measure for Measure* (1.4.77). Yet Wall transforms the specific meaning of the lines to something more general. This accords with his reflection that 'the observations that the Bard makes throughout his works (sonnets included) are so universally true and have transcended the ages as none other, that he truly is timeless'. And Wall also recognizes the impact of citing Shakespeare in a seemingly low-brow genre:

1. It makes [a country audience] think you are smarter than you really are.
2. Americans aren't as big a boobs as people think and a surprising number know the references down to the act and scenes. (2009)

So, for Wall, Shakespeare offers a way to appeal to a wider audience. With good reason: precisely because it invokes emotive themes and truths, modern country is a huge and complex commercial enterprise, and the factors that lead to a song's or artist's success are various. In his detailed statistical study of these factors, Charles Jaret cites 'musical and lyrical content, the singer and level of promotion' but also notes 'a random element' that can give a track 'a chance to be heard and possibly a chance to become popular' (1993, 183–84). Perhaps Shakespeare offers just such a random, unexpected element. As such, any engagement the music has with Shakespeare can be as much about economics as it is about emotion.

Continuities between the two, and with Shakespeare, have a long history in country. As Robert Sawyer notes, the early country music star Hank Williams was known, and marketed, as 'both the "Hillbilly Shakespeare" and "The Shakespeare of the Common Man"'. Such comparisons simultaneously 'deconstruct the difference between high and low', 'serve as oxymoronic public relations tags', and betray a 'comparison' between artists that 'may actually have historical validity':

Both Hank and Shakespeare had problematic relationships with their fathers, who struggled painfully to make something of themselves in . . . emerging market conditions.

Both artists' works share these concerns, by, for example, challenging 'standard definitions of masculinity'. Sawyer has also described how more modern country artists, such as John Michael Montgomery, have referenced *Romeo and Juliet* as 'a barometer of superior love, but also as a benchmark that the songwriter's lovers can surpass'. Elaborating on this model of appropriation, Sawyer points to the song 'Romeo', written by Dolly Parton, Mary Chapin Carpenter and others, and performed by Parton with Billy Ray Cyrus. The song combines elements of Elizabethan diction that unsettle expectations of modern 'standard' English expression, with a strident sexuality that similarly destabilizes expectations about 'the standard objectification of women by men'. Such reversals, notes Sawyer, 'may also call to mind Parton's own proto-feminist endeavors' as a successful show-business entrepreneur and artist (2005, 7–8, 4–5). Evidently, Shakespeare and country work on and rework each other in powerful ways.

COWBOY JACK CLEMENT

Continuities and also discontinuities between Shakespeare and country have resurfaced most recently in Robert Gordon and Morgan Neville's 2007 film *Shakespeare was a Big George Jones Fan: Cowboy Jack Clement's Home Movies*. Cowboy Jack Clement is an engineer, record producer, singer, musician and songwriter involved in the Nashville country scene. His career began at the legendary Sun Records studio in Memphis, as owner–producer Sam Philips's 'right hand man', in the words of one of the film's contributors. Jack went on to work with a huge range of artists including Waylon Jennings, Jerry Lee Lewis, Charley Pride and Johnny Cash, and founded his own studio, the Cowboy Arms Hotel and Recording Spa, to which the luminaries of 'Outlaw country' who were unwelcome in staid Nashville repaired for good times and to cut records. Cowboy Jack's collaborations with Johnny Cash have suffered critical disdain, being described as 'cloying pop songs' (Dawidoff, 1997, 187). Yet he enjoyed success with poignant tracks such as 'Let's All Help the Cowboys (Sing the Blues)', which compared performing Shakespeare to singing emotionally candid country songs (and which was recorded by Jennings for his 1975 album *Dreaming My Dreams*). *Shakespeare was a Big George Jones Fan* assembles present-day footage of Jack discussing his life and career, his incomplete earlier TV specials and 'home movies' featuring stars he has worked with, concert performances, and animated sequences, some including Shakespeare. Throughout, Shakespearean allusions and references abound, offering rich material to explore Cowboy Jack's, and country music's, relationship with Shakespeare. As such the film sustains Cowboy Jack's marginal status as a novelty pop-culture figure, but also repositions him in the contexts he occupies, or aspires to occupy, repositioning Shakespeare along the way.

The first animated Shakespearean sequence follows a scene where Cowboy Jack and friends sit round a table with the country star George Jones, for whom Cowboy Jack wrote several hit songs. Cowboy Jack sings a jokey number, ending with the line 'I've been flushed from the bathroom of your heart'. Jones responds ''s better than some of the stuff I'm hearin''. The film then cuts to what seems to be a moment later in the same scene, creating a sense of Jack changing the subject abruptly:

COWBOY JACK	I had a dream one night, 'bout Shakespeare.
[to George Jones]	An' he was a big fan o'yours.
GEORGE JONES	'Bout who?
COWBOY JACK	Y'know, William Shakespeare. An' he was a big George Jones fan.
JONES	You gotta joke comin' up, I'll bet.
COWBOY JACK	No, no, that's it! What we need around here is some high-class dreams, y'know.
JONES	Yeah.
COWBOY JACK	Shakespearean dreams.

At this, the screen wobbles into a dream sequence, or hallucination, with an animated Shakespeare, and a photo of Cowboy Jack's face, both in space suits orbiting the earth. The film's end credits reveal Shakespeare is voiced by 'Chance Martin (The Voice in Black)', a play on Johnny Cash's persona, befitting Martin's deeply Cash-ish low vocal tone. In the animated sequence, this space-cowboy Shakespeare grumbles in those low tones, 'Oh, OK, I'm just a dream', to which Cowboy Jack responds: 'No, no, but that's what I tell people.' Despite being 'high-class' (or sky-high) Shakespeare seems to empathize with an all too earthly need for circumspection, feints and obscurity: 'That keep y'out of trouble doesn't it, Cowboy?' Cowboy Jack concurs, even as he jokily diminishes his own credibility further: 'Yeah, if I tell 'em I got a time machine, they'll put me in the loony bin.' Satisfied with this, Shakespeare and Cowboy Jack resolve to go and drink some beer.

From this ahistorical reanimation of Shakespeare, suspended in time and space, the film then cuts to the present day, as Cowboy Jack explains his own conception of Shakespeare to the camera. He confesses he is 'captivated by Shakespeare himself', suggesting he is somehow in thrall to a far greater artist, yet he adds he feels some equalizing connection exists between them across time and space. Shakespeare 'seemed like he was a whole lot like me, sort of', a 'music hustler, or something': he 'writes his stuff, casts it, n'gets his friends to show up and sells tickets'. As Cowboy Jack's use of 'seemed', 'like', 'sort of' and 'or something' indicate, he is wary of stretching the comparison too far, but this outward wariness doesn't stop him doing so. Perhaps it is another joke, another feint, mystifying how and why he makes popular music and reducing Shakespeare's stature to do so. Yet even if this is the case, the final comment stands as both a canny summation of the early modern stage's hucksterism and the economics of contemporary country-music production, as practised by Cowboy Jack, in his 'lodge'-cum-studio. The joking tone is muted further as the film intercuts between Cowboy Jack's explanation and a performance from a much earlier 'Never-Finished TV Special'. Here he sings Hamlet's 'To be or not to be' soliloquy with some poignancy, intimating his own mortality and unrequited aspirations to the accompaniment of a gently fluttering piano. Cowboy Jack's nostalgia for the past – his own, and Shakespeare's – vies with a sense of how old he has grown in the 2000s. 'To be or not to be' hardly articulates the emotion: what *was*, what *is* and what *will be* are juxtaposed.

Shakespeare and Cowboy Jack's relationship deepens as the film progresses. In a DVD chapter entitled 'Sigh No More Ladies', Cowboy Jack sings to a guitar-toting, cowboy-hat-wearing animated Bard-in-a-bar, setting a song from *As You Like It* to a country tune, but rewriting the closing lines: 'converting all your sounds of woe/into songs that make some money'. Shakespeare is here an honorary Good Ol' Boy, enjoying Cowboy Jack's legendary hospitality. Shakespeare is in good company: this hospitality and 'self-confidence' were also extended to a star as big as Paul McCartney, as Cowboy Jack allegedly advised the former Beatle when he visited Nashville, 'Let's do "Yesterday" and I'll show you how to cut that sucker right' (cited in Larkin, 1993, 83). In a later chapter in the film, called 'Lighten Up Shake', Shakespeare and Cowboy Jack are shown as such good buddies that Cowboy Jack develops his informal revision of the canon. Still in the same bar, Cowboy Jack continues to muse on Hamlet's soliloquy, but suggests to Shakespeare that it is 'too morbid'. Shakespeare responds in the manner we might expect Jack expects him to: 'Well, Cowboy, that stuff really sells, y'know.' Cowboy Jack couches his (re)production advice in gentle terms: 'Well, I wouldn't want you to change it, but, er, write s'more happy stuff man, y'know, get outta the pits.' Shakespeare mumbles, but manages to admit 'maybe nobody understands me'. Cowboy Jack offers a way out: 'Maybe not, but you'll have more fun.' Shakespeare decides that *this* is what he really wants, and that Cowboy Jack's approach has merit:

SHAKESPEARE	Well, that's what I wanna do. T'have more fun. I never had that much fun.
COWBOY JACK	Remember man, we're in the fun business. If we're not havin' fun, we're not doin' our jobs.
SHAKESPEARE	He knows it and I know it, now we gotta convince . . .
COWBOY JACK	. . . the world . . .
SHAKESPEARE	. . . that's right, the world.

Exhausted by having collaborated on a scheme for a new, pan-historical popular aesthetic, relevant both to the Globe and the global village they have floated above (or simply done in by the beer), Cowboy Jack promises to meet Shakespeare in a couple of weeks for another 'good time', and nods off to sleep. Shakespeare sends him on his way with the inevitable 'Good night, sweet prince'.

Shakespeare as artist and as body of work figures in various and contradictory ways in this film, but these contradictions say much about any relation to both country and popular music. He appears as an object of whimsical fun, lost in space, or just a guilty dream or playful hallucination: this might undermine his cultural authority. But this doesn't seem to be Cowboy Jack's or the film's sole aim. Shakespeare may be out in the vacuum of space, but he's also deep inside the material and mind of this popular music maker. If Shakespeare can only be communicated with through altered states or dreams, is he nevertheless part of this music's subconscious? Joking aside, giving Shakespeare 'Johnny Cash's' voice equates the expressive powers of two artists Cowboy Jack evidently respects. And since Cowboy Jack insists to George Jones that he's gone beyond joking, that first animated sequence actually works to offer a serious balancing out of the earlier jokey song.

To put this another way, and to begin to invoke a theorist who might help us interpret these scenes, Cowboy Jack resorts to comedy as a means to distort the profundity of his dream, in order to make that dream expressible. Sigmund Freud repeatedly observed the 'very far-reaching agreement' between 'joke-work' and 'dream-work': both condense and thereby relate seemingly disparate phenomena, displace or rearrange seemingly normal positions, and represent seemingly unmentionable things indirectly (1905, 215). As he suggested: 'Dreams . . . are often most profound when they seem most crazy.' Wearing what Freud terms 'a fool's cap' means 'forbidden speech' can be 'tolerated', and spoken 'without peril', since the fool's 'unwelcome words' are 'clearly nonsensical': in a suitably Shakespearean allusion, Freud exemplifies this with reference to Hamlet donning 'a cloak of wit and unintelligibility' (1900, 575). As his own version of Hamlet, Cowboy Jack is self-consciously aware that confessing his dreams makes him appear even more foolish, insane even, but he does so all the same.

These Shakespearean dreams still express aspiration, in two related senses, then. First, when Cowboy Jack terms these the 'high-class' dreams we 'need', he implies Shakespeare's cultural authority is worth aiming at for those who don't have it. Second, and *almost* conversely, these are dreams about what sort of producer of popular culture, and even consumer of popular music, Shakespeare would have been. Cowboy Jack insists on Shakespeare's status as a commercial entertainer – in these terms they relate. Cowboy Jack realizes he and Shakespeare are both bound up with particular modes of cultural production – the 'fun business'. When Cowboy Jack assumes that Shakespeare would have been a 'fan' of popular music in general and George Jones in particular, Shakespeare's discernment and authority legitimize Jones, Cowboy Jack, and country and popular music more generally. But recognizing these aspirations need not mean that the film simply casts popular music as some 'low class' cultural form, irredeemably remote from high art such as Shakespeare's, and requiring his seal of approval. Instead, the film and Cowboy Jack create continuities between Shakespeare and popular music. In its own surreal way, their joint extraterrestrial circulation bears out what Karl Marx and Friedrich Engels famously observed about class relations. Though alienated from the fruits of their labours (or just *looking* like aliens), these (cultural) workers of the world (or Globe) can 'UNITE!' because 'The working men have no country' – or *are* country through and through (1848, 258, 241). Perhaps articulating these commonalities represents Cowboy Jack's wishful dreams. But they are no less significant for that, as Freud's appropriately musically minded analysis of dreams reveals:

> Dreams are not to be likened to the unregulated sounds that rise from a musical instrument struck by the blow of some external force instead of by a player's hand; they are not meaningless, they are

not absurd; . . . On the contrary, they are psychical phenomena of complete validity – fulfilments of wishes . . . constructed by a highly complicated activity of the mind. (1900, 200)

Casting Shakespeare as a big George Jones fan may seem wilful and desperate. But as we saw with some rap Shakespeare, articulating these continuities also attests to pop's creative power, a power that, like jokes and dreams, can deform accepted progressions and hierarchies of time and status, making possible 'collocations' and '*simultaneity in time*': 'In the unconscious nothing can be brought to an end, nothing is past or forgotten' (Freud, 1900, 424– 25, 733). And the dreamlike, unearthly, yet very material association of Shakespeare and Cowboy Jack again confirms their status as cultural producers in the context of a common 'business'. To recollect Marx and Engels' famous observations, in the outlandish transgressions and revolutions impelled by industrialized commodity capitalism, 'All that is solid melts into air' (1848, 223).

But does Shakespeare's presence in Cowboy Jack's high-class dreams represent his difference from or connection to popular music like country? Does the fact that Cowboy Jack has to create their relationship through wish-fulfilment, cultural labour and the work of dreams prove that it is possible or impossible? As Freud observed, that's the problem with dreams – it is hard to interpret them without reproducing their ambiguity:

'No' seems not to exist so far as dreams are concerned. They show a particular preference for combining contraries into a unity or for representing them as one and the same thing. Dreams feel themselves at liberty, moreover, to represent any element by its wishful contrary; so that there is no way of deciding at a first glance whether any element that admits of a contrary is present in the dream-thoughts as a positive or as a negative. (1900, 429–30)

Yet as Freud also noted, analysis (whether psychoanalytic or cultural, we might add) does not invent but only recovers relationships that dreams distort or displace, yet cannot deny or determine: 'The new connections are, as it were, loop-lines or short-circuits, made possible by the existence of other and deeper-lying connecting paths' (1900, 385). The film offers evidence for this interpretation. Early on, the singer–songwriter Kris Kristofferson describes Cowboy Jack's identity in terms that suggest these continuities are not simply Cowboy Jack's dreamy invention: 'Cowboy Jack Clement, to me he was like a Shakespearean character, he was kinda a cross between Falstaff, y'know [laughs] and, er, God knows what'. Kristofferson goes on to imply this parallel is not simply laughable, but apt: 'But to me he symbolizes what attracted me to Nashville at that time, which was just the love of creation'. Cowboy Jack's Shakespearean status derives both from his roguish affability and his technical ingenuity, qualities as at home in the Nashville of a certain era as the film imagines they were in the early modern theatre. Voicing the film's Shakespeare with a Johnny Cash sound-alike audibly rein-forces these continuities. The DVD commentary begins with Cowboy Jack and 'Alamo Jones' (Chance Martin, in reality) trying to outdo each others' Johnny Cash impersonations, staking a claim to his identity:

CHANCE MARTIN: Hello, I'm Johnny Cash.
COWBOY JACK: No, you're not. Hello I'm Johnny Cash.
CHANCE MARTIN: No, I'm Johnny Cash.

But in the logic of the film, both men are also playing roles to stake a claim to Shakespeare's voice. And if anyone can do a Johnny Cash, then anyone can *do*, play or perform with (a) Shakespeare. Though Shakespeare speaks in the distinctive accents of a popular musician, this doesn't necessarily underwrite Shakespeare's universal articulacy, but can be seen to affirm both his continuing translatability, *and* the way popular music acts as a medium in which to perform such translations. Again, the film seems to manifest this. On the Shakespearean dream sequence, Cowboy Jack notes this interanimation of Cashs and Bards is a 'good combination'. This allows Alamo Jones aka Chance Martin aka Johnny Cash aka Shakespeare to affirm, with the positive logic of dreams, where there's no word for 'No': 'Yeah, it sure is.'

CHAPTER 6

SHAKESPEARE AND THE SIXTIES

Having looked at what happens to Shakespeare in specific genres of popular music, the next two chapters discuss his relations with popular music in particular periods. As we have seen, there are some problems with this approach. To separate music into periods can be no less arbitrary than to separate it into genres. But by looking at Shakespeare in appreciably distinct moments in the history of popular music, we might see how *he* changes. This chapter focuses on Shakespeare's representation in the popular music of the 1960s; it tightens that focus further by (mainly) considering that music in one location (the United Kingdom); and begins even tighter, by concentrating at first on one group in particular in that location and period: the Beatles.

SHAKESPEARE AND THE BEATLES

It is not nostalgic to suggest that as 'the first pop musicians to challenge the clear distinction between high and low cultural spaces', the Beatles were 'experimental, eclectic' (Frith et al., 2004, 77, 79). The band's experimentalism was in part facilitated by their genesis and existence as 'patient burrowers and cunning foragers', beetling around in the 'detritus' of a 'trash-laden pop scene'; in part by their connections with their audiences; and in part by their willingness and ability to rework those audiences' expectations (McKinney, 2003, 3). As Ian Inglis puts it, 'they were *given* a multiplicity of voices by the community within which they were active and successful' (2000, xvii). Consequently, rightly or wrongly, tongue-in-cheek or not, contemporaries also perceived that the band represented a new form of peculiarly *national* popular-cultural identity:

> For several decades, in fact since the decline of the music-hall, England has taken her popular songs from the United States, either directly or by mimicry. But the songs of Lennon and McCartney are distinctly indigenous in character. (Mann, 1963, 59)

Writing in 1964, Brian Epstein, the Beatles' then-manager, similarly identified their grounded character, but noted their eccentricity: 'They are British, but un-English in that they accept barriers of neither class nor sex' (1964, 93). All these characteristics are evident in the ways the group engaged with and changed an icon of national identity – Shakespeare. These engagements in turn reveal the Beatles' changing sense of themselves as artists, and the changes at work in the musical period they dominated.

As recipients of a post–Second-World-War British education, the Beatles were exposed to Shakespeare. Paul McCartney observed: 'By going to grammar school I knew I'd fairly soon have Latin phrases or know about Shakespeare' (Miles, 1998, 13). Yet this exposure did not cause contempt or passivity. Even prior to the bohemian excitements of art school, they were positioned, or positioned themselves, as active consumers of high culture such as Shakespeare, but also as producers, or reinterpreters, of the theatrical arts he embodied. McCartney intimated as much when recollecting his school days to one biographer: 'We did *Hamlet*, which I immediately started to eat up. I became a director in my own mind' (Miles, 1998, 41). In the band's earliest days, McCartney remembered, they 'once tried to write a play' (Miles, 1998, 39).

This active engagement laid the foundations for commonalities between the band and Shakespeare. Stephen Bretzius has intricately traced some of these commonalities, in terms of allusions and cultural effects. They are related by the 'sheer popularity' of their lyrics, and the ways they all 'harnessed . . . tremendous cultural and historical energies'(1997, 121). The Beatles performed or registered complex rhetorical and cultural shifts, as Shakespeare did. Beatles' songs implicated auditors in a 'quasi-Shakespearean fusion of first and second person, *me* and *you*'(122). The band's inclusive words 'unsettle gender in lyrics', just as Shakespeare 'delimits early modern culture in part by cross-dressing and unsexing the sexual difference upon which it is grounded'(132). So both the Beatles and Shakespeare evoke 'Bottome-sque dissent' against early modern and modern Elizabethan establishments, even as they speak to and for changing nations (129).

Beyond academia, these connections have inspired, and been manifested by, musicians influenced by the Beatles. In a 2008 interview, the musician Chris O'Neill recollected how he had begun touring songs that would comprise an inventive musical project he named 'A Bard Day's Night'. As this title intimates, O'Neill's work imagines what might have happened if the Beatles had travelled back in time and met

Shakespeare. O'Neill acknowledged that his earlier experiences of the Beatles and Shakespeare might have made it difficult to connect them in this or any way. As a Liverpudlian, he 'always loved the Beatles' and 'grew up with them'; but though he also 'always loved English' he did not study Shakespeare at school, and confessed he wasn't 'switched on' academically. Yet having played George Harrison in the 1994 Beatles biopic, *Backbeat*, O'Neill was looking for medium-sized theatres to do gigs with his Beatles tribute act, The Backbeat Beatles (in which he plays the role of McCartney). He saw the Globe on the internet, featuring an image of 'four guys with lutes' on the stage. Though he thought it would be 'great to do a gig there', he was resigned to his separation from the world of Shakespeare: 'I'm never gonna play there'. Nevertheless, in a 'dream-state' during a restless night's sleep, O'Neill followed a 'train of thought: how'm I gonna get a gig at the Globe Theatre?' He kept returning to the image of 'four guys playing lutes', and the image became confused in his mind with the four Beatles. After conceiving his title for a time-travel Shakespeare–Beatles jam session, says O'Neill, the connections became ever more obvious: Shakespeare created 'something worth remembering'; so did the Beatles; Shakespeare was the 'spokesman of a generation'; so were the Beatles. In his own way, O'Neill had rethought both Shakespeare and the Beatles: where once four lads shook the world, there were now 'five lads that shook the Globe'. The congruences began as visual and musical ('four guys playing lutes'), but became verbal (in the puns O'Neill used as song titles, like 'Maccabeth', or 'To Be or Not to Let It Be') and cultural. O'Neill describes the Beatles' early venue, The Cavern, as *their* Globe; they were all provincial, not elite, and 'related to their audiences'. O'Neill's songs, featuring uncanny replays of Beatles-esque melodies and arrangements with lyrics from the plays and poems, bear out his belief that the two merge 'very easily'. O'Neill has suggested the sonnets work best of all, which is perhaps inevitable since he is reviving their initial Italian incarnation as songs. But the tone of other Shakespearean excerpts is reinvigorated too, by their synthesis with the Beatles. For example, O'Neill sets Ariel's songs from 1.2 of *The Tempest*, 'Come unto These Yellow Sands' and 'Full Fathom Five', to a string arrangement and melody that evokes 'Eleanor Rigby'. This connection ably borrows from the Beatles to reinforce Ferdinand's melancholy and loneliness.

However, back in the 1960s, it might have seemed as though the Beatles themselves saw Shakespeare as a competitor, not a comrade-in-arms. This is particularly apparent in the band's parody sequence of the Pyramus and Thisbe scene from *A Midsummer Night's Dream* (5.1.108–363), broadcast on UK television as part of *Around the Beatles*, in the spring of 1964. If we want to understand Shakespeare's place in the popular music of this time, especially the Beatles', we need to ask: why this scene, and why then? There are several answers.

THE BEATLES' *DREAM*

We have seen how Cowboy Jack Clement gets to grips with Shakespeare in dream-states, to communicate fantasies about himself and the Bard. For their part, the Beatles give us a fragment of Shakespeare's *Dream*, at a moment when their own fantasises were materializing. In his allusive, idiosyncratic history of the group, Devin McKinney argues that in 1964, 'at least in its first months', the Beatles were enjoying their burgeoning success, honeymooning with their fans, and living 'sweet dreams, mass dreams unprecedented in size and spontaneity' (2003, 87). Writing in 1964, Brian Epstein himself recorded the significance of the year:

> The group of young musicians who could neither read music nor write it, and who are known as the Beatles, conquered the United States of America on February 7th, 1964, and by implication – since America is the heart and soul of popular music – the Beatles ruled the pop world. By May this year the Beatles had become a world-wide phenomenon. (11)

Fresh from their television appearances on the US Ed Sullivan Show, 1964 was the moment of their desired ascension:

> What the Beatles touched off was dreamlike in particularly deep and intricate ways. Their mania became a huge, open arena for the unregulated discharge of submerged energies – their own, and the audience's. (McKinney, 2003, 87)

Through this performance of Shakespeare, the Beatles signal their awareness of the time's *Dream*/dream-making, playing up their status as players. Their parody draws attention to the significance of impersonation to popular music: the Beatles acted as much on record or in their films as they do in this Shakespearean burlesque, and as such are conscious of their power and status as marketable performers, and their audience's role in sustaining them. As Wes Folkerth notes, throughout the performance, they keep their 'trademark Beatle boots' (2002a, 77). How better to signal their cultural power than by taking off Shakespeare? At the time, associates were willing to confuse the two: 'I don't know whether it was William Shakespeare or Ringo Starr who said: "When this business stops being fun, I'm giving it up"' (Epstein, 1964, 112). Epstein's confusion of Shakespeare and Starr may itself be a bit of ironic 'fun' – implying Starr, the non-writing drummer, is no Shakespeare – but it reinforces the kind of cocky connections the band themselves suggest in their *Dream* parody. Like Cowboy Jack, the Beatles think they are in the same 'business' as the Bard. But in this case, these connections not only relate to but also overwrite Shakespeare, at a time when he was enjoying his own moment in the spotlight in April 1964, in celebrations for the quatercentenary of his birth.

But, again, why this scene? Annabel Patterson influentially suggested that the mechanicals' play-within-the-play offered a 'revaluation of those "unpresentable" members of society, normally mocked as fools and burdened like asses, whose energies the social system relies on' (1989, 69). As such, they offer inversionary laughter within the context of a performance licensed by political authorities. If the play-within-the-play does this in the *Dream*, then the Beatles, the New Elizabethans' rude mechanicals (or working-class artists who performed for 'royalty'), do this with Shakespeare: his elevation is reduced, and their status is confirmed, through their 'comic festive energy' (Folkerth, 2002a, 77, 79).

And this scene is certainly comic. The sequence begins with a flourish blown by three trumpeters in silhouette; this is replaced by a drawing of the Globe; this is followed by the raising of a flag. While these scenes appear to be a condensed visual echo of the opening of Laurence Olivier's 1944 *Henry V*, any gravity is deflated from the start. The silhouetted trumpeters turn out to be three of the Beatles, dressed in an approximation of Elizabethan garb, who smile and laugh; the flag is hoisted by Ringo, dressed like his bandmates, who then fires a cannon which triggers sound effects of smashing glass, tumbling masonry and boinging springs. These scenes and sounds position the sketch in relation to the TV shows of Eric Morecambe and Ernie Wise, ascendant in the 1960s, and often featuring the Beatles, or recall the radio comedy of *The Goon Show* (broadcast on the BBC Home Service, 1951–1960), of which the band was especially fond, a series produced by the Beatles' own producer, George Martin. Peter Sellers of the Goons would return the favour and confirm the link in suitably Shakespearean form, with his 1965 version of the Beatles' 'A Hard Day's Night'. Reciting the lyrics in the style of Olivier's 1955 Richard III, full of twitches, wry (or malevolent) smiles and dramatic (or hilarious) pauses, Sellers traded on his impersonation skills to evoke Richard/Olivier's ability to make innocent words sound sinister. The humour involved might seem to poke fun at the idea that the Beatles' words could possess Shakespearean grandeur: part of the comedy comes from the incongruity. But Sellers's take on the lyrics prove uncannily apt for Richard, the consummate grafter, who works like, and is compared to, a dog. This version reached the UK Top 20, and was performed by Sellers dressed as Richard for a Granada TV special, followed by the band singing the suitably ironic, or simply suitable, 'We Can Work It Out'.

The scenes and sounds of the Beatles' *Dream* sequence therefore signal the band's working knowledge and familiarity with the medium of television, and also a breezy anarchy and iconoclasm, impelled by the same cultural confidence that empowered a generation of new, working-class, provincial and demob-happy entertainers in the post–Second-World-War period. So Sinfield argues:

'The 1960s' is of course a myth; but that is an important thing to be, since what we think and do depends on the stories we tell ourselves. . . . It wasn't quite bliss to be alive, but it made a change. (1989, 283)

The Beatles seemed to embody this change. Ian MacDonald has suggested that British pop culture of the time 'represented an upsurge of . . . expression into a medium till then mostly handed down to the common man by middle-class professionals' (1995, 22). This 'upsurge of . . . expression' had material foundations. The significance of youth, and so of the popular music that 'sprang' from its cultures, was an 'economic phenomenon': 'the new consumer society in which hitherto underprivileged and silent groups now had, if not a voice, certainly purchasing power' (Marwick, 1996, 131, 123). Franco Zeffirelli's 1968 film version of *Romeo and Juliet* sought to capture – or neuter – some of this youthful energy on the big screen, and as noted above, Buhler has described the ways this film influenced pop music in the period and after (2002).

But, in the sketch, while parody dispels gravity and iconoclasm reigns, Ringo is still mortified by the unintended effects of his cannon's charge, and makes for the exit. His escape is blocked by crowds of Beatle-maniacs, holding balloons and placards, and singing 'We love you Ringo'. When the beat in the Beatles loses his cool, his audience helps him get it back. This aligns the Beatles' cultural confidence to parody high cultural figures like Olivier and Shakespeare with their fans' desire to let them do so. In moments like this, the Beatles come to represent a newly reconfigured nation of the young and creative, a nation now seeing itself on screen, and hearing its vernacular performed or repeated on record. As MacDonald observes, it wasn't just sex that began in the early 1960s: 'An extraordinary thing began to happen to pop music in 1963: the audience started to take over the role of formulating what was performed' (2003, 192). In this case, the fans also create a spatial and temporal continuity between the TV set with its mock-up of an Elizabethan stage, and the world beyond, as they march into and populate the studio. The 'do-it-yourself participatory element' of youth and popular cultures at this time is here made evident (Marwick, 1996, 132). As this scene rehearses a vision of the popular significance of the early modern stage via modern media, whose very workings are visible, the powerful presence of the audience is palpable, and significantly gendered and sexualized: young women, as groundlings, reach out to touch their idols' feet and trousers. Yet young men, elevated in boxes, rain only abuse down on the players. They attack the Bard and ridicule the parody ('load of old rubbish'), referencing the idioms of popular music to do so ('Roll over Shakespeare'). The elevated male malcontents also deride the pretensions of the performers, betraying regional tensions latent in this emerging aesthetic: 'Go back to Liverpool'. These interjections police a range of divisions that the Beatles transgressed in their performative experiments, here and elsewhere: divisions between province and metropolitan centre, between popular and high culture, and between 'authenticity' and 'performance'. Yet the sketch also deliberately unsettles sexual and gender identities. Throughout, John/Thisbe engages in homoerotic winks with Paul/Pyramus, yet has blacked-out teeth and a gruff voice; when Paul/Pyramus declares 'out sword' and moves to stab himself, he brandishes a pathetic blade.

All saucy stuff, but the Beatles were not the first English musicians in the decade to present such a cheeky take on the Bard. In one verse and chorus of the song 'Flash Bang Wallop!', from the 1963 musical *Half a Sixpence*, Tommy Steele offered a risqué summary of *Romeo and Juliet* where the heroine bawls, and the hero tumbles, tears his tights and bends his rapier, in knockabout Music Hall style. Steele's dalliance with

Shakespeare was part of an effort to establish himself as a mainstream entertainer who could have a career beyond the vagaries of rock 'n' pop. This motivated his appearance as Feste in a 1969 version of *Twelfth Night* for ATV (directed by John Sichel), alongside esteemed British thespians Alec Guinness (as Malvolio), and Joan Plowright (as Viola).

In comparison, for all *their* cheeky appeal, the Beatles were cruder, coarser, more cutting and provocative. This meant that the audiences' aggressive interjections are not uncontested, and even seem scripted, as if the band and their collaborators (the audience, and their TV producers) sought to express and confront these tensions. One female audience member hits one of the men; and when Paul hits the Wall, one male audience member shouts 'Hit him back wall', to which Pyramus/Paul responds, off-script: 'He should not, 'cos this is Thisbe's cue, and she comes in and we look through the . . . Shuddup!' So these audience inter-jections do not simply attack Shakespeare, or appropriations of him, policing various divides. They also allow the band to reinforce the cultural and material success of *their* identities as performers who can transgress such divides. One male audience member shouts of or to Ringo, dressed as a mangy big cat, 'Feed that lion!' Ringo's response moves from past to present in terms of grammar and in its reflection on his current status, for it begins in an approximation of early modern English syntax, but ends with a knowing sneer: 'And know that I, one Ringo the drummer am, for if I was really a lion, I wouldn't be making all the money I am today, would I?'

And yet, as this summary has suggested, the parody is not entirely iconoclastic; nor, as Folkerth notes, does it show Shakespeare 'simply having his cultural capital appropriated' (2002a, 79). The sequence presents popular musicians taking on high culture, animated by the social changes around them, but their commingling of cultural and class dis-tinctions is mindful of its transgressions. The timing of the broadcast locates the performance around significantly Shakespearean and hence national cultural anniversaries, even as it might be seen to supplant or re-envision the forms of culture and nationhood being commemorated. Lennon, for one, would celebrate Shakespeare's big day as his own with a Literary Luncheon at Foyle's, promoting a book, *In His Own Write*, while also implicitly doffing a Beatle-cap to a literary forebear. His gar-bled fragments of prose, poetry and playlets, contained (per)versions of Beckett and Wordsworth ('I Sat Belonely'), but also what might be considered an approximation of the Henriad, in the father-son wranglings of 'Henry and Harry' (the father wants the son to follow in the family trade; the son doesn't want to; the father ends up buried by the mother – maybe *Hamlet* is the more appropriate reference?).

By this scene's close, when Paul/Pyramus and John/Thisbe lie down holding hands, saying 'Adieu, Adew, I do like to be beside the seaside', Shakespearean language is metamorphosed into popular song: this is *both* a parody and a bond. To McKinney, the Beatles always made audiences ask: 'Subversion or elaboration?' (2003, 94). This question resounds here. Subsequently, following bows and catcalls, the sequence finishes by reinvoking *both* the continuities and discontinuities between Shakespeare and popular music and culture that the sketch explored, as Lennon speaks to the camera:

> Enough of this [?] rubbish, we'd like to bring on something good now, some girls, hee hee [he leers], we'd like to bring on the Vernon Girls, and two of the girls from the film *The West Side Story* [sic], the Jets . . .

As The Beatles' cultural significance burgeoned, so their engagement with Shakespeare was sustained, albeit in fragmentary and no less estranged forms, as if his status could only be apprehended or overcome through circuitous or piecemeal means. McCartney himself seemed diffident about tackling the Bard:

> In September 1966 Paul was even asked by Kenneth Tynan to write music for the songs in the National Theatre production of Shakespeare's *As You Like It*, starring Laurence Olivier. Paul wrote back thanking him, saying he had given the matter some thought but he couldn't write music to Shakespeare's words; perhaps he could write the 'Ballad of Larry O' for them. (Miles, 1998, 124)

Though Shakespeare is 'conspicuously absent' from the 'gallery of notables' on the cover of the group's 1967 album *Sgt. Pepper's Lonely Hearts Club Band*, he figures as a truncated echo in the reference to 'Billy Shears' in the segue between the titular song and the second cut, 'With a Little Help from My Friends', whose opening lines themselves echo *Julius Caesar*'s 'Friends, Romans, countrymen, lend me your ears' from 3.2.74 (Bretzius, 1997, 121–22). Other echoes and fragments abound. McCartney cites *Hamlet* in Richard Lester's 1964 film of the group, *A Hard Day's Night*. The 'fool on the heath' from *King Lear* becomes 'The Fool on the Hill' on 1967's *Magical Mystery Tour*.

The apocalyptic dying fall and fade-out of 'I Am The Walrus' from the same album features a fuzzy, random, radio excerpt that captures fragments of lines from a BBC performance of the same play:

OSWALD   O untimely death! Death!
EDGAR   I know thee well – a serviceable villain . . .
              Sit you down, father. Rest you. (4.5.249–54)

This last appropriation is especially provocative: what might we make of Shakespeare's place (or displacement) in 'I Am the Walrus'? Perhaps the significance of the allusion is reduced because it is so random: Shakespeare might as well be anyone. But this randomizing is itself a telling kind of artistic democratization, evoking the era. As the Beatles' career and work progressed into the later 1960s, and aligned with the counter-cultural energies they sometimes represented or gave voice to, randomness itself became a legitimate aesthetic mode:

All you had to do was toss a coin, consult the *I Ching*, or read a random paragraph from a newspaper – and then start playing or singing. Anyone could do it, everyone could join in. (MacDonald, 1995, 210)

So while the capture of a radio fragment may be random and accidental, its subsequent recording in the studio and broadcasting is deliberate and conscious: 'the perfectly random can produce sense as spontaneously as it generates chaos' (McKinney, 2003, 240). For the very *gesture* of randomness resisted orthodox cultural discourses and taxonomies; though idealized or stylized, it signalled spontaneity as opposed to prejudiced premeditation, feel over thought, and irreverent informality against staid conformity.

As the decade developed, the increasing importance of randomness in 'chance-generated music events' also reflected the increasing importance of hallucinogens like LSD to creative processes (MacDonald, 1995, 21). Precisely because the Shakespearean allusion here is random, and is technologically and aesthetically possible in a pop song of this time, it suits a track variously described as 'vicious, excremental, and running over with grue' (McKinney, 2003, 201), and 'a damn-you-England tirade that blasts education, art, culture, law, order, class, religion, and even sense itself' (MacDonald, 1995, 214). Is Shakespeare 'vicious' and 'excremental', and so opposed to those 'institutions', or is he part of them? Is he present in fragmented form because those institutions were, or were being, fragmented? Would the fragments ultimately cohere, but in *new* forms?:

> The Beatles' psychedelic music represents a state of mind different from ordinary reality: a magical, all-beautiful, all-loving vision in which opposites are peacefully reconciled. Whether that state of mind is ultimately a delusion is up to the listener. (MacDonald, 2003, 98)

PSYCHEDELIC SHAKESPEARES

Given these questions and contexts, it should come as little surprise to observe that Shakespeare came to figure heavily in popular psychedelic and counter-cultural musics of the late 1960s and early 1970s.

Some of these figurings were politically forthright. Lanier notes that on *Dangerous Songs!?*, Pete Seeger combined words from Ariel and Hamlet in the developing genre of protest song 'to meditate on the problem of post-revolutionary complacency' (2006, 69). The decade's counter-cultural appropriations of Shakespeare reached something of a peak in Johnny Mandel and Mike Altman's 1970 track 'Song from M*A*S*H (Suicide is Painless)', used in the TV series and film of the same name. Though the song could be read as advocating passive acceptance of fate, it cited Hamlet's own ruminations on self-destruction to reflect on the confusion and depredation caused by America's involvement in the Korean War, and, much more topically, in Vietnam.

Yet, in keeping with the period's more benign and blissful popular pseudo-philosophies, other figurings read Shakespeare, and especially his 'old . . . pre-modern' language, through a less confrontational post-Romantic prism (Lanier, 2006, 69). This turned Shakespeare into a pioneering poet for consciousnesses attuned to what psychedelic sages termed 'the Universal Symphony', audible under the influence of drugs, or when the repression of 'straight' society had been overcome (Thompson, 1967, 293). This meant that even where a band was not overtly political, they could pose aural challenges to orthodox tastes, invoking Shakespeare to do so. Pink Floyd's 1967 'Astronomy Domine' opens with an aggressively distorted blues-inflected guitar riff, features close-miked, treated voices swooshing through the soundscape, and a heavy tom-tom pulse throughout. Folkerth suggests that through this sonic abrasion come lyrics and rhymes communicating between planets and periods: 'the band moves beyond space and into Shakespeare's magical worlds' (2006, 404). As the song puts it: 'Floating down the sound resounds around the icy waters underground, / Jupiter and Saturn, Oberon, Miranda, and Titania'. The rush of hallucination echoes in this melting and remembering of Shakespeare's words.

A subgenre of late-decade Shakespeare-referencing psychedelia also developed that elevated him to the status of a laureate for childlike innocence and pastoralism (as opposed to jaded, over-civilized and alienated urbanism). Preluding tracks like The Sallyangie's 1969 'Midsummer Night's Happening', Donovan's 1967 album *a gift from a flower to a garden* was one standout among the odes for literal and figurative inhabitants of a paradise apparently regained that cited Shakespeare. This featured 'Under the greenwood tree', a version of the song from *As You Like It*, with 'words by William Shakespeare, a tribute', as the sleeve notes put it. Echoing the appeal made to the Beatles, in his autobiography Donovan recollects that he was approached by 'Sir Laurence Olivier' to 'compose melodies' for a production of the play at London's National Theatre. While the use of Olivier's title might only hint at Donovan's reverence for the Bard and his 'modern' interpreters in the 'classical theater', what is clearer is the singer's pleasure at being connected with Shakespeare and such institutions: 'I was delighted to be asked' (Leitch, 2005, 176–77). Yet as the song closes, Donovan, like Jaques in the scene, adds his own 'invention' (2.5.44) to the original lyrics to express a 'come hither' inclusivity (2.5.5):

> Will you, won't you, won't you join the dance . . .
> Do the Willy the Shake . . . we do the Willy the Shake.

These putative ad-libs are not given in the sleeve-note lyrics: Donovan's words and Shakespeare's remain separate in textual form. Yet on the track, Donovan interferes with and rewrites Shakespeare, even while claiming to respectfully extrapolate from his characters' seemingly sensual and earthy interests. Shakespeare is casually turned into a popular dance ('the Willy the Shake'), with punning intimations of sexuality dispelling any of the scene's residual 'melancholy' (2.5.10). In this new green world where 'love is crownèd' (5.3.35), there are only intercoursing friends, and no enemies but 'winter and rough weather' (2.5.42).

Another remarkable track in this vein released in the same year was the Byrds' 'Mind Gardens' from their aptly titled album *Younger than Yesterday*. Here David Crosby sang of the fatal perils of cultivating a fearful and defensive sense of self, cut off from nature, others and the elements, when walled against 'the slings and arrows of outrageous fortune' (*Hamlet*, 3.1.60). As the song's free-flowing *raga* melodies spiral amidst multi-layered and reversed acoustic guitars, Crosby resolves to tear down the walls he has built around his ego, and endure. L.A.-hippy clichés aside, the psychic and sonic openness of this psychedelia attains harmonies the alienated Hamlet can only contemplate: the gardens of *his* mind are 'unweeded', possessed by 'things rank and gross in nature' (1.2.135–36).

So Shakespeare became a guru for altered psychic and social states. Suiting the period's social flux (or at least the myth of it), this usage had been current for some time, admittedly. In 1962, on the hook of the single 'As You Like It', Adam Faith repeatedly invoked the Shakespearean play title to promise his beau that whatever alteration was desired of him, he'd willingly perform it, whether cutting his 'kooky' hair, or changing his 'crazy' attire. Chiming with a comedy involving extensive role-play, and an artist who had himself adopted a pseudonym (and who had released 'Who Am I?' the year before), the track mingled assertive self-fashioning with sanitizing self-negation, set to an unthreateningly light-orchestral backing. It also fitted the beginning of a period when pop addressed the yearnings (and demands) of its audience as never before: Faith is assuring fans he bends to their wills. Yet by later in the decade, the Shakespearean shifts and fashionings achieved were of a different, more intense, order. When Angela Carter described the dissolutions in conventional identities she perceived around her in 1967, she referenced the same play (and the Beatles), but extolled the performative energies of *all* popular culture:

Mutability is having a field day. . . . One passes oneself off as another, who may or may not exist – as Jean Harlow or Lucy in the Sky with Diamonds or Al Capone or Sergeant Pepper. . . . This holiday from the persistent self is the perpetual lure of fancy dress. Rosalind in disguise in the Forest of Arden could pretend to be a boy pretending to be a seductress, satisfying innumerable atavistic desires in the audience of the play. And we are beginning to realise once again what everybody always used to know, that all human contact is profoundly ambiguous. And the style of the sixties expresses this knowledge. (316–17)

At such times, in addition to the putatively comic bucolia of *A Midsummer Night's Dream* and *As You Like It*, *The Tempest* also became a key text, appreciated for its perceived transformative and redemptive qualities. The sleeve notes for the Zombies' British psychedelic classic *Odessey and Oracle* contained a (mis)quote (from 3.2.138–41) that conveys the scope of shifts in sensibility:

> Shakespeare said
> 'Be not afraid;
> The isle is full of noises
> Sound, and sweet airs that give delight and hurt not.
> Sometimes a thousand twanging instruments
> Will hum about mine ears; and sometimes voices'. . . .
> Thanks to Will Shakespeare . . . for his contribution to the sleeve
>   notes.

Evidently, 'Will' shared the Zombies' informal (and undead) state, in an isle (or British Isles) full of perfumed airs, noises and sounds. Of course, Shakespeare never 'said' these words – Caliban did. This misattribution not only aligns creator and creation, writing and speaking, past and present, informal 'Will' with canonical 'Shakespeare'; it also (re)constructs a fantasy nation-state where even enslaved characters of questionable humanity feel popular music's power.

Yet even at its most flowery, flaky extremes, the period's pop was still about power of more material kinds – economic muscle and markets, hit making and hype. In Derek Jarman's words, the most important product came to be the 'authentic', self-possessing, individual, what he memorably called the 'millions of the fuckers who were being taught to become themselves' (1996, 75). However else Shakespeare was used, at times he came to provide the cultural accreditation for this, as can be heard in Nik Cohn's account of lunch with Nick Venet, the manager of the Beach Boys:

> 'I'm known as the Gutsy Greek,' he told me. 'I got where I am by hustle, bustle and elbow-grease.' Everything he said was ornate, an attempted proverb . . . I was most impressed, liked him enormously. 'Baby,' he said. 'Unto thine own self be true.' (Cohn, 1969, 99–100)

As victim and plotter, unable to heed his own advice or recognize its flaws, Polonius seems an odd choice as a business guru. But since the heroes, drugs and inspirations were changing, so were the terms of engagement with Shakespeare. By the mid-1970s, David Bowie's drug-fuelled descent into paranoia, disillusionment, crypto-fascism and occultism produced a notable example of this:

> In 'Station to Station', the Thin White Duke – Bowie as a cocaine-frozen Prospero lost in his (magic) circle, tall in his room overlooking the ocean (Prospero's island 'cell' transported to the coast by Los Angeles) – despairingly reviews his repertoire of illusions. (MacDonald, 2003, 145)

Whether it is a side effect of the drugs (on the character or the performer) or not, in the cold, dark funk of this song Shakespeare resounds, if only in fractured, half-remembered ways. Having once performed the track 'Cracked Actor' while singing to a Hamlet-esque skull, here Bowie howls a dissolute, corrupted version of Prospero's lines about the 'stuff' that 'dreams', and nightmares, are 'made' of (*The Tempest*, 4.1.156–57). The strained Shakespearean echo indicates Bowie's 'vexed' (4.1.158) state of mind as he turned his back on Los Angeles, and commenced his musical 'struggle towards Europe': citing a totemic, canonical, dead white male was part of that (Wilcken, 2005, 14).

That said, revivals of the aesthetics and aims of psychedelia, as in Manchester of the late 1980s, would sustain earlier uses of the 'rough magic' and 'heavenly music' of this play (5.1.50–52). The Stone Roses' B-side 'Full Fathom Five' not only invokes Ariel's song of 1.2.399–405, but literally reverses the A-side, 'Elephant Stone', to do so, slyly turning it into something psychedelically rich, strange and suited to altered perceptions that blurred temporal and cultural contexts. In other words, the song's retrogression reminds us of the changes back and forth between the 1980s and the 1960s, and between both periods and Shakespeare. Much was abjured, broken and lost in the 'certain fathoms' (5.1.55) of these backs and forths. Yet as ever with Shakespeare and popular music, what seemed frozen, drowned or dead, was not.

CHAPTER 7

SHAKES-PUNK: 'DEFORMED, UNFINISHED', AND ROTTEN

As we have seen, for various very good reasons some genres and examples of popular music are less willing and able to relate to Shakespeare than others. Punk could be considered like this, implacably opposed to institutions like Shakespeare. But is that opposition *so* implacable? This chapter explores what happened to Shakespeare during the conflicted and challenging punk and post-punk eras, and why. Punk involved developments in popular media other than music but these other media *used* music. Equally, punk confronted reactionary and repressive shifts in the West's late twentieth-century social climate. As such, this chapter situates several key figures in relation to these shifts, figures like Johnny Rotten and Elvis Costello, later groups like Titus Andronicus, and film makers like Derek Jarman. All these artists approach Shakespeare in innovative ways, yet all do so within the context of punk: its upsurge (the Sex Pistols), its possibilities (Jarman), and its aftermath (Costello and Titus Andronicus). Throughout, we will see how ambivalence towards Shakespeare took different, provocative forms, which might be characterized as 'Shakes-punk'.

DEFINING SHAKES-PUNK

Before we think about Shakes-punk, it is worth admitting that punk itself is difficult to define. It didn't happen in one place, and its impact and influences were not, and have not been, fixed to one time. As Jon Savage notes of punk's early days, in the mid to late 1970s, there could be 'as many contradictions as there were groups' (1992, 133). This chapter does not try to ignore these contradictions, or paper over them. This is because as far as motives could be ascribed to so heterogeneous a scene, in the United Kingdom at least, the contradictoriness appeared *deliberate*, a poised but unstable attempt to cut up, bring together and demystify existing cultural signs and values:

> Punk announced itself as a portent with its polysemy of elements drawn from the history of youth culture, sexual fetish wear, urban decay and extremist politics. Taken together, these elements had no conscious meaning but they spoke of many things: urban primitivism; the breakdown of confidence in a common language; the availability of cheap, second-hand clothes; the fractured nature of perception in an accelerating, media-saturated society; the wish to offer up the body as a jumble of meanings. (Savage, 1992, 230)

In its musical beginnings, punk involved a 'deliberate *un*learning' (Savage, 1992, 82). The conventional narrative of punk's history runs that in place of the pomposity of prog-rock and the falseness of teeny-bop, punk offered a back-to-basics stripping down to rock 'n' roll's bare bones. Given some of the movement's dependence on unflashy barre-chords and simple song structures, privileging wilful imperfection over deadening polish, this is as accurate as it is paradoxical: lots of punk was, in Savage's words, 'reversing into tomorrow' (1992, 55). Even where such pseudo-primitivism was muted, punk 'established a Year Zero rule of elementary aesthetics in the service of a "won't get fooled again" outlook' (MacDonald, 2003, 200). This was a genre explicitly 'bent on negation' (Marcus, 1993, 177). What hope would a figure like Shakespeare have in a scene like this? Was he to be ignored, reviled or perceived as one of many jumbled symbols and icons to be debased and negated? This would seem to be the case on the Wipers' 1981 single 'Romeo': the titular hero roams an apocalyptic cityscape doomed never to meet Juliet because she doesn't exist. Alternatively, since punk revived older modes such as Dada and Situationism, did it manifest another paradox, that negation sustains what is negated, including Shakespeare? As Freud suggested: 'Negation is a way of taking cognizance of what is repressed' (1925, 438). When the Stranglers mused on the decline of centuries of icons whose Romes have burned on 1977's aptly titled 'No More Heroes', they included Shakespeare in the list of the fallen. Yet was this song a lament for the old, or a triumph of the new? Dick Hebdige noted punk's 'large claims for illiteracy', but also that 'literary sources turned out to be firmly though implicitly inscribed in the aesthetics' of UK and US punk (1996, 19, 27–28). Might these sources include Shakespeare?

However we answer these questions, it will become evident that things became both more complicated and more propitious for Shakespeare as punk fragmented and mutated into what can only accurately be described as post-punk:

> Punk threw the record industry into confusion, making the majors vulnerable to suggestion, and fluxing up all the aesthetic rules so that anything abnormal or extreme suddenly had a chance.
> (Reynolds, 2006, xxi)

Post-punk cultivated a 'sense of possibility' in terms of art and ideology, being 'informed by often hidden, but definite gender politics' (Savage, 1992, 418–19). Post-punk amplified and broadcast punk's chaotic heterogeneity (musically and otherwise) but also its passionate intensity: to Simon Reynolds, looking back from the twenty-first century, the music created in the United States and United Kingdom in the period 1978–84 represented 'a counter-culture that was fragmented yet shared a common belief that music could and should change the world'. As such, because of this dissemination and this belief, 'punk had its most pro-vocative repercussions long after its supposed demise' (2006, xv–xvi).

We can get a sense of the post-punk period's play with Shakespeare, and with eclectic cultural influences, from a couple of initial examples. Released on Manchester's idiosyncratic Factory Communications, Kevin Hewick's 1982 track 'Ophelia's Drinking Song' featured loose-limbed percussion from another Factory luminary (A Certain Ratio's Donald Johnson), and a guitar treated with chorus and phase effects, playing 'mostly a drone in [the chord of] E'. This created a watery, dissolute sound suiting the lyrics which combined Shakespearean elements with counter-cultural traces: 'You make me dive into a river of drugs . . . I sing Ophelia's drinking song, until I choke on weeds and mud'. The notion that the hardly hearty Ophelia might actually have had a drinking song may seem ironic, especially since Hewick admits that though he 'loved Shakespeare at school', 'I didn't do any research on it or anything, didn't even consult the play'. But Hewick now suggests he was inspired to 'mix up . . . unconnected things' when conceiving the track, things which hint at histories of excess and obsession, auto-destruction and self-expression: his father's copy of Mario Lanza singing the drinking song from Richard Thorpe's 1954 film *The Student Prince*; Marianne Faithfull's performance as Ophelia in Tony Richardson's 1969 produc-tion of *Hamlet*; and the notion that 'death comes as a merciful release' to

Ophelia in the play (2009). As the song's lyrics put it: 'the mad air is flushed from out of my lungs, by the compassionate water'.

Aside from this punkish eclecticism, we can also sense the emphatic and explicitly self-conscious form of post-punk engagements with Shakespeare in the title of the Mekons' 1979 album for Virgin: *The Quality of Mercy Is Not Strnen*. This title deliberately strained Portia's words compelling Shylock to act mercifully in *The Merchant of Venice* (4.1.181–202). The record's cover showed a 'chimp typing out Shakespeare' (Marcus, 1993, 246–47). Was this anarchic popular music cack-handedly learning the art of garbling the qualities and 'strength' of heavenly high culture (like Shakespeare), mocking the idea that such culture's edifying mercies might gently 'rain' from Olympian peaks on dumb beasts cowering 'beneath'? Or did the title and accompanying image parody the band's status as alienated artists mercilessly co-opted by mass production and commerce? As Reynolds notes, by signing to a major label, a band 'whose whole point was amateurish charm' had 'inadvertently ended up with a career on their hands' (2006, 119–20). But this makes it hard to tell whether the Mekons were contrasting their co-option in capitalism with Shakespeare's perceived autonomy, or comparing their mutual misrepresentation in an age of mechanical reproduction. Whatever the implications, the Mekons' semi-destructive, strained continuity with Shakespeare actually set up a later connection. A 1982 compilation of the band's material issued by CNT would complete Portia's lines in its title, though still misquoting them: *it falleth like the gentle rain from heaven – The Mekons Story, 1977–1982*. Is this disdain, distinction or homage, or both? But let's not get ahead of ourselves. These issues of Shakes-punk's hybridity, ambiguities and unsettlement initially concentrated around the group that did most to first make punk popular and notorious: the Sex Pistols.

THE SEX PISTOLS

In his survey of appropriations of Shakespeare in popular music, Wes Folkerth recalls the perhaps 'mythic story' that when John Lydon performed as Johnny Rotten with the Sex Pistols, he 'reportedly borrowed heavily from the mannerisms and especially the posture of Sir Laurence Olivier in his 1955 film portrayal of Richard III' (2006, 387). Folkerth goes on to note that though this 'revelation' might be less than reliable given the band's propensity for media baiting and misinformation, the

'visual juxtapositions' between Rotten and Richard are 'striking', especially in Julien Temple's 2000 film about the band, *The Filth and the
Fury* (2006, 387). They certainly are, and then some. Temple's film
generates constant visual and *aural* juxtapositions between Richard
and the Pistols, especially Rotten. But what are the effects of these juxtapositions on Shakespeare and the group? The connections begin with
the title credits, which mimic those used at the start of Olivier's film,
retaining the sketch of a family tree, parchment appearance, gothic
script, and illuminations of red and white roses. Yet the cod-historical
mimicry is pointed, as the reworked preface shows:

HERE NOW BEGINS ONE OF THE MOST FAMOUS AND AT
THE SAME TIME INFAMOUS OF THE LEGENDS THAT ARE
ATTACHED TO THE CROW^DN OF ENGLAND

This erasure certainly signals the film's and the band's eruptive desire
to evoke history from below: the lineages traced here are of popular
cultural dissent, not rulers; crowds, not crowns. This might seem to use
Shakespeare's play only to aggressively overwrite and displace it. In
turn, this would chime with punk's anti-establishment stance. In the film,
Johnny Rotten protests he was 'fed up with the old ways'. Those old
ways include cultural institutions like Shakespeare, and educational
methods that compounded rather than mitigated the alienation and lack
of entitlement endured by someone like Lydon/Rotten, as he puts it
in the film:

I question everything, I always have done. We were doing
Shakespeare. A teacher would give me a hard time and he wouldn't
tell me what I wanted to know. I'd ask outright questions, and
you're not supposed to do that. You're just supposed to accept – it's
Shakespeare, it's great, you're not.

From this perspective, Shakespeare is used in education (and elsewhere)
to silence dissenting or critical voices, and diminish the stature of those
with them. Yet as Sinfield has suggested, just as social structures can
generate both 'acquiescence and revolt' so 'rock subculture was partly
produced by', 'in specific opposition to', and as a 'defence' *against*
school, since 'the extension of schooling trapped all young people . . .
while allowing only a proportion of them to feel more than occasional
pleasure, pride or dignity' (1989, 31, 157). So this silencing prompted

Rotten's vocal reaction: 'That's not good enough for me'. This response and the context generating it may have involved asking why Shakespeare is now made central to education, and considered so 'great', at the cost of modern readers' self-esteem. But Rotten didn't hate Shakespeare: he wanted to know more, just on his terms. And at times during his education (and before John Lydon *became* Johnny Rotten), it would seem Rotten found himself in circumstances more conducive to a deeper appreciation:

I learned most of my studies with the teachers in the pub. I would sit with them in the pub during lunch break. Sometimes they wouldn't go to class, either. . . . We talked about Shakespeare. Reading Shakespeare, I found his characters vivid. They thought very differently back then – far more emotional and less on the logical, thinking side. I loved *Macbeth* – a gorgeous piece of nastiness. The characters did what they felt, not exclusively because they were evil, but because they didn't have the inclination to behave any another way. They just fitted in with the times. Plus it was much easier to use murder as a solution then.

As a teenager, I found the language of Shakespeare a little difficult until it was properly explained. I actually got an inkling of it at William of York [Lydon's school] with Mr. Prentiss. He explained that, although slightly buttered up, that was the way people talked then. Once I got into the poetic beat of it, I began to understand the gist of Shakespeare. At Kingsway college, they explained to me that it would lose its point and purpose to modernize the prose. It's the same logic as to why you can't live out a seventies punk rock environment today in the nineties. It's not valid now, and it doesn't connect with anything around it. You had to get into the dream of it – a vision complete unto itself. (Lydon, 1994, 64)

This account from Rotten's autobiography reveals many aspects of the Shakes-punk phenomenon. As we've heard, popular musicians from Cowboy Jack Clement to the Beatles apprehend Shakespeare in or as some kind of dream-state. In his final sentence, Rotten does something similar. For him, and others, dreams combine, mix up and offer alternatives to reality. This meant that Shakespeare was not entirely deplorable to an inchoate anarchist like John Lydon, but could actually be profoundly appealing. The appeal is complex, though. In some ways

Shakespeare is sufficiently disconnected and discrete from the decrepit period Rotten finds himself in to offer an opposition to that period. In other ways Shakespeare is close enough for Rotten to make productive connections with his work. To Rotten, Shakespeare's characters show a merciless but energizing disregard for moral niceties, and so reflect an earlier period where it was obvious those niceties were not universally maintained. This contrasts with the hypocritical, repressive and restrained state Rotten resists. Yet Rotten intimates that this Shakespearean energy is proto-typically punk, an aesthetically arranged savaging of superficial order and pleasantness.

The complexity continues. Rotten is insightfully wary of making any ahistorical links between his circumstances and Shakespeare's. But, ironically, he makes a connection between what people do to Shakespeare when they try to modernize him with what people try to do to punk when they seek to perpetuate it: this both admits and denies the desirability of joining Shakespeare and punk. Rotten also accepts the need to historicize Shakespeare – he and his characters fit with his 'times', and the language is 'difficult' because alien and old. Shakespeare's meanings are context-specific and isolated ('complete'), not universally applicable. But the language expressing those meanings has a 'beat' and 'gist', a compelling ideological and musical force. As such, he is willing and able to use Shakespeare as an authoritative resource – an inspiration? – to reinforce his own attempts to articulate the 'beat' and 'gist' of 'the way people talked' in his own time. What's good enough for Shakespeare is good enough for Rotten. One might then wonder precisely which 'times' Shakespeare fits with best, which is partly Rotten's point.

The Filth and the Fury only makes it harder to tell. In the film, Rotten goes on to suggest that he found in Shakespeare a source for a new identity. This indicates continuity, not distinction, empowerment, not disenfranchisement, and as much is signalled in the dialogue he performs with Richard's description of himself in Olivier's film:

RICHARD   And that so lamely and unfashionable
           That dogs bark at me
ROTTEN   I got news for you – dogs barked at me! In a way that
           whole persona, of say, Richard III, helped when I joined
           the Sex Pistols. Deformed, hilarious, grotesque . . .

If the Pistols did want to destroy and reshape their society, Rotten and Temple emphasize that there were Shakespearean precedents for this desire. Rotten asserts the punk dictum of 'don't accept the old order, get rid of it' to footage of Richard topping another stooge. *The Filth and the Fury* insists on these political and aesthetic links. Richard's self-ascription as 'Deformed, unfinished' (1.1.20), echoed by Rotten above, is itself treated with echo effects and overdubbed onto footage of the Pistols performing a gloriously ramshackle version of the Modern Lovers' 1972 proto-punk anthem 'Roadrunner'. Deformed, unfinished, *rotten*. This describes the band's attitude, and their followers', on stage and off: a defiant, vital response to a nation that deemed them monsters (like Richard), and to the corporate excesses of a music business that sought to silence or soothe but never broadcast alienation. Welcome to Shakes-punk.

For, with many others, Shakespeare fuelled the fire of that alienation, as the likes of Rotten and Temple saw something in his work that cultural gatekeepers sought to regulate. Richard is an insistent and significant presence in the legend the film relates, and the play provides a narrative structuring device for the Pistols' story. As Rotten observes: 'You put all this together and it makes for high drama.' Footage of London in 1976, with piles of uncollected rubbish, riots and racism, is juxtaposed with Olivier's Richard announcing that 'Now is the winter of our discontent' (1.1.1), a phrase that re-entered media circulation at the time and became more significant as the decade drew to a close. This emphasizes that what Rotten calls 'the germ, the seed' of the Pistols was 'generated' in a moment of civil war, 'total social chaos'. When the Pistols are shown playing 'Holidays in the Sun', described by Rotten as 'our crowning glory', we see footage of Richard's coronation. When the Pistols tour, Olivier's armies clash. When punk fans pogo, gobbing at each other, we hear Richard's wry words, wooing Anne: 'Why dost thou spit at me? (1.2.144). And when the band degenerate on stage in San Francisco, we watch Richard writhing in his death throes.

If this seems a stretch, the Shakespearean connotations of the group and their aesthetic were not lost on their successors. On 'Last in the House of Flames', Luton's goth punks UK Decay conjured images of anarchic conflagration and self-destruction that explicitly echoed *Macbeth*'s sense of toil and trouble, while also contributing to the period's chronicles of domestic degeneration. As Rotten indicates, in these troubled times, tragedies had currency. So for their antipodean version of post-Pistols punk-rock in 1982's *Junk Yard*, the Birthday Party took on Shakespearean concerns in 'Hamlet (Pow Pow Pow)'. The song begins as a grisly tribute to the hero, with Nick Cave acting the perverse cheerleader by spelling out Hamlet's name letter by letter, followed with an abrasive, drawn out 'yeah'. The music is no less abrasive, fizzing with Rowland S. Howard's feedback-heavy buzz-saw guitars and an up-and-down bass run stuck on repeat. Among these harsh and frantic sounds, this Hamlet embodies both modern stylings and Shakespearean features, as a wounded killer on the prowl, in love and in mourning, driving a Cadillac, carrying a gun, and wearing a crucifix, a new Old Testament avenger. Fittingly, given Hamlet's introspection, as the song winds down, the shots evoked in Cave's vocal do not just signal external violence, but introverted suffering – the self-destruction of shooting up, and the junkie's restless need for a fix, which the itchy, jerky, trapped, repetitive soundscape of *Junk Yard* mainlines. Denmark was a 'prison' for Hamlet (2.2.246); so is this song and the pain it evokes: 'In Cave's work, most of the characters are in a sense prisoners – of an obsession, or a claustrophobic environment' (Reynolds, 1990, 70). Here Hamlet becomes an archetypal, alienated, inspirational rocker in the Gene Vincent mould. But there are other connotations. Whatever the Birthday Party's own dark indulgences, this Hamlet also figures as the Pistols' Sid Vicious, dead from an overdose while out on bail for the murder of his lover Nancy Spungeon in 1979. This is no mere tribute but a funeral blues for the deaths and death of punk.

These tragic Shakes-punk figurings would return in a different form in the 1993 film *The Punk and the Princess: Romeo and Juliet with Attitude*, directed by Mike Sarne, a one-time '60s popster. Featuring a character called Shakespeare no less, this is a transposed but redemptive version of the fatal Vicious-Spungeon clinch:

> Rockers hunt punks in Notting Hill and an unemployed teenager falls for an [American] heiress . . . playing Juliet in a pub theatre – after poolroom duels and apparent death by heroin, love conquers all. (Howard, 2007, 306)

So the film does what Shakespeare and the Pistols couldn't, cleaning up and selling out both as a result. The most cynical example of this kind of post-Pistols punkish Shakes-ploitation came with the 1981 'The Skinhead Hamlet', written by Richard Curtis, later the author of *Blackadder* and umpteen romantic comedies. Though purporting to translate the play into a modern vernacular, the expletive-laden text was as much an Oxford-educated author's dig at the superficially coarse idioms and fans of punk as it was a knowing burlesque of Shakespeare (and the piece's reactionary sneer is obvious). Yet there were others working at the time, like Derek Jarman, who proved more willing and able to progress beyond punk's dead ends and their cynical exploitation, exploring instead the challenging possibilities of the Shakes-punk connection.

DEREK JARMAN

Jarman's profound relations with Shakespeare and the early modern period are unquestionable.[1] Yet his relationship with the punk period was more problematic. It can legitimately be argued that Jarman had a deep 'ambivalence' towards punk's 'violent youthful energy', and disliked 'some of the arbitrary and philistine attacks on previous art' that certain punk practitioners performed (Wymer, 2005, 56). But because he was a polymathic aesthete, Jarman couldn't fail to be influenced by developments in subcultures around him, especially when those subcultures generated art forms such as music that could have an impact on film, his main medium. Jarman admitted there was 'very little music' in *his* youth, and people's obsessions with the technologies of 'sound systems' were 'faintly ridiculous'; but, he noted, 'on film, of course, it's another matter' (1992, 219). There were practical reasons for his interest: through the 1980s, Jarman's film aesthetic developed in direct relation to the financial and stylistic possibilities offered by the burgeoning medium of music video. Beyond these practicalities, for Jarman, music in film could provide aesthetic and social harmony, or ironically evoke their absence: 'I never wanted to be strident, rather I wanted to be in tune, to sing songs' (1996, 72).

Again, this urge for musical and existential harmony might be seen to set Jarman at odds with punk's definitively disharmonious aesthetic and ideological noise. Yet Jarman shared many of punk's aims: 'I'm out to destabilise and destroy' (1996, 166). In part Jarman wanted to 'destabilise and destroy' cinematic as well as sexual propriety, both of which he found oppressive because so closed and closeted. Sexuality, like cinema, was about process, not product; creative chaos, not stultifying perfection; animated irresolution, not terminal conclusion: 'The filming, not the film' (1992, 200). Whatever else such views represent, these are resolutely punkish values, and at times they found a focus through what Jarman wanted to do with Shakespeare, or, rather, what he *didn't* want to do: he hated the 'Lego theatrics with the Royal Seal' of Kenneth Branagh and his ilk (1992, 147). So despite coming from an earlier generation, Jarman 'felt . . . kinship' with London's punk scene: 'I just liked the

energy of the whole thing, and whether it was misdirected wasn't worry-
ing me. . . . It was socially engaged, and very naive sometimes, but
deliberately so' (quoted in Savage, 2009, 664, 663, 666). Jarman was
caught up in, and caught, the moment. As Michael O'Pray puts it, the
cultures of punk offered a 'convenient home' for Jarman, though 'his
sympathy was tempered by scepticism' (1996, 96).

Scenery from his 1976 film *Sebastiane* served as part of the backdrop
to a Sex Pistols' gig at Butler's Wharf in the same year. Jarman filmed
some of the earliest footage of the Sex Pistols, which later resurfaced
(uncredited) on Julien Temple's *The Great Rock 'n' Roll Swindle* (1980).
By early 1977, Jarman had begun 'collecting fanzines and things' produced by the burgeoning scene (quoted in Savage, 2009, 662). Most
strikingly, Jarman's *Jubilee* (1978) combined imaginings of Elizabeth
I and her magician John Dee with explosive expositions of the cultural
and actual violence of later-century London life, and featured performances from punk luminaries from the city and its discontented suburbs –
Toyah Wilcox, Helen Wallington-Lloyd, Jordan and Adam Ant. As such,
to Savage, *Jubilee* 'captured the mood of Punk England better than anyone could have predicted' (1992, 377). Yet while recording the vitality
of this scene, Jarman also observed its limits. *Jubilee* ends with one-time
iconoclasts signing up to major labels, punk co-opted for commerce: 'the
moguls really were still in control and it was never really going to upset
anyone' (quoted in Savage, 2009, 663). This was Jarman's justifiably
bleak summation of punk's fate in the 1980s: 'it did end in repression,
with Margaret Thatcher's England', a society ravaged by neo-liberal
monetarist policies (quoted in Savage, 2009, 664). Jarman himself
accepted that 'Jubilee's no "fun" at all':

> A bitter chill blows through the film. For an audience who expected
> a punk music film . . . it was difficult to swallow . . . and most of the
> music lay on the cutting-room floor. (1984, 26, 172)

Some critics have argued, in turn, that the 'punk nihilism' Jarman
expressed coloured the rest of his work (Bersani and Dutoit, 1999, 59).
Whether Jarman's Shakespearean films are nihilistic is debatable, but they
certainly remained punkish, meaning culturally and politically engaged
and enraged, and he sustained Shakes-punk to channel that rage.

The Angelic Conversation (1985) counterpointed the sonnets (read by
Judi Dench) with the cries of birds and a soundtrack from the unclassifiable
electronic ensemble Coil, who had grown up alongside and out of the

influential industrial-noise cultural terrorists Throbbing Gristle. Such films queered Shakespeare, in all senses, at a time when queerness provoked repression. To Jarman, though, this was a *restitution* of Shakespeare, not a travesty. Not long into *The Last of England* (1987), Nigel Terry, providing the voice-over, intones lines Jarman would adapt in his memoirs, echoing Ben Jonson on his contemporary and rival (1618, 265):

> The swan of Avon dies a syncopated death . . . The household gods have vanished . . . the oaks died this year. On every green hill mourners stand, and weep for *The Last of England*. (1996, 189)

As these words suggest, Shakespeare's dying fall is attuned to the rhythm of the times, but this is nothing to celebrate on what Jarman would elsewhere term 'this desolate island', the United Kingdom in the post-punk, Thatcherite 1980s (1992, 19). The film's obsessively repeated, fractured and chromatically polarized images consolidate this, with scenes of post-industrial wastelands, rough trade shooting up, flares in the dark, and visual echoes of the distant past. In this environment, Shakespeare has been made homeless and redundant by the brutalities of 'exhausted institutions', the philistinism of 'malevolent bureaucracies', and a market-led and heritage-peddling cultural narcolepsy. This is a land of dope and the always tainted glory of a dying empire, battling enemies perceived within and without, mired in a past that snuffs out the future. As Wymer suggests: 'Jarman's hatred of Thatcherism was partly because her particular brand of Conservatism wasn't actually conserving anything' (2005, 6). By his own admission, Jarman argued that if his films appeared conflicted or provocative, they were nonetheless 'made in an older tradition', a tradition punk both derided and revived, and that included Shakespeare (1996, 81). This was the Jarman who affirmed, on screen and page, that 'The past is present' (1996, 175). *Jubilee* itself was, he would suggest, a 'healing fiction', a continuity that 'harked back' to Middle English poetry like *Pearl* and *Piers Plowman*; but it was no less 'socio-political' or punk for that (1996, 188). So *The Last of England* suggests that it wasn't the irreverent anarchy of movements like punk that offed the Bard – the endless hymning of the pomp and circumstance of '*Little England*' and the 'cosmeticised' heritage of UK PLC did for him (1996, 81). Phenomena such as punk, says the voice-over in phrases that allude to both the early modern stage and the fanzine culture of the 1970s, allowed the disenfranchised to 'recreate ourselves', by 'sniffing glue instead of . . . Masonic brandies'. Whether fleeting or degenerate, such recreations exposed the 'lies flowing through the national grid', proved 'there are more walls here than Berlin', and broke 'the silence of an English suburb'.

The continuities, possibilities and problems created by Jarman's Shakes-punk cinema arguably converge on his 1979 version of *The Tempest*. Wymer suggests this film is an 'introspective psychodrama', 'sublimely indifferent' to issues of post-colonialism, and not 'consistent' in portraying queer sexuality; in turn, Wymer downplays the idea that the film can be seen as a 'punk subversion of Shakespeare' (2005, 73–75). Yet the popular music Jarman incorporates into the film's climax, 'Stormy Weather' sung by Elisabeth Welch, suggests why we might query this view. Rather than subverting Shakespeare into some 'alternative' form, Jarman extrapolates from punkish possibilities in the play.

As a veteran of Broadway's 'Negro' shows of the 1920s, Welch had a long career during which she worked with pre-eminent African-American entertainers such as Josephine Baker and Paul Robeson, and with innovators of popular song such as Cole Porter and Irving Berlin. Welch's classy performance is hardly punkish, and of course predicts turbulence on and off screen: will Ferdinand and Miranda's love last; will life get easier for the gaily dancing mariners, on screen and off? However sweet the song, we end in the shadow of future tempests, which will divide anew. That said, the camera pays Welch 'loving attention', and her shimmering performance, flanked by adoring sailors, is a joyous spectacle comprising, privileging and animating the different cultural, sexual and class identities post-punk accommodated (Chedgzoy, 1995, 204). Jarman himself thought Welch's singing 'an enchantment' – she magics up alternative ways of being (1984, 191). If we can read Caliban as the image of some bestialized colonial other (termed a 'thing of darkness' at 5.1.278), here an artist in an African-American tradition conjures the 'Sounds, and sweet airs', that torment him (and us) with 'delight' (3.2.139); if the climax of Shakespearean romance is hetero-sexual union and familial reunification, here same-sex couplings occur with gay abandon; and if the low-ranked mariners were 'All lost!' in the storm in 1.1, here they are exuberantly revived.

These kinds of alchemical mixtures of Shakespeare, film, ideology and music reverberated in mutations of the punk culture Jarman once chronicled. In 1983, the dub-inflected group New Age Steppers released a reggae cover version of 'Stormy Weather' on their third album, *Foundation Steppers*, featuring vocals from Ari Up of the Slits, 'a cosmopolitan group of aggressive, politicized females' (Savage, 1992, 486). The Slits themselves articulated a 'naïve idealization of noble savagery' that made them sound and look like female Calibans – naked but for loincloths and mud on the cover of their 1979 album *Cut*, and making a wondrous, spacious noise therein (Reynolds, 2006, 84). Jarman's Miranda, the *Jubilee* veteran Toyah Wilcox, would eventually offer her own Shakes-punk amalgam on her album *Ophelia's Shadow*, which gave voices to women from Shakespeare and beyond.

In other contexts the power of the Shakes-punk hybrid Jarman articulated in his *Tempest* was also self-evident. Michael Armitage's 'low-budget reggae production' of the play at the Oval in Brixton in 1981 featured an all-black cast, 'Reggae, Carnival, African dance & drumming / Music by Wasimba', and was 'received with immense enthusiasm' by 'a mostly black audience salted with punks'. This production offered a 'droll way of dealing with colonialism and (in)subordination in the play', and ended with 'cast and musicians joined in concert' by the audience's prolonged clapping at the finale (Clayton, 1986, 523–24). Here a Shakespeare play *became* a popular, punky reggae party, with the audience as theatrical and musical collaborators, animated by common cultural and political concerns: 'for white punks in Europe, reggae in the 1970s became the musical form with which to voice protest' (Frith et al., 2004, 196).[2]

Such scenes confirm that many punks and post-punks combined politics and art, thrived on manifestos and dictums, and blended confrontation with context. Theirs was 'a new music' that also offered 'a new social critique', with both music and critique borrowing from older intellectual and cultural forms (Marcus, 1993, 2). So when Scritti Politti's Green Gartside was archly reworking Derrida and Barthes into pop songs, why couldn't literary theory be affected by music? Some was. The range of essays, influences and ideas brought together in a book like *Political Shakespeare: Essays in Cultural Materialism*, first published in 1985 and edited by Jonathan Dollimore and Alan Sinfield, reflected an established leftist bent developed from Raymond Williams's work. As such this collection was a defiant riposte to the discriminations developing under Margaret Thatcher's reign, a context that Jarman and others so perceptively represented. But the original 'Foreword' to the collection also reads like a post-punk agenda, being irreverent, anti-institutional, demystifying, conscious of process, committed to progress, and dedicated to ripping things up and starting again, in literary criticism and beyond:

[T]he relevant history is not just that of four hundred years ago, for culture is made continuously and Shakespeare's text is reconstructed, re-appraised, reassigned all the time through diverse institutions in specific contexts. . . . cultural materialism does not pretend to political neutrality . . . On the contrary, it registers its commitment to the transformation of a social order which exploits people on the grounds of race, gender and class. (1994, vii-viii)

In retrospect, Dollimore has suggested: 'As for punk itself I think we kind of looked on in awe' (2009). Yet when Dollimore and Sinfield constructed a new literary critique of Shakespeare (again, borrowing from older forms), their vision was, like punk's, 'determinedly *in* the world', and thus deeply implicated in the context in which it was made (Savage, 1992, 295). In other words – never mind the bollocks, here's the cultural materialists.

ELVIS COSTELLO

What happened next to Shakes-punk? We can tell this story by considering an artist who grew out of and beyond the punk era: Elvis Costello. Costello's allusions to Shakespeare allowed him to explore the boundaries of popular music, the personal or political issues that can be aired in it, and how. The implications of Costello's post-punk relationship to Shakespeare are both contained in and explode from a track, 'Mystery Dance', on his first album, *My Aim Is True*. In the lyrics, the restless, murderous Romeo 'Mystery Dance' reimagines could feasibly have grown from Shakespeare's play. But Costello confuses matters – Romeo, not Juliet, is high (spatially and emotionally), and set to jump from a window into a net she holds: 'neither character is content to play out the script as Shakespeare's playtexts suggest' (Buhler, 2002, 259). Whether Juliet's net sustains or captivates is unclear, but this reversal keeps Romeo alive long enough to demand that he isn't dead and shouldn't be buried. This implies his vitality, perhaps, and fits in with the music's and the play's edgy, trebly pitch:

> The song summons the urgency and inexperience of adolescent love not only through its reference to Shakespeare's young lovers, but through its 1950s-style rock-and-roll arrangement. (Folkerth, 2006, 391)

Costello's Romeo acts and speaks with a sense of dissatisfaction: perhaps expressing the confused angst of a teenage rebel without a cause, but more probably evoking the frustrations aroused by mystified furtive fumblings in the dark, as later lines hint. Significantly, in a song that is highly – *awkwardly* – personal, dealing with private parts and places, Shakespeare offers some protection, allowing intimate matters to be brought to light through impersonation. Just as Declan Patrick Mac-Manus, at different times in his career as Elvis Costello, would assume personae (D.P Costello, Howard Coward, Napoleon Dynamite), so he would return to this use of Shakespeare in later work.

Yet the frustration in 'Mystery Dance' also comes from Costello's dissatisfaction with his Shakes-punk creation, this fusion of *Romeo and Juliet* with the knowing neo-primitive musical style. The named characters disappear in the subsequent chorus and later verses, replaced by a more personal, but also more abstract, 'I' and 'you'. Romeo may live on (not least in popular song, as this song shows), but his survival stultifies, and has to be escaped. And the ideals of love generated by writers like Shakespeare and perpetuated by popular music might be potent, but they also mystify reality, creating hopes that we cannot fulfil however much, as the song's chorus suggests, we try and try. By 1982, Costello would confess his dissatisfaction with the myth-making in such music: 'There's a dishonesty in so much pop . . . all that starry stuff' (cited in Frith, 1998, 163). And as he pricked the mysteries of Shakespeare, so Costello deconstructed pop. One way to do this was to make his songs deliberately wrought, highlighting their artistry: 'Even at their most emotionally intense Costello's songs are self-conscious, (a self-consciousness reflected, most obviously, in the drawing-attention-to-itself cleverness of his word schemes)' (Frith, 1998, 171). This is part of the reason Costello paradoxically cites *and* departs from Shakespeare here: to demystify him, and to attain critical distance from a medium like pop that might echo his myths.

But 'Mystery Dance' nonetheless remains stuck on the aggravations of sex and love, and how we represent these. The song's close confirms this. Here the vocals are almost hooked on one insistent note and phrase, and the tune is unresolved, with Costello's narrator continuing to express dissatisfaction with a mysterious something and their inability to do something else anymore. Because the last line repeats, the impotence and obsession increase: do the deferred satisfaction and lingering frustration take other forms? 'Mystery Dance' was one of the songs on the demo tape Costello sent out in 1976, as he courted the music industry. With this song, in this format, Costello advertised himself and his ambition: as Buhler notes, the song's starting riff echoes the opening of the *other* Elvis's 'Jailhouse Rock' (2002, 259). As such, the 'Mystery Dance' he performs is a commercial as well as a sexual transaction, but if the King is implicated in this, so too is the Bard: how better to convey writerly enterprise than by appropriating from, and linking yourself to, Shakespeare? Moreover, with this bold move, Costello distances himself from the pub-rock proto-punk scene that nurtured but limited him. With the benefit of hindsight, Costello could reflect ironically on this frustration and ambition, as a tale told in the liner notes of the 2003 reissue of 1981's *Trust* reveals:

> The rowdiest but slightest cut on the record, 'Luxembourg', had its origins in an R'n'B number, 'Seven O'Clock', written for Canvey Island's finest, Dr. Feelgood. The final draft of the lyrics picked the hapless dukedom as an object of scorn, but only after the original, equally wordy text had been rejected by Dr. Feelgood's frontman, Lee Brilleaux, after one perusal, with the immortal line: 'What's this then, fucking Shakespeare?'

This kind of humbling would have its effects, but only momentarily:

> Sometimes doing an old song is like returning to the text of a play . . . It's not invalid, just because it's old, otherwise nobody would be acting Shakespeare. (Not to say that everything I do is Shakespeare!) (cited in Davis, 2005)

Not *everything*? As his career progressed, Costello would move beyond this coy diffidence, invoking Shakespeare again and again to bring about the comparable kind of distinction in or from popular music that 'Mystery Dance' heralded so ambiguously. With the collaboration with the Brodsky Quartet on *The Juliet Letters*, Costello 'distanced himself from youth-centered pop culture and from mass-market appeal' (Buhler, 2002, 259–60). This album was inspired by a newspaper article about a scholar replying to letters sent to Juliet Capulet in Verona. As such, it speaks of desire and the need for 'correspondence' in several ways: between the letter writers and whoever they hoped would read their writing; between Costello and the Quartet, and so between the worlds of classical and popular music; between Costello and music itself (he learned to write it during the collaboration); and between Costello and the status of Shakespeare.

Beyond the title and its source, the Shakespearean allusions are subtle, but significant. In 'Romeo's Seance', the hero is lost and alone in an empty house hearing unplugged radios, imploring Juliet to respond through the static of time and space, stuck in a modern age that has no place for either of them. When she does respond, he tells us the music we are hearing is of her creation: some communication does occur. Suitably the track opens with a single violin melody, answered and in part echoed by the rest of the quartet. Yet the 'you' Romeo calls at the song's end includes us, his listeners, as well as Juliet, and he can only repeat his request for us to hear him, uncertain whether we will. While this song seems to give life to long-gone lovers in an uncaring world, it also implies Shakespearean figures are displaced *from* that world. Other tracks suggest this dislocation is no bad thing. 'Damnation's Cellar' debates the dilemmas caused by constructing a machine that will bring back figures from the past: in a move that privileges mass culture over high art, we're told Shakespeare will have to wait his turn behind Liberace and Laurel and Hardy. In the end, with the prospect of Hitler's revival, the machine is destroyed. So, though the album aspires to create correspondences, it also records failed communications, not least with Shakespeare. His spirit lives on but it is ghostly or fuzzy, as in 'Romeo's Séance', or something to be secured in 'Damnation's Cellar'.

If communication with the spirit of Shakespeare was frustrated on that album, Costello sought to exorcize more ghosts with his later forays into classically scored visions of the Bard, especially *Il Sogno*, his 2004 work with the London Symphony Orchestra and Michael Tilson Thomas, otherwise known as 'Ballet after Shakespeare's A Midsummer Night's Dream'. When packaged as an album, this piece indicated Costello's ambivalence about positioning himself within and beyond pop, and about using Shakespeare to do so. Superficially, the easy assimilation of Shakespeare, classical music and Costello was apparent. The sleeve appropriated the visual format and even the typographic fonts of a classical recording. The liner notes allowed him to lay bare the workings of his composition and its genesis, and betrayed an excess of details about how themes, motifs and movements in the music interplayed, juxtaposed and recurred, with second-by-second accounts of moments in the score. At times these served as Costello's paraphrasing commentary on the play, but because the score takes what Costello terms 'certain small liberties' with Shakespeare's text, *Il Sogno* is as much a vehicle for Costello's continuing ambitions as it is a faithful reproduction of Shakespeare, and the synopsis in the liner notes is in part a knowing justification of this (Costello, 2004, 8).

The fact that Costello felt such justification was needed is telling. For even as he advertised his talents in an unfamiliar area, he also admitted his difficulties in learning to comprehend orchestral and ballet production. His notes consider the 'confusion and delusion' of the characters in the woods' dream-world, and the 'opposition and confusion' inherent to the play (2004, 13, 11). Yet perhaps he felt this too. Like 'Mystery Dance', the score ends in melodic irresolution, with the ballet's seemingly happy conclusion unsettled by musical echoes of earlier strife, and their potential repetition. This is an insightful reading of the play. But in this irresolution we can also identify Costello's self-consciousness about the difficulties involved in being a 'popular musician' taking on Shakespeare in classical music, and the conflicts within musical forms and in Shakespeare's text these difficulties expose. Taking liberties with Shakespeare, the score does the same with classical music, ironically disclosing its limits.

Significantly, Costello's liner notes emphasize the play's rude mechanicals are artisans – skilled craftsmen, not just figures of fun. This suggests a degree of sympathy between this composer and these subjects, and an awareness of the problems (and opportunities) of using classical music to accommodate their presence: 'I wanted to distinguish the different forms of existence in the play with contrasting music' (2004, 4). The artisans first appear to folk music melodies, played on a non-classical instrument, the cimbalom. This challenges but also expands the classical instrumentation that might soundtrack the social scope of the play. Later, the music for the artisans' play-within-a-play echoes motifs first heard in the court scenes, and so suggests that high cultural forms can be appropriated by apparently lower-ranked performers, just as Costello is doing. But the appropriations are not *just* echoes. As Costello admits in the liner notes, so many of the album's 'grander orchestral gestures', used to evoke the court, are coloured by 'an element of pomp and musical parody'. Elsewhere, at times the 'classical music' produced has a jazzy swing that seems to accomplish things mere massed strings can't: brushed cymbals and pulsing bass signify the temporary resolution of problems between Lysander and Hermia, and sweeping saxophones herald the magic glide of Puck and the other 'swinging fairies' (2004, 4).

Il Sogno shows that Costello can position himself in a musical tradition beyond pop, and he scrupulously tells us he can. But in that scrupulous telling, he confesses, with characteristic wit, both how easy and hard it has been to fit into his new environment: 'When a very serious French publication inquired, "Who is your favourite dancer?" I had replied honestly, "Cyd Charisse."' (2004, 4). Given Costello's audible unease with the medium he is adopting, perhaps Shakespeare acts as a defence of or license for his musical experiments. Yet by scoring Shakespeare, Costello takes conflicts, confusions and oppositions from the *Dream* and works them into his own relation to non-popular music. These conflicts and oppositions are textual, musical and social. In other words, even at this remove from the scene and sounds of punk, Costello sustains a critical edge, extrapolating from Shakespeare's play.

When he has gone back to his original milieu, Costello has also shown himself able to appropriate Shakespeare for political as well as personal impact. Folkerth suggests that when Costello wrote 'Miss Macbeth' from 1989's *Spike*, he had in mind Lady Macbeth's memory of ripping a child from her breast and dashing out its brains (2006, 380). Certainly, the song's lyrics evoke a morbid, unloved and so possibly loveless female figure, tormented by children and bad dreams as she torments others, bleeding infants white with pins. But elsewhere on *Spike*, and angered as the 1980s dragged on, Costello conjured comparable monstrous females, that provide another context for this allusion to Shakespearean psychic and political violence. 'Tramp the Dirt Down' fantasizes about dancing on the grave of a baby-kissing, greedy demagogue who performed her own kind of bloody voodoo on a deferential and misinformed public, and who became, as we have seen, a hate-figure for punk and its offspring: Margaret Thatcher.

SHAKES-PUNK NOW

As punk's cataclysmic Year Zero has receded into the more distant past, the music's appropriations of Shakespeare have sustained but also rethought previous iconoclasm. In other words, whatever the ironies of relating to an older musical movement to create new sounds, some later punk-influenced artists have continued punk's antipathies to previous cultural forms, including Shakespeare. The Sheffield punk-pop group Arctic Monkeys snarled about Montagues and Capulets in the middle eight of their raucous 2005 breakthrough single 'I Bet That You Look Good on the Dancefloor': this dreamed of clubs throbbing with amplified noise and hormones, full of dirty deeds but devoid of romance in the Shakespearean sense – there's no room here for fusty lovers, or the long-dead author who created them.

Yet Shakes-punk lives on in various, still politicized, forms. The Washington DC-based Taffety Punk Theatre Company 'are mostly aging punkers, or alt-rockers, or post-punkers, whatever we're calling it these days, who are also classically trained actors'. They confess their desire to 'do theatre without abandoning the things that drew us all to punk rock'. This involves making connections between the Shakespearean stage and the aesthetics and animation of punk subcultures, spin-offs, gigs and scenes: 'We are always using our early experiences (from playing in bands, or setting up shows, or even just seeing shows) as a touchstone to reflect on what we're doing in the theatre.' David Polk, a company member, suggests: 'Going to see a play is just like going to see a band. The stories told are the same, just the medium is different.' Marcus Kyd, another company member, explains the connection:

> I came up with this wacky notion that punk is older than itself. I used to think about who in the classical world was a punker without knowing it. Shakespeare was definitely on the list. Moving the theatre at Shoreditch across the Thames in the middle of the night is just one bit of evidence for that.

For Taffety Punk, showing that Shakespeare was a 'punker' involves several elements. They reformulate his image: the flyer for their staging of *Troilus and Cressida* at the Folger Shakespeare Theatre in 2009 promised 'We Will Rock You', and depicted a sword-swinging figure whose chest was adorned with the anarchist 'A' so beloved of punks, and whose shield bore the legend 'ANARCHY' itself. The Company also try to do for Shakespeare (especially his rarely performed plays) what fanzines do for punk groups: compensate for mainstream ignorance, challenge perceptions of what is acceptable, and foster a 'DIY aspect'. To Polk, as with Akala in another context, making these kinds of connections is vitally inclusive and entitling:

> The folks who come see our shows are often not normal theatre-goers. Theatre has been held on a pedestal for so long as the realm of those who can afford high prices. By bringing theatre and punk together, I feel like we've shown that theatre is for everyone. (Kyd and Polk, 2009)

Shakes-punk also survives beyond the theatre. In 2008, some 400 years after he first graced a stage, Titus Andronicus was on the road again.

This time, though, it was in the form of a US band bearing his name, and touring an album called *The Airing of Grievances*. The collection is a heady, punk-infused collision of musical and literary influences, with the group's musical forebears including the Clash, the Pogues and the Jesus and Mary Chain. All these and more are audible in their dense, explosive, bass heavy sound, which often pitches intricate or soaring melodies over a squall of instrumentation, recorded with lots of 'bleed' to intensify the noise and blur distinctions between parts. The band consciously play with their punk and post-punk influences. One divided track – or two related tracks – toys with a punk rallying cry: 'No Future Part I' and 'No Future Part II: The Day After No Future'. The idea that it is possible to have a sequence of 'no futures', exploring what it means to live on after an apocalyptic moment, suggests how the band see themselves surviving in the United States post-9/11. Yet this also extends a punk past that expressly disdained the notions of nostalgia and longevity. In effect, the group imply the punk project is incomplete and unresolved; things are still up for grabs, and work is to be done. The album evokes this in its first track, 'Fear and Loathing in Mahwah, NJ'. This tips a nod to the chemically-enhanced gonzo prose of Hunter S. Thompson, but also cultivates punkish sonic extremes. It begins with a reverb-laden vocal filtered to give a limited tonal range, backed by a listless acoustic strum. This has the air of an illicit, home-taped bootleg. But cosy domestic security is shattered by the first of the many explosive expletives that stud the album, as the whole band kicks in. As the track progresses, the mood and noise change again. These unsettling and unsettled shifts signify yet more irresolution and restlessness.

Beyond citing gonzo, the band also showcases a literary and cultural heritage with a longer, or more ostensibly refined, history. These references are rarely reverential though, as indicated by this extension of John Donne's opening line from the tenth of his 1633 'Holy Sonnets' (1996, 313) in 'Albert Camus':

So, Death, be not proud
because we don't give a fuck about nothing
and we only want what we are not allowed.

Vitality and desire vie with mortality and prohibition. Reverential or not, these influences, and these themes, are evident in the album's division into literary chunks ('Prologue', 'Part I', 'Part II' and 'Epilogue'), and, inevitably, in the many Shakespearean allusions.

Apart from the band's name, the most notable first allusion occurs at the end of 'Fear and Loathing', with Doug Johnson's reading of Aaron's unrepentant lines from the last act of *Titus Andronicus*, lines that conclude:

> But I have done a thousand dreadful things
> As willingly as one would kill a fly,
> And nothing grieves me heartily indeed
> But that I cannot do ten thousand more. (5.1.141–44)

This track doesn't just cite Shakespeare (or Thompson) but *recites* Shakespeare, over a fading but residual electronic hum of feedback. Why? What is Shakespeare's role in this latest renaissance of a punk aesthetic? In interviews, at times the band has been as nonchalant as it has been explicit about the way it assimilated Shakespeare:

> As far as the name is concerned, it started out just as a cool-sounding name. I have found that when a person wants to be in a band, he or she spends a lot of time accumulating a mental file of words or phrases that would be cool band names. *Titus Andronicus* was, to my mind, the best one that I'd come across. (quoted in Lindsay, 2008)

But the group's engagement runs deeper than this. 'Fear and Loathing' includes embittered lyrics addressed to someone smugly self-satisfied in their ability to express:

> Fuck You! . . . If you're the poet you say you are and beauty's in everything you see, then how can love exist in a world run by people like you? Because when there's suffering you're there. From southern trees, you hang them in the air.

These lines do several things. One is to create an equivocal dialogue with a 'poet' like Shakespeare, someone renowned for the perceived universal beauty of his words, yet someone also instituted as a nauseating paragon of White Male cultural authority of the kind currently running the show so poorly in most corners of the globe. Yet set against this figure, and this aggression, are Aaron's lines. The recital suggests, then, that like Johnny Rotten, the band identifies with a 'villain', and revels in his unrepentant energy in opposition to those who'd repress him. Just before Aaron's words, the final line of the track runs, 'Now let's never speak of it again, right?' Irresolution becomes more pointed here, an opening-up set against a closing-down. Letting Aaron's words live on, and 'speak . . . again', is a cutting riposte to those who silenced other voices, and hung up black skins (like his) on 'southern trees'. Another relationship to Shakespeare therefore becomes possible: he anticipates and stages the violence in modern Western culture, and can usefully be incorporated into a musical mode where that violence is addressed.

The group's complex relationship with Shakespeare is also evident in a track that is itself called 'Titus Andronicus':

> Throw my guitar down on the floor. No one cares what I've got to say anymore. I didn't come here to be damned with faint praise. I'll write my masterpiece some other day.

These lyrics echo both Alexander Pope's 1735 'Epistle to Dr Arbuthnot', and Antony's oration in *Julius Caesar*:

> I come to bury Caesar, not to praise him.
> The evil that men do lives after them (3.2.75–76)

The burden of literary prestige evident here only intensifies this song's frustration with an inability to express: it's all been said before, master-pieces are now impossible, and there'll never be another Shakespeare. But the band is also motivated by engaging critically with someone like Shakespeare, so rather than being debilitating, he and other authors prompt new work in new forms. As with the reference to Donne, noth-ingness and oblivion don't inhibit the band, but impel it. This implies continuity, rather than simply conflict, between these new forms and a literary past. For the group, the sonic violence of punk-inflected popular music offers the potential for healthy self-expression comparable to a genre like tragedy: 'In the Aristotelian sense of "catharsis," I will say that I hate to imagine what kind of person I would be if I didn't get to scream my lungs out fairly regularly' (quoted in Lindsay, 2008). More than this, the punk aesthetic empowers artists (and listeners) because it privileges process over glossy commercial product, and prizes inclusive incompletion over false and fatal certainty:

> That is what punk is, I suppose – not having a lot, but reaching as far as possible with what you have, and beyond. To that end, the

failures are always more exciting than the successes, so we wanted our album to have a very human quality to it, to make it clear that it was made by regular people, not by gods, as someone like, say, Led Zeppelin would want you to believe. (quoted in Lindsay, 2008)

For Titus Andronicus, *Titus Andronicus* is uniquely relevant, because it is so stylishly violent, so unformed (or deformed), so open to (popular) influence, so *punk*:

Shakespeare obviously is a very classy entity, more or less the pinnacle of human achievement and excellence. At the same time, *The Most Lamentable Romaine Tragedy of Titus Andronicus* is not really all that far removed from, say, *The Texas Chainsaw Massacre* so it was an odd contradiction in the literary world – basically a generic slasher flick that happens to be the work of the greatest mind that ever walked the planet. That seemed like the kind of line that I wanted our band to straddle; that line between the more cerebral, thoughtful elements of the human condition and the part of us that just wants to see blood and brutality. If *Titus Andronicus* the play could have both those, I wanted Titus Andronicus the band to have them too. As for the text, *Titus Andronicus* the play is basically a piece of crap, at least compared to the likes of *Hamlet* and *Richard II*, but I think that the monologue that we used . . . comes pretty close to redeeming the whole thing. It is very beautiful in its sheer wickedness and its lack of remorse. A very pure thing, you know? I wanted our album to have that same kind of attitude, that sort of take-no-prisoners thing. (quoted in Lindsay 2008)

In its fervid Shakes-punk syntheses, the band more than achieves its aims, discovering something 'deformed' and 'unfinished' in Shakespeare *and* punk, as Johnny Rotten and Derek Jarman did, and taking their discoveries in new directions. What might follow?

NOTES

1 On Jarman's relationship to the Shakespeare and the early modern period, see Wymer, 2005, 1–17, 85–86; Chedgzoy, 1995, 177–221; Hawkes, 1996, 103–16; and Ellis, 1999, 288–315.
2 On the links and tensions between reggae and punk, see Hebdige, 1996, 27, 29, 63, 66–70, 132.

CHAPTER 8

PREDICTING RIOTS?: SHAKESPEARE, POP AND POLITICS

By now, it should be apparent that understanding how Shakespeare and popular music relate requires thinking about those relations in particular historical and social contexts. Before moving on to consider how challenging and provocative it can be to think about these contexts on a global scale, it is worth looking at one recent, specific example of those relations. This will resituate earlier discussions about the politics of popular music as it is consumed and produced. It will also recollect previous ideas about how popular music engages with Shakespeare, not simply through allusion or citation, but also through visual referencing in the media that now embody and market such music. To address these issues, it is necessary to consider a song, that song's music video, and the repackaging of that video.

THE KAISER CHIEFS

In 2005, the Leeds-based band Kaiser Chiefs released a single called 'I Predict a Riot' on the independent rock label B-Unique. The song became a hit that contributed to a remarkable upturn in the band's fortunes after many years of struggling in small venues with little success. Using a first-person narrator, and elements of Yorkshire dialect that are at once local and anachronistically old-fashioned ('I tell thee'), the song purports to diagnose the ills of a boozy post-millennial Britain. Here, we hear, people are 'lairy' and towns 'scary', a 'friend of a friend' gets beaten for 'looking the wrong way at a policeman', and the narrator himself is 'attacked' by a 'man in a tracksuit'. This is the state of a nation where girls 'with no clothes on' freeze but for a covering of 'chip fat': 'not very sensible'. The narrator bemoans that none of this would ever 'have happened' to 'Smeaton', an 'old Leodiensian' (the Latinized name for someone from Leeds, a Leeds Rugby Union club, and also the name of Leeds Grammar School's magazine). To an insistent one-note two-chord riff, the chorus chants: 'I predict a riot'. On its second outing, the chorus is prefaced by a bridge: 'and if there's anybody left in here / that doesn't want to be out there / I predict a riot'.

The lyrics are ambiguous, to say the least. The narrator disdains the indecorous and grotesque insensibility of a perceived underclass of drunks and louts, male and female. Such misbehaviour is opposed to a nostalgic and idealized construction of a well-educated, bourgeois figure and their culture. But the narrator is no less appalled by the malfunctioning mechanisms of social control: the police themselves are as heavy-handed as the thugs they are meant to punish. To complicate matters further, the chorus and the bridge prompt questions that unsettle these already unstable positions. Are they expressed by the same narrator? Who will be rioting, and who is predicting it? Is the drunken mass potentially seditious, or will unrest be motivated by those well-heeled types discomfited by that mass? Does the jabbing chorus register an insistent fear for a more degenerate future, or promise a backlash against an errant state and its licentious subjects? And who is on the inside and the outside (of what)? Is violent drunkenness happening 'out there', or is 'out there' a zone excluded from the clique of potential *bourgeois* rioters?

This may seem remote from Shakespeare, but these questions become important, and more relevant to Shakespeare's relationship with popular music, when the song is broadcast in other forms of media, notably its music video. Directed by Stylewar, the 2005 video is shot throughout in grainy, grimy black and white, with shades of German Expressionism, or even the late nineteenth-century 'song-slides' used by sheet-music sellers as 'pictures telling the story', a 'necessary sales aid' pre-dating '1930s jazz shorts' (Frith, 1988, 12). In other words, it is full of visual references to film's and modern popular music's early days. The setting confirms this retrospective feel: the video opens in a smoggy, provincial, industrial town, stuck in the early 1900s. The band is shown setting up its instruments in the street, to perform what the MTV generation would recognize as an 'unplugged' session, but what is more traditionally termed 'busking'. They are watched with interest by a similarly street-based but much more sinister quack physician peddling snake oil whose side effects seem to include people turning into animals. He notices how the band draws a crowd, and leaves his calling card in an instrument case. The band visits him at his suitably foreboding residence, and he outlines his plans for its world domination. Playing on the necessary migrations modern English musicians like the Kaiser Chiefs must undertake, the band then heads off to make its fortunes in London, in a carriage piloted by its diabolic svengali. The band's first venue in the capital? Shakespeare's rebuilt Globe in Southwark, where a poster advertises its star billing, complete with mug shots. But as the band enters the theatre grounds, and without its knowledge, its manager flips the poster around to reveal the boys' new image, complete with animal ears, tufts and noses: they are now 'The Fabulous Furry Freakshow'. In a move towards a more orthodox 'performance video' inserted into the narrative trajectory of the piece, a stage curtain then lifts to reveal the band and theatre audience – including a dancing policeman – going wild. The manager gets his comeuppance for bestializing the band after the performance. To the sound of crackly, suspenseful piano music, one band member reveals he recorded his antics with a camcorder. Defeated, the manager runs away. The video makes no reference to Shakespeare beyond the scenes at the Globe. But as we will see, the band's performance location there, these scenes, the video, its repackaging and the song as a whole can nevertheless be read as offering a significant exploration of Shakespeare's relationship not only to and with popular music in general, but more specifically to the politics of modern popular music.

After its initial rotation on the usual music television outlets, the video was included on a 2005 Kaiser Chiefs' DVD, *Enjoyment*. The DVD juxtaposes different chronological moments, in a manner that mimics the song. And just as the video looks old and references cinematic history while using modern digital technology, so the DVD presents other videos, performance footage, earlier promotional material and a mockumentary about the places the band visited on a recent tour, including London, Manchester, Glasgow and San Francisco. In addition, through fake reportage, the band members are shown as children and also in the year 2030, reflecting on their careers. This reformatting makes the band's interactions with constructions of Shakespeare even more explicit and complex.

To stock footage shots of a recent but not current London from the air, the wry tones of the actor Bill Nighy insistently encourages political apathy in viewers, by describing how 'your government and its royal family will do all the deciding for you'. As various military bands march past Buckingham Palace, the voice-over observes, 'I predict an uprising'. But riot is not an option. We are told any attempt at 'toppling the government' would be 'futile'. Significantly, the original 2004 promotional video for the song 'I Predict a Riot' (directed by Charlie Paul) featured a mass pillow fight in a small music venue: orchestrated in and by a gig, politicized violence has no punch. Instead, the DVD's viewers are charmed by ironic shots of a thatched cottage ('London is known for its busy Oxford Street, still with its quaint shops'), London Bridge (a rural stream), and an 'autumn daffodil'. This is, we are told, 'UK Shire Limited', where 'Tourists . . . jig the night away', and fans 'flood' to see bands like Kaiser Chiefs, 'as if sheep or eels perhaps'. What is Shakespeare's role or place in all this? Each performance and iteration of, or context for, the song complicates any response to this question, as does the band's consistent play with temporality and chronology – while we know *where* we are, we're less sure *when* this is.

In the first instance, the video repositions the politics and poetics of the song's lyrics. In the video, 'in here' now means within the Globe; 'out there' the world beyond. The revellers in the theatre are now no longer alienated observers reflecting on a degenerating society, but a potentially riotous assembly fired up with a call to arms by performers in from the provinces. This is nothing new for rock 'n' roll, which, from its advent, has been characterized by its capacity to stimulate pleasurable *and* political energies: 'pleasure frequently *is* the politics of popular music' (McClary and Walser, 1988, 287).

Yet the public disordering of personal and political bodies had been seen as fundamental to the consumption of popular music even before this. One of the nineteenth century's most stalwart defenders of folk music, Sir Hubert Parry, attacked mass-produced songs popular with (sub)urban consumers in these terms:

> The modern popular song reminds one of the outer circumference of our terribly overgrown towns. . . . It is for people who live in those unhealthy regions, people who have the most false ideals, who are always scrambling for subsistence, who think that the commonest rowdyism is the highest expression of human emotion; for them, this popular music is made, and it is made, with a commercial object, of snippets of slang. (cited in Frith, 1983, 34)

Parry set commercially motivated, unhealthy, linguistically errant, geographically marginal 'rowdyism' against a cultured core of 'emotion' expressed through honest art and standard discourse. He wasn't alone. In the words of Sir John Herschel, another nineteenth-century commentator:

> Music and dancing (the more's the pity) have become so closely associated with ideas of riot and debauchery among the less

cultivated classes, that a taste for them, for their own sakes, can hardly be said to exist. (cited in Frith, 1983, 39)

But the Kaiser Chiefs' relationship with Shakespeare posits an even longer continuity of aesthetic and civil disobedience located in the suburban spaces of a city, reviving concerns about the riot and debauchery associated with the early modern stage. This continuity has recently received attention in Paul Du Noyer's history of the capital's music. This reveals the connections within a specific location across time – between the 1500s, the 1800s, and London pop's present – and also reminds us that Shakespeare's audiences were 'raucous, not reverential': 'good tunes were a prized aspect of the entertainment' (2009, 6). These audiences' theatres were a quintessentially socially and geographically marginal phenomenon, positioned as eccentrically distinct from the more regulated centre, because they were surrounded by and in league with brothels, bear pits and taverns. Such stages and their crowds confirmed the worst fears of Elizabethan anti-theatrical commentators, such as Thomas White, sermonizing in 1578 about the 'continual monument of Londons prodigalitie' (cited in Chambers, 1923, IV: 197).

Part of the early modern theatre's problem was the uncontrollable animation it was perceived to provoke in its audiences. Anthony Munday opined in 1580: 'Whosoeuer shal visit the chapel of Satan, I meane the Theater, shal find ether no want of yong ruffians, nor lacke of harlots, vtterlie past al shame' (cited in Chambers, 1923, IV: 211). A year earlier, Stephen Gosson had complained vehemently about the crowd's 'heauing . . . shoouing . . . ytching . . . shouldring . . . ticking . . . toying . . . smiling . . . winking'; in 1582, he observed a comparably active 'foming . . . fretting . . . stampinge' (cited in Chambers, 1923, IV: 203, 213). In 1583, Phillip Stubbes was animated in similar ways, and used almost exactly the same flurry of paralleled verbs to describe public dancing, as if he was both appalled and fascinated by what his prose could and could not order: 'such laughing and fleering, such kissing and bussing, such clipping and culling' (cited in Chambers, 1923, IV: 223). The implications of such animation were as dangerous then as those of rock 'n' roll would be later: politically compromised as modern popular music might be, what begins as 'foot-tapping' could end with 'state-smashing' (Christgau, 1970, 366).

The bestialization of the band and its consumers makes these political, cultural and historical collocations in this 'continual monument' ever more suggestive. As the band embodies and excites animalistic urges, so the early modern stage accommodated and created what anti-theatrical commentators like White called 'monstrous birds' and 'helhoundes' (cited in Chambers, 1923, IV: 197). Such associations play upon the spatial and social connections between dog-fighting, bear-baiting, bestial audiences, and unruly theatres in the entertainment zones of early modern London's suburbs. And the video certainly stages the potency of live performance *in* the theatre. This not only advertises the Kaiser Chiefs' vitality, but also reveals the dissident potentials of Shakespeare and the popular medium he worked in. As Bill Graham, the veteran American rock promoter, observed:

> In actuality rock and roll has become so successful that the majority of fans don't go to see the artist but to be in the presence of the artist, to share the space with the artist. (cited in Goodwin, 1988, 269)

This video shows popular music fans sharing a vital 'space' with artists they adore. But this is also a Shakespearean space, a 'symbolic topography' of Liberties and liberty (Mullaney, 2007, 26).

SHAKESPEARE AS BRITPOP?

Does this make Shakespeare a radical rock 'n' roller, a subversive Britpop icon? Described by John Harris, 'Britpop' 'referred to the idea that young British musicians [of the late 1990s and early 2000s] were knowingly reconnecting their music to a fleetingly forgotten heritage, stretching from the rock aristocracy of the 60s . . . to the more cerebral elements of punk rock', with 'the articulation of quintessentially British experiences', and an urge for 'commercial success'. They were thereby reacting to the 'brief American domination of alternative rock that took root in 1992' (2003, xv). To reference Shakespeare in this context might signal a triumphalistic, nationalistic or commercial impulse. But it also registers a desire to reconnect with a still older cultural tradition, manifesting what Lanier describes as 'nostalgia for some lost Elizabethan communalism', a 'romanticized past' in an age of mass cultural consumption: this is the 'Globe myth' (2006, 166). Such myths are reductive, trite, misinformed and misinforming: 'Shakespeare has never before been so persistently if crudely exploited as a form of national and cultural capital' (Dollimore, 2001, 154). Yet Lanier also observes that 'like all myths', this one 'gives expression to cultural aspirations that cannot be entirely reduced to bad faith':

For as much as the new Globe gestures in the direction of continuity with British heritage, it also uses the Globe myth to try to mark a break . . . with some of the exclusionary legacy of Shakespeare the high cultural icon. The participatory, not-quite-raucous, not-quite-reverent flavour of Globe performances, the felt collectivity and intimacy of the audience and actors, elements that mark the experience as distinctively *popular*, spring as much from the myth the building evokes as from its particular arrangement of space. (2006, 166)

If the Globe is an ambiguous location, we can see and hear elements of these ambiguities in the Kaiser Chiefs' performance. The DVD as a whole parodies the notion of the United Kingdom's heritage industry as a form of social control, a false consciousness. The Globe might stand as one iconic location for this nation-making industry and the false consciousness it promotes. By situating themselves in the Globe, and predicting a riot there, the Kaiser Chiefs deconstruct that heritage industry, the version of history it presents, and these only seemingly 'national' cultural constructs. This makes Shakespeare bold and bolshy, because he is made continuous with popular culture past and present.

Yet such imperatives and yearnings might also be an equivocal reaction to the medium of popular music itself. Frith suggests that the technologies that facilitated the production and dissemination of popular music to wide audiences have also 'made possible the apparent privatisation of the musical experience', as people consume music *en masse*, but alone: 'We can . . . write the history of twentieth-century popular music culture in terms of a movement from collective to individual activity' (2004b, 27). With this in mind, the representation of the Kaiser Chiefs' live performance attempts to re-energize collectivity, invoking Shakespeare's Globe as a site of mass-consumed popular culture in which to do so. For Frith, since music is 'a universal human practice', it follows that experiencing music is 'an essentially humanising experience, a kind of ideal sociability' (2004b, 27). Live music, especially, joins audiences and performers in the 'immediacy of sound' (Frith, 1983, 5).

However, the song's lyrics record popular unrest as much as they encourage it, and the unrest predicted in the lyrics is only ever a prediction, unrealized and dissolute in its genesis and direction. The video *simulates* but does not *stimulate* subversion, performs live*ness* but is not a *live* performance. And even as the video stages collectivity, this does not in itself, or in actuality, subvert the cultural or political status quo. Nostalgically alluding to Shakespeare's status as popular (and high) cultural power only confirms the band's (and the audience's) lack of agency in the present. The Kaiser Chiefs are a renowned good-time 'festival band', playing live at large-scale summer events. But, again, as Frith observes, such generations of collectivity are compromised: 'Here we have a gathering of fans and musicians hoping for the unexpected, and the proximate threat of drugs and drink and anarchy, but all, in fact, tightly controlled' (2004b, 45). For Adorno, precisely because popular music operates as an immediate 'social cement', it also manifests the 'repression and crowd-mindedness' of 'anthropophagous collectivism'. Consumers' decisions to conform to buying what they are offered embodied a dehumanizing 'jitterbug fanaticism and mass hysteria' whose consequences were chilling to someone who had survived Nazism (1941a, 460–61, 466). This is compounded by the fact that the band, like any other, *consists of* commercial artists, and commercial interests have consistently staged and exploited pseudo-subversive collectivism for profit. As an advertisement for Columbia records appealed to fans in 1967: 'The Man can't bust *our* music . . . Know who your friends are. And look and see and touch and be together' (cited in Buxton, 1983, 428). What was true then is truer now: with the rise in downloading, and the fall in profits from sales of albums and the like, one of the music industry's strategies has been to rebrand itself as a *live* music industry.

Is this, as the band ironically suggests on another song, 'The Modern Way'? The video for *this* song tells the story of 'William Green', a man who learns to perform tricks with tennis balls, and ascends to the heights of celebrity (to the extent that the band performs on his TV show, playing *in* a huge tennis ball). But Green's creativity is explicitly linked to commercial exploitation: sales of balls rocket, and shops are forced to put up posters saying 'Sold Out', intimating both Green's success as a *commercial* artist, but also his failure as a *credible* performer. The Kaiser Chiefs' status as long-struggling, provincial 'indie rock' emphasizes these concerns. Indie rock is constructed by fans and practitioners as different from mainstream commercial rock, but it is also 'defined by its concern for the scale of consumer capitalism, rather than by its radical rejection of an economic system' (Keightley, 2004, 129). Indie rock offers a 'logic of authenticity', exclusivity and independence from mainstream mores and modes, yet it is produced by, and marketed through, these only ever relational positions (Hibbert, 2005, 56).

However, the band also knowingly signals its own co-option as part of both the heritage and music industries, and the nation they purport to manufacture. The group found fame in the years after Britpop's critical and commercial bubble had burst: perhaps its staging of sites and sounds so bound up with 'British' identity also parodies anyone who tries to wrap themselves in a flag to sell culture – high or popular. The video might seem to record a movement from innocence (the band performing *al fresco* and authentic in the provinces) to bitter experience (the band misrepresented in the city). But any romantic nostalgia, for the band's, Shakespeare's or pop music's past, is complicated. The Northern English industrial landscape in the early scenes is not idealized, but visually and materially grim. The use of the camcorder to expose deceits shows a modern technology winning out. In this regard, the forms of 'I Predict a Riot' offer an ironic take on claims made for and by popular music, in a manner not dissimilar to the cultural production of the early modern theatre: 'a commodity that speaks, and that speaks about the conditions of its own culture and its own production' (Mullaney, 2007, 58). For the Kaiser Chiefs, and for Shakespeare, as cultural producers occupying the Globe, this reveals a relative autonomy, a critical distance, from their context:

> It was a freedom, a range of slightly eccentric or decentered per-
> spectives, that gave the stage an uncanny ability to tease out and
> represent the contradictions of a culture it both belonged to and
> was, to a certain extent, alienated from. (Mullaney, 2007, 30–31)

A pop band performing or predicting a riot at the Globe might be a politically compromised gesture. But as Lanier's reading of the rebuilt theatre suggests, such gestures speak to 'popular discontent with the atomization and alienation of modern life', and so realize a 'yearning for some social alternative . . . which might be harnessed to more pro-gressive political ends' (2006, 166–67). So though Germaine Greer, another renowned commentator on Shakespeare and popular (counter-) culture, would misattribute (and misquote) William Congreve's words, a point she made in 1969 still serves as an apt conclusion to this exploration of one site of Shakespearean sound: 'Music hath charms to tame the savage beast, as Shakespeare noticed. Music hath alarums to wild the civil breast, as well' (339).

CHAPTER 9

ROCKIN' ALL OVER THE GLOBE

Describing Shakespeare's place in the modern world, Michael D. Bristol influentially observed:

> Shakespeare is a term with extraordinary currency in a wide range of discursive practices as a complex symbol of cultural value . . . it refers equivocally to a particular man, an author, a body of works, a system of cultural institutions, and, by extension, a set of attitudes and dispositions. (1996, ix)

Even more than in his own day, Shakespeare has now hit the 'big-time'. Bristol exemplifies Shakespeare's current status with reference to popular Western music stars: 'No less than the Beatles or Liberace, Elvis Presley or Mick Jagger, Shakespeare is big-time in the idiomatic sense of cultural success, high visibility, and notoriety' (1996, 3). Hence, for Bristol, Shakespeare emerges as the biggest international pop star of all: 'even more versatile as a cross-over artist than Madonna' (1996, 90). Bristol's analogies consolidate the connections *this* book is trying to make. But if we're thinking about global star status, why restrict ourselves to Western pop? Where critics have attended to Shakespeare and popular music, the music they have focused on has tended to be Anglo-American – *Shakespeare and Popular Music* has thus far proved just as guilty. Yet just as Shakespeare wrote 'in an age of unprecedented intercultural exchanges' (and staged these), so now he is both subject and object of production and consumption in different places around the world (Sousa, 1999, 8). Not without strains and conflicts, this makes Shakespeare 'global' *and* 'local', and complicates how we understand and discriminate both these terms.[1] Crucially though, in this regard his status concords with the current character of popular music: as globalized commodity, as product of globally diverse local populations, and as a technological and musical synthesis of global and local musical forms. Discussing appropriations of Shakespeare in contemporary films from and for global markets, Mark Thornton Burnett suggests: 'The local is not always to be found where one might conventionally expect it' (2007, 48). This chapter tries to begin to realize this in other ways, as it situates Shakespeare in relation to the sounds made in the global-local contexts of what has come to be known as 'world music'.

SHAKESPEARE AND 'WORLD MUSIC'

As Wolfgang Arming observed in 1979, in the later years of the twentieth century, Western-produced recorded music became 'more international', with the 'land of origin' becoming 'less discernible' (cited in Wallis and Malm, 1984, 160). Simultaneously, local popular musics from around the globe became more available to international consumers, as 'world music'. What separated the 'world music' marketed at the end of the twentieth century and after from ethnographic recordings made by anthropologists and researchers in previous years? Beyond a marketing boom, perhaps not much:

> International pop music in the 1990s may be packaged quite differ-
> ently from international pop music in the 1950s, with greater respect
> shown to its formal qualities and local history, but what's on offer to
> the consumer, the musical pleasures promised, aren't so different:
> in the context of the denunciation of Western pop artifice and dec-
> adence, the authentic itself becomes the exotic (and vice versa).
> (Frith, 2000, 308)

This interchange between the 'exotic' and the 'authentic' as a response to bland *in*authenticity is no innocent process, and affects the words we use to describe the music produced and consumed around the world: 'As the transnational corporations plunder the musical assets of the Third World, "world music" can hardly be a neutral term. But it is not a settled, univocal one either' (Middleton, 1990, 293). This explains the prolifera-tion of cognate terms such as folk, roots, 'ethnopop, New Age, *sono mondiale*, and *musique métisse*', all of which reproduce but also challenge 'world music's' commercial, 'Euro-American, postcolonial' construction and its imposition on non-Western 'Other' musics (Guilbault, 2004, 176, 178). Given these issues of locality, exploitation, resistance and authenticity, Shakespeare's status in the marketplace of the global village is a beguiling one. When quoted or sung, does he offer 'local' artists a passport to 'global' exposure? Does his place in 'local' musics prove or problematize his 'global' presence? Does the synthesis of Shakespeare and 'world music' combine two cultural forms that are 'others' in relation to the mainstream idioms and idiocies of Anglo-American pop, cultural forms that are, in turn, sufficiently alternative to attract alienated, jaded consumers? Finally, are these two others privileged by their supposed difference because it conveys 'authenticity': 'world musics' as the sound of specific locales, Shakespeare as the universally appreciated voice of everyman?

Such questions touch on, but fail to express, the complexity of what Shakespeare means in 'world music', and how such music makes Shakespeare mean differently. We can draw out two points though, which will have some bearing on this chapter. First, as it is made, marketed and consumed, 'world music' is as much a local, national or regional as a global phenomenon, and evokes the contradictions of this. As Simon Frith argues:

> Even the most nationalistic sounds – carefully cultivated 'folk' songs, angry local dialect punk, preserved (for the tourist) traditional dance – are determined by a critique of international entertainment. (1989, 2)

Given what we know of Shakespeare's role in the constructions of many locales' or nations' identities, his place in the conditions that produce this critique is important.[2] Second, the material forces that impel global consumption (of music, and all else), also cause new connections between cultures and people. This is less bland than it sounds: given the legacies of colonialism and the realities of neo-colonialism, these connections can be as discordant as they are harmonious, and we can hear this in what happens in the relations between 'world music' and Shakespeare, once an empire's poet-in-chief.

SHAKESPEARE AND 'FOLK': ONE NATION UNDER A GROOVE?

Even when we think about 'world music' then, we need to consider the locations in which that music has been made and consumed: one person's 'world music' is the sound of someone else's home or heritage. At risk of reinforcing the Anglocentrism of this book further, it is worth observing that the sound of one nation's musical heritage has proved particularly significant for Shakespeare, especially during a period when that musical heritage has been seen to be threatened by commercial pop. As Julie Sanders observes, composers such as Edward German, Gustav Holst and Ralph Vaughan Williams positioned Shakespeare 'alongside songs and dances from the folk tradition', informed by early twentieth-century pastoralism that encouraged 'a general identification of Shakespeare's plays with a specific notion and understanding of "Englishness"' (2007, 189). Sanders also observes that much of this pastoralism, and its attendant nationalism, stemmed from the work of the great collator and reviver of English traditional music, Cecil Sharp.

In 1916, after holding summer schools on English country dance in collaboration with the Shakespeare Memorial Theatre at Stratford-on-Avon, and after contributing folk music to a performance of *A Midsummer Night's Dream* earlier in the decade, Sharp was well placed to work on celebrations for the Shakespeare Tercentenary. As his biographer notes, despite Sharp's aversion to 'most forms of pageantry', he recognized such celebrations could be a 'useful means of introducing English folk music and dances' to a wider audience. In other words, Shakespeare provided a means for once-popular music to become popular again. Sharp's vision of this popularity was global:

> Accordingly, when the New York Centre of the English Folk Dance Society was invited to provide an English 'Interlude' in Percy Mackaye's *Masque of Caliban*, to be performed in the New York Stadium, Cecil agreed to compose the scenario and to direct the performance. (Karpeles, 1967, 133)

Enacted before 'some twenty thousand spectators', this 'Interlude' saw several hundred performers combine various traditional English country dances and songs with the representation 'of an Elizabethan May-Day Festival on the outskirts of an English village' (Karpeles, 1967, 133). The performance was, in Sharp's eyes, a success, and united the huge and diverse audience:

> I felt more proud of being an Englishman than I have ever felt before. And the spirit of the tunes and dances was such that participants became infected by it and for the one moment they became English, every Jew, German, French, Italian, Slav one of them. (cited in Karpeles, 1967, 133)

Sharp uses Shakespeare and popular music to make the world one. Given the time and place, Sharp overwrites New York's status as a quintessential melting pot (without even mentioning the 'Americans' living there), and attempts some peace-making here, with currently conflicting nationalities merging. But this merging and pacifying occurs under England's flag. Emboldened by the Bard, English folk soundtracks the construction of a new global identity, based on the fabrication of an older, local scene. Whether you judge this infectious Englishing to be unifying and inclusive, or imperialistic and oppressive, depends on whether Sharp's conceit subsumes your idea of national identity (and this could apply whether you are English or not).

Sanders persuasively suggests that Sharp's identification of Shakespeare and English traditional forms fed into the artists who grew from the United Kingdom's folk revival, citing a song by Martin Carthy that alludes to Lady Macbeth's sleepwalking in 5.1, 'Perfumes of Arabia' (with Dave Swarbrick, on *Skin and Bone*). Sanders finds other evidence of this link in Carthy's work with the Royal Shakespeare Company (2007, 189–92). And Sharp's sense of Shakespeare is sustained, albeit in a muted, different form, by John Boden, a modern musician working in the English folk tradition. In addition to covering 'The Rain it Raineth Every Day' from *As You Like It* with John Spiers from the group Bellowhead, Boden has provided music for productions of *Hamlet* at the Globe, for *The Merchant of Venice* at the Royal Shakespeare Company in Stratford, and for stagings of *Julius Caesar* and *Macbeth*. These diverse settings have taught Boden that, for an English folk musician, Shakespeare is still a powerful 'potential source' of material, offering a 'body of shared stories', and 'words and phrases that are always good in a song'. As such, Shakespeare is a 'reference point' providing a cultural shorthand about tragic love or troubled youth that artists can cite in an 'efficient manner', and which audiences will appreciate (2009). Boden is echoed by Richard Thompson, a veteran of the English folk-rock scene, who suggests that songs from the plays are 'easy to sing' and 'accessible to all', but with 'subtleties and layers of meaning' (2009). Boden's and Thompson's descriptions of Shakespeare's value don't share Sharp's nationalistic fervour, but the idea remains that Shakespeare brings a touch of commonality to particularly local types of music. And the connection is all the stronger because it works both ways. Boden, for one, is 'fascinated' by how Shakespeare seemed to incorporate 'elements of folk song', and how he has acted as a 'conduit for the folk tradition' (2009). Realizing this connection means we can also hear how artists like Boden and Thompson have redefined what we anticipate from both English folk musicians and Shakespeare.

Performing in Stockholm in 2000, Richard Thompson, backed by Danny Thompson, did a cover of 'The Story of Hamlet'. After admitting the aesthetic authority of Shakespeare's tragedy backed by solemn minor chords, the song shamelessly affirms that it has dumbed down the plot for its audience, and goes on to portray Elsinore as a brutal, bestial world with jazzed-up riffing, demotic lingo and some wittily outrageous and hilarious rhymes. This represents an obviously irreverent take on Shakespeare. Yet Thompson's cover also challenges expectations of what he, as a musician with a folk background, can or should do. In this regard, the song's history is significant. It was originally composed by Frank Loesser for his rewritten score for the 1949 film version of Cole Porter's 1936 Broadway musical *Red Hot and Blue*. In simple terms, while it might not appeal to folk purists (and Thompson has never insisted on courting *them* in his career's peregrinations through popular song) it comes right from the heart of twentieth-century popular/commercial music. Brilliantly, the next song on the album featuring this track is Thompson's version of Britney Spears's 'Oops! I Did It Again': perhaps this continues the pop précis of Hamlet's mistakes. Elsewhere, for Thompson, Shakespeare fittingly becomes an ally against restrictive cultural orthodoxies. On 2003's 'Outside of the Inside', Thompson takes on the mentality of a religious fundamentalist, someone who finds Charlie Parker bestial, Einstein heretical, Botticelli needlessly arousing, and Shakespeare (with Isaac Newton) a noisy distraction from purer pursuits. Only a narrow-minded persona would make these mistakes. And only an artist open minded about Shakespeare and global musical traditions – local to the 'old world', or New York – would be able to challenge our expectations of both.

IN PERFECT HARMONY?

Moving from the local to the global then raises other issues. Sometimes the contexts for the post-colonial commingling of Shakespeare and global musics have been close to the initial locations of the Shakespearean stage. Paul Sirett and Paul Joseph's 2004 musical *The Big Life* merged a version of *Love's Labours Lost* with ska and other West Indian musics to chronicle the lives of black Britons' histories, in the years following the arrival of the *SS Empire Windrush* in 1948. Reviews suggest that the 'largely black British audience' appreciated not only the way in which its musical heritage and migration experiences were staged, but also how using Shakespeare to map that heritage and those experiences publicized them (Ritchie, 2005, 5). Moreover, Shakespeare's presence in a 'ska musical' might legitimate such music, but it also contributed to the arrival of the first black British production in the commercial theatre establishment of London's West End, and the ongoing acknowledgement of black Britons' contributions to and places in their new home. So this staging commemorated the completion of a circle, linking metropolis to former colony, pasts to present.

Some recordings and productions have similarly evoked the world's newly accessible – or exploited – musical environments, suggesting Shakespeare has a place in them, and creating a harmonious hybrid between such environments and the Bard. A 2005 BBC Radio 3 adaptation of *Pericles* 'took place in a "world" culture of different accents designed to chime with the production's "world music" score' (Greenhalgh, 2007, 187). Comparably, in the theatre, Tim Supple was commissioned by the British Council to stage a 2006 version of *A Midsummer Night's Dream* that incorporated the talents of Indian musicians alongside actors, acrobats and dancers, with the cast speaking in the array of languages and dialects of the Indian subcontinent and Sri Lanka (including English). In the globe-trotting performances of this celebrated production, the musicians and their instruments were onstage throughout, foregrounding this *Dream*'s desire to present mixed modes of expression that were at once global and local, Shakespearean and modern, verbal, non-verbal and musical. This production itself echoed Habib Tanvir's 1993 adaptation of the play, *Kamdeo ka Apna, Vasant Ritu ka Sapna*, which featured the 'musical folk-theatre form of Nautanki' once hugely popular in India's northern states (Chaudhuri, 2007, 96). Hybridizing has occurred in films too, with some juxtaposing Shakespearean plots with non-Western scores.[3]

Beyond India, other post-colonial locations have offered confident and innovative takes on Shakespeare. Ladysmith Black Mambazo, the South African ensemble specializing in the vocal genre *isicathamiya*, contributed a version of Sonnet 8 to the 2002 compilation *When Love Speaks*. Embodying both the grievous sufferings and hopeful future of their nation, the group sought to answer the poem's opening question: 'Music to hear, why hear'st thou music sadly?' The group's harmonized, contrapuntal adaptation reflected both the sonnet's words and its country's aspirations, at once unified and particular ('all in one one pleasing note do sing'). The adaptation also exemplified the universalist strains of some discourses of 'world music', *and* of some Shakespearean appropriations in a global context: 'being many, seeming one'. The ensemble and its style of music were apt agents for this collaboration. Ladysmith Black Mambazo has made great efforts to 'cross over', bringing South African music to the globe, by working with Paul Simon on his *Graceland* album, and with the P-Funk legend George Clinton on 'Scatter the Fire' from its album *Two Worlds One Heart*, whose title signals the kinds of connections the group tries to forge. Its efforts paid off: the group won a Grammy award for its album *Shaka Zulu*, in the 'Best Traditional Folk Recording', the first time a non-US musician had won an unshared prize in this category; in 1994, it accompanied Nelson Mandela when he accepted the Nobel Prize; and in 2009 it won another Grammy. These are remarkable feats, since the roots of the band's music are linguistically, sonically and socially distinct, bound up with the cultural and political history of working-class Zulu-speaking communities. But when did cultural and historical distinction ever prevent *Shakespeare* being hailed as a universal voice, in his own time or after? Since Ladysmith Black Mambazo's music is influenced by the gospel of missionaries, it blurs distinctions as Shakespeare does: 'The quasi-tonal harmonic language of *isicathamiya* . . . allows *isicathamiya* musicians to appropriate and re-appropriate western musical forms continually' (Taylor, 1997, 71). When they collaborate, who appears as the more global or 'universal' here – Shakespeare or Ladysmith Black Mambazo? The beat of whose lyrical expression sounds stronger? Arguably, both the group and the Bard emerge healthily from this transfusion: the latter's (admittedly problematic) status as lyricist for the world is maintained, while the former's global aspirations and inclusiveness are furthered.

Ladysmith Black Mambazo has shown how Shakespeare can be made to speak differently in new, global locations. Comparably, when contemporary popular music accommodates global sounds, these sounds can reinvoke latent strains or connections in Shakespeare's words. In an unreleased track for his stage show *A Bard Day's Night*, Chris O'Neill set the balcony scene from *Romeo and Juliet* (2.1.43–234) to a Beatlesesque piano-led melody. Yet the middle of the piece features a sitar break, followed by O'Neill's own words. With this incorporation and seguing, O'Neill reilluminates the passage from the play. This scene shows us Juliet as a 'fair sun' shining through a 'window', and we, like Romeo, see her as 'the east'. Yet O'Neill's song, inspired by the Beatles' own dalliances with Indian tunings and instrumentation, lets us *hear* a version of what we perceive on stage and read on the page: we witness the union of two lovers, set to the union of Western and Eastern musics, underscoring the union of old and new lyrics.

But these kinds of hybrids are not always so harmonious, and their implications are not always so clear, for our ideas of both Shakespeare and 'world music'. We can get some sense of the complexity of popular music's global production, dissemination and reception, and how this has impacted on Shakespeare, by considering a little-known 1965 track by the Shake Spears, called 'Do the Shake Spear'. The band began as the Dynamics in what is now the Republic of Zambia but what was once British-controlled Northern Rhodesia. In 1964, the band moved to Belgium and became the Shake Spears, recording for the Ronnex label. In 1965, they moved again, this time to England.

The track is a basic 12-bar blues, enlivened by the repetition of a ribald saxophone riff at the start, and its intrusion throughout. The opening line signals the song's novelty: 'Here's a new dance that the people can do'. In a response to the lead vocalist's call, the dance is immediately named and copyrighted by the backing vocalists, in a phrase that repeats throughout the track: 'shake spear, shake spear'. This dance is, we're told, very inclusive and easy, soundtracked as it is by this 'song with a beat for me and you'. Moving from the universal to the personal, the singer invites his listeners to get better acquainted with the dance, the song and him:

> So move in close, 'cos ya gotta be near, shake spear, shake spear,
> I want you with me baby when we do the shake spear . . .

Should any resistance remain, we are provided with a how-to guide, in the manner of the popular dance songs that 'bossed pop right up until the Beatles broke' (Cohn, 1969, 84):

> Bend your back forward move your arms to and fro, shake spear,
>   shake spear,
> Shake it shake it baby and let yourself go, shake spear, shake spear,
> Do it nice and easy now and don't lose control, shake spear, shake
>   spear,
> A little bit of rhythm and a lot of soul.

It is hard to miss the overt and insistent references to Shakespeare here, but what functions do they serve, and how can we contextualize them?

The band's name, and the song's, fragment Shakespeare's; though corny, this is a disjunctive respelling that generates other possible interpretations of the Bard. Some of these interpretations are bawdy: the spear being shaken 'near' the singer's 'baby', and even the act of doing 'the shake spear', are blatantly sexual. This is a cheeky, if obvious, way to fiddle with the figure of Shakespeare, though of course, puns weren't beneath *him*. As Samuel Johnson observed, quibbling with words was Shakespeare's own obsession, and his plays would repeatedly 'sacrifice . . . propriety' for this 'fatal Cleopatra', the tempting, exotic and estranging coupling of sounds and meanings that spelled death for everyday, established understanding (Johnson, 1765, 274). But the band and song do more than remind us of the Bard's coarser word play. The cultural and actual locations of 'Do the Shake Spear' create their own meanings, in terms of how the song relates to Shakespeare and the global context of its production and marketing.

This song, and its play with Shakespeare, were produced in a post-imperial moment. The Republic of Zambia came into being in October 1964, but the winds of change and anti-colonial protest were gathering before this. By making Shakespeare sexual, could the band be heard to exploit the perceived primal, libidinal energies of the supposed 'Dark Continent' it had grown up in but left behind as it sought fame back in the colonial centre? In other words, like a set of modern-day fatal Cleopatras, the Shake Spears bring what sounds like the rhythms of Africa to slay and seduce those who don't know how to shake their spears. The band appeared willing to exploit its African past in the name it traded under while at EMI: Teeny and Tony and the Bush Babies. By doing this, was it vocalizing its power to shake up staid European culture, inciting people to 'let' themselves 'go', through the medium of songs and dances that could disturb the repose of one of that culture's icons?

Alternatively, by making this play with Shakespeare, did the group seek to signal its sophistication, and its *separation* from its African roots? Perhaps the band is diminishing (or mocking) the possibility that an upstart, spear-shaking nationalist would even know who Shakespeare was. For though the dance might allow people to 'let' themselves 'go', the song also regulates and cautions against losing 'control' – psychological, sexual or colonial. This regulation is written into its musically formulaic structure, metrical consistency and rhyming couplets: the five-beat line meets the twelve-bar blues. In this way, mingling Shakespeare and 1960s' pop showed how far this band had come in its diasporic return, as it presented its cultural credentials to the burgeoning music scene in Belgium and the United Kingdom. At the time of the quatercentenary of Shakespeare's birth, there was money and interest in this kind of Shakes-ploitation tie-in, even beyond the Beatles: the Reflections' 1964 song '(Just Like) Romeo and Juliet' sold over four million copies. In these terms, it may have been more appropriate to discuss this song in another, earlier chapter, one more focused on the music of that period. Moreover, perhaps it was inappropriate to discuss Shakespeare's relation to 'world music' with reference to a song that audibly rehearses Anglo-American musical norms. But these norms are not discrete or stable – because based on *African*-American models, they are inherently influenced by global musics, and the global spread of local musics. And so offering a definitive reading of 'Do the Shake Spear' is difficult precisely because of the various geographical and cultural contexts this seemingly banal song occupies: the genesis of the Shake Spears was international, and, as such, though generic, 'Do the Shake Spear' is literally *world* music, but music of a world where the dislocations and complications caused by colonialism are still evident.

These dislocations, and the grievous legacies they evoke, continue to demand attention. But so too do the connections they provoke. To modify the comments from Bristol at the start of this chapter, perceived globally, *a* Shakespeare remains one of popular music's *most* popular, and certainly most prolific, recording artists. As one half of the internationally renowned Jamaican reggae-dancehall team Sly (Dunbar aka Drumbar) and Robbie (Shakespeare aka Basspeare), *this* Shakespeare has been involved in writing, performing, producing or remixing literally thousands of tracks for globalized markets and audiences. Just as Sly Dunbar's first name sustains the lineage of the American R & B-funk star Sly Stone, as an icon of African-American musical consciousness, so Robbie Shakespeare's identity as a post-colonial, international artist appropriately resonates with a history in which Shakespeare spoke of and for an imperial core imposing its cultural and political authority on the identities of those on the supposed margins. Yet as Robbie's remixed and alternative surname suggests, such cultural and political authority is made rich and strange in the impersonations, synergies and hybridities of the world's contemporary popular musics. This is less Shakespeare in love, more Shakespeare as *dub*. And Shakespeare's expressive, diasporic, centripetal, lyrical legacy lives on, not least, for example, in the form of Robbie's cousin, a Jamaican-born, Los Angeles-based reggae performer. His stage name? Black Shakespeare.

143

NOTES

1 See Burt, 2003b, 14–36; Orkin, 2005; and White, 2007, 5–10.
2 See Joughin, 1997; and Bristol, 1990.
3 See Sanders, 2007, 158; and Burt, 2003a.

CHAPTER 10

FANS, FANS, FANS, LEND ME YOUR EARS: LISTENING TO LISTENERS

Shakespeare and Popular Music argues that part of the meaning and pleasure of popular music might be generated through its relations with Shakespeare. But to comprehend the relationship between Shakespeare and popular music, some attention should be paid to how *audiences* relate to Shakespeare in popular music. That is the aim of this chapter.

POP'S USES AND USERS

People have been interested in audiences for a long time. Plato realized that even when authorities tried to control the form and production of music, they could not dictate whether listeners found pleasure in what they heard, especially if that music was *popular*:

> Take someone who has right from childhood till the age of maturity and discretion grown familiar with a controlled and restrained style of music. Play him some of the other sort, and how he'll loathe it! . . . Yet, if he's been brought up to enjoy the strong appeal of popular music, it's the disciplined kind he'll call frigid and repellent. So as I said just now, on the score of pleasure or the lack of it, neither is superior nor inferior to the other. (1970, 290)

In different ways, modern analyses of popular culture, especially those that use ethnographic approaches, have also insisted on the variety and importance of consumers' interpretations of and responses to the culture they consume.[1] As a critical reaction to Adorno's *apparently* deterministic approaches, analyses of popular *music* have done something similar, acknowledging the diverse ways in which people understand their music. But that '*apparently*' is important. Adorno recognized that the 'functional interpretation' of 'light music' mattered: 'it should be shown that the same components and the identical drive structures to which light music adjusts take on totally different meanings depending upon the given state of social progress' (1932, 426). In other words, how a song was contextualized by producers and consumers in specific times and places was worth remembering. Later commentators like Simon Frith have affirmed this more clearly: popular music is not '*just* a product (an exchange value)' but also a 'use value' (1983, 101). As Frith observes: 'It's not where pop songs come from that matters, but where they get to . . . Once a pop song is launched on the world, all sorts of things can happen to it' (2004a, 106–7). Evidence abounds signalling this plurality in consumption. For those running the popular music industry for profit, it has been and still is very difficult to market to audiences with unpredictable patterns of consumption, even though creating something that '*holds meaning for the public*' motivates all levels of the production process (Hennion, 1983, 185). In fact, whatever Adorno says about standardization, the more 'apparently homogeneous' the product, the more 'potentially productive the role of reception' as 'cultural power' devolves among 'users': in other words, people make the same thing different (Middleton, 1990, 61, 97). The industry is 'organized around the realities of overproduction' precisely because of this (Frith, 1983, 62). And *what* an industry. In 1999, it had a worldwide turnover of $38 billion, with the US music industry worth $15 billion alone. Such statistics may not be as bloated a decade on, given the rise of online file sharing and downloads. But financial commitments by producers and consumers, in whatever forms, continue to evince other investments: 'these figures do not just describe a major industry, a source of revenue and of trade links, they also describe a source of meaning and pleasure' (Frith et al., 2004, ix). In this rests popular music's simultaneous power and need, its give and take: 'Understanding rock and roll requires asking what it gives its fans, how it empowers them and how they empower it' (Grossberg, 1986, 114). As Frith argues, 'if the power of popular music lies in its popularity, then the particular choices that the people make are significant' (1983, 62). Nonetheless, some critics discussing Shakespeare and popular culture, especially popular music, have sometimes tended to downplay issues of intentionality and reception – how producers and consumers of popular music use Shakespeare, and why. So Lanier observes:

> When popular culture cites Shakespeare, the overriding concern is often not what the passage 'really' means. Rather, it is often more focussed on passages as instances of Shakespeare's cultural authority. (2006, 53)

Comparably, when discussing Madonna's use of the word 'cherish' in the song of the same name as a reference to *Romeo and Juliet*, Buhler downplays the issue of whether 'this is an intentional allusion or not' (2002, 258–59).

This shows a now orthodox and understandable literary-critical disregard for the intentional fallacy: it is misguided to limit how we interpret a work based on the motivations we attribute to its creator. But such comments also rest on a series of assumptions: that, to echo Lanier, a Shakespearean passage can *really* mean something definite; that those citing or alluding to such passages don't necessarily do so in the full knowledge of that definite something; and, lastly, that whether an allusion is intentional or not is of little 'concern' when we think about the responses of consumers to these passages, allusions and intentions.

To rethink these issues, perhaps we would do well to recognize that Shakespeare's presence in or relation to popular music may mean more to some audiences than others, where 'meaning' something signals not just semantic but also intellectual or emotional value, based on audiences' awareness of intentionality. In other words, what will we learn about Shakespeare and popular music by exploring how listeners understand their relationship? Audiences' responses are particularly apparent in the theatre, where people react fairly immediately (or not at all) to what they see and hear. As a composer for Shakespearean productions, John Boden admits the challenge of making music that fits the staging and the audience. Boden asserts that he starts with the assumption that the songs in the texts are 'the least well-known' aspects of the play. And whether communicating with directors or playgoers, Boden recognizes he has to 'mediate' the way he talks about the music – he can't assume musical knowledge, but he can 'manipulate' audiences to take them on the 'journey of the story', with Shakespeare and the score reinforcing each other (2009). People like Boden, actively involved in making links between Shakespeare and popular music, have to modify their intentions when facing consumers of what they produce. The uses and users of such music cannot be ignored. But this is not only true in the theatre.

LISTENING TO LISTENERS

In their work on media and audiences, Karen Ross and Virginia Nightingale assert:

> Audiences are unnatural phenomena. They do not exist in nature, but are created in the course of human interactions – with each other and with the technologies we invent. (2003, 1)

Nightingale and Ross underline this point in other work, observing that 'the conjunction of time and space' is vital for locating audiences (2003, 5). Like texts, they exist in specific contexts. To understand what specific popular music audiences make of Shakespeare in *their* popular music, I conducted some online research, signing up to various fan sites dedicated to musicians whose works scholars have suggested reference Shakespeare in significant ways: the Indigo Girls, Bruce Springsteen, Elvis Costello and Bob Dylan. Once signed up, I posted the following request, edited here, as 'an academic researching the relationships between Shakespeare and popular music':

> As I'm sure you know, [Artist(s) X] have/has a long and rich heritage of engaging with Shakespearean imagery and themes . . . What I'm really interested in, though, is how you guys as fans respond to these kinds of relationships and allusions. It seems to me the fans' perspective is missing from a lot of accounts of 'Shakespeare and Popular Music'. So I'd really, really appreciate it if you or your subscribers/contacts could spend a few moments thinking about and hopefully responding to these questions (if they seem lame, by all means go off topic!): Do you notice/care about the allusions to Shakespeare in [Artist(s) X's] songs, and if so, how do they make you feel about [Artist(s) X] and/or Shakespeare? Why do you think [Artist(s) X] incorporate these kinds of links to Shakespeare in songs?

Wherever and however it is conducted, this kind of activity is fraught with problems. Using an online medium cannot alter the reality that researcher status and bias, sample size and constitution, and mode and context of address and response all merely consolidate the impossibility of attaining unmediated, 'authentic' reactions to questions like these (Morrison, 2003, 111–130). Nonetheless, cultural researchers have suggested that the internet contains audiences with particular characteristics:

> Online fan communities are . . . expansive self-organizing groups focused around the collective production, debate and circulation of meanings, interpretations and fantasises in response to various artifacts of contemporary popular culture. (Jenkins, 2003, 281)

This makes this kind of research as valuable as it is problematic.[2] Moreover, these characteristics have a particular relevance to a study of Shakespeare and popular music. Because this 'collective exchange of knowledge cannot be fully contained by previous sources of power', online communities and the interpretations they generate can undermine 'traditional forms of expertise' (Jenkins, 2003, 283). As we'll see, these forms include the traditional expertise and value invested in Shakespeare. What follows, then, summarizes fans' responses on the sites to this request. On reading these responses, we might remember Sheryl Garratt's warmly wry comment on her own infatuation with the Bay City Rollers, and others' infatuations since: 'A fan's mind is a curious thing' (1984, 405).

Surveying fans' responses to these questions and requests, several significant themes – not to say curiosities – emerge. Some fans were adamant about Shakespeare's influence on, and significance to, the popular music artists they consumed, and comparisons with Shakespeare emerged as a key indicator of such artists' worth:

> I firmly believe that had Shakespeare never existed, per se, then we would never have had Bob Dylan . . . the early writings of Bob Dylan ooze with Shakespearian style, tempo, and invective. Many of Dylan's early love songs have literally been re-writings of Shakespearian sonnets . . . in many ways, Dylan managed to capture and mimic the Bard of Avon's poeticness . . . Dylan even managed to capture the 'pathos' that Shakespeare did so well. It is no small surprise to me that Dylan's first album, entitled *Bob Dylan*, was actually ready for release under the title of *Shakespearian Dreams* . . . Columbia Records pulled the title as they feared that it would

not [appeal] to the US market . . . most of the albums carrying the Shakesperian Dreams title were destroyed, however several copies were salvaged and are now amongst Dylan collectors most sort after and prized collectibles. There is very little doubt or arguement that Dylan, or rather Dylan's style of writing would never have come about had Shakespeare never existed. (Thickboy, 2008)

Similarly, some fans accepted the notion that Shakespeare and popular musicians might be related, but mainly in the sense of a shared heritage or universal appeal:

If, as I do, you rate Dylan as a literary great, then he is continuing what Leavis calls the great tradition, quoting and requoting, citing and alluding, as TS Eliot suggests, to paraphrase, there is nothing new under the sun . . . i.e., we are all subject to what we have heard, read and seen, and as Schubert says, again to paraphrase, music goes on for ever, every room still holds the vestiges of every note that sounded there. (Stephenoxford, 2008)

Shakespeare content is not exclusive. The imagery and content is the same as countless other writers. His work is one of a very few early works so it seems like it was original but it was far from it. The human spirit, youthful angst, soul searching of springsteen's work is classic, not original. What they both really do share is the unique way they wrote for their time. (Kipp, 2008)

I think that as someone said earlier they both share the empathy that allowed them to write in such a way that so many people could/can relate to . . . common themes that affect the 'everyman'. (Cybercat, 2008)

But these kinds of responses, happy to correlate Shakespeare with popular music in specific ways (that ironically emphasize their shared universality), were not frequent. Far more frequent were responses that sought to *diminish* the significance of such correlations:

you can't judge Shakespeare or anyones influence for that matter on [an artist's] references. "Shakespeare he's in the alley" doesn't mean anything other then Dylan knows who the guy is. (Jookyle, 2008)

Consequently, some respondents would only make such correlations in heavily ironic terms:

> is that shakesteen or shakin steven or springspear. wow this is a deep and meaningful subject. (Cathy, 2008)

The connections evoked (but ridiculed) by these playful neologisms are precisely what this study has aimed at. Clearly, then, to insist on the profundity and complexity of Shakespeare's connections with popular music might be to mishear or overlook the way fans consume the music in which those connections only *appear* evident. For some fans, the notion that Shakespeare was a presence in their stars' work was, if not unconscionable, at least unremarkable or even ludicrous. As such, their comments were critical or sarcastic:

> [Elvis] Costello is very much steeped in musical history and, despite his verbal dexterity, reflects little in the way of literary history. I think he's said in interviews that he's never been a big reader. . . . Witty, brilliant and intelligent, yes, but allusive to high culture? Not really. (Westinghouse, 2008)
> I love a good wind up. (NorthSideJimmy, 2008)
> You're pulling our leg I believe. Bruce [Springsteen] and SHAKESPEARE?? The only connection between Incident [on 57th Street] and Shakespeare being the words "Romeo and Juliet" if you ask me. When Bruce wrote that song way back when I don't believe he even knew about someone like Shakespeare, shitty school education and all . . . Perhaps meanwhile he'll know a bit about him PERHAPS . . . (Sixty9chevy, 2008)
> [Springsteen] learned more from a three-minute record, baby, than he ever learned in school. (Misadventure, 2008)

One respondent even contrived an elaborate and brilliant spoof of the questions, 'to further the cause of important scholarship':

> Do you notice/care about allusions to Shakespeare in Costello songs/albums
> (a) No
> (b) Yes

(c) What's an allusion, dude? Is it like that thing that you see when you're in the desert but like it isn't like really there or something?

and if so, how do they make you feel about Costello and/or Shakespeare?

(a) Tired

(b) Mildly aroused

(c) Whoa, this is some seriously strong shit, man. What was the question again?

Why do you think Costello might incorporate these kinds of links to Shakespeare in his work?

(a) Because it makes him look big and clever

(b) Because there are only so many Bret Easton Ellis references he can get away with

(c) Because the clever chicks really go for all that literature shit and some of them are like seriously hot, you know? (Perry, 2008)

Quite apart from deflating academic pretension in good-natured (and doubtless well-deserved) ways, such responses restated the difference between Shakespeare and popular music that many commentators have observed, consolidated or problematized. Why? Some respondents wanted to construct their icons as inherently antipathetic to a Shakespeare they perceived as high-cultural, accessible only to the educated. By this, making and enjoying popular music emerge as practices actively opposed to and dismissive of Shakespeare and what he represents. So some respondents maintained the very value distinction between high-elite and low-popular cultural forms that conservative critics (and Adorno!) try to uphold.

Work on other aspects of popular culture has revealed similar phenomena. Ien Ang analysed 42 letters written in response to an advert placed in a Dutch magazine asking for people's views on the US soap *Dallas*. Ang identified in the responses a persistent strain of what she termed 'the ideology of mass culture', a perception that glossy, commercial, American cultural products like *Dallas* were bad for individuals and communities, or at least not as good for people as improving media and art. But Ang's study proved influential not simply because she recognized that it was people who disliked *Dallas* who reproduced this view. She discovered that even those who professed their affection for

Dallas showed how consumers could 'internalize' and repeat the negative 'judgements' of mass culture in their responses:

> The dominance of the ideology of mass culture apparently even extends to the common sense of everyday thinking: for ordinary people too it appears to offer a credible framework of interpretation . . . Its norms and prescriptions exert pressure on them, so that they feel the necessity to defend themselves against it. (1985, 278, 276, 281)

Perhaps a comparable defensiveness coloured some of the reactions I recorded. Still, some respondents *were* willing to acknowledge a more general debate about the ways Shakespeare related to popular music:

> I've never bothered to try to pick them [Shakespeare references] all out but they don't get by me when I hear them, at least not the more noticeable ones. (Mamablue, 2008)

This comment was particularly suggestive because it intimated that references to Shakespeare are something for consumers of popular music to 'get' (or not 'get'). This might reinforce the notion that Shakespeare represents occult or exclusive knowledge. However, the respondent had other ideas, and perceptively outlined something of the diversity of intentions in and responses to Shakespeare in popular music:

> I think that there's a reason why Shakespeare is seemingly timeless. I think that when you borrow from him, whether people know you're borrowing or not, the sentiment of the lines is never lost on the audience, no matter how many centuries later. I think that if you're able to say, 'hey that's a Shakespeare reference' makes you anything from an interesting conversationalist at a totally geeky party, to completely pretentious. I do dig Shakespeare but as far as popular music references to him are concerned, I don't think you need to always know the origin to get the line. ([The Indigo Girls'] Swamp Ophelia's one exception) (Mamablue, 2008)

What begins as another testimony to Shakespeare's universal, timeless, translatability becomes a sense that popular music can be autonomous from, but not necessarily opposed to, Shakespeare. Moreover, in specific instances, knowledge of both enhances the pleasure a listener gets from both. This reinvests some consumers with particular powers:

> Shakespeare is attached to products capable of being appreciated by a special class of consumer capable of appreciating *both* the subtleties of pop allusion and consumption *and* reference to a different cultural register. (Lanier, 2007, 97)

ON FANDOM

Despite his reputation for downplaying the diversity and depth of consumers' responses to popular culture, Adorno may be helpful here. In his work on popular music, Adorno tried to describe the stages of reception that happened as people recognized a popular tune. We might relate the stages he identified with the ways some respondents dealt with their recognition of Shakespeare in popular music. First, according to Adorno, people have a 'more or less vague experience of being reminded of something ("I must have heard this somewhere")'. Then people experience a 'moment of actual identification', when 'vague remembrance is searchlighted by sudden awareness'. What Adorno says about recognizing a pop song can be seen as analogous to what some respondents said about hearing a Shakespearean reference *in* a pop song.

After this comes what Adorno called 'subsumption', as people fine-tune their recognition: 'the interpretation of the "that's it" experience by an experience such as "that's the hit 'Night and Day'"'.' When listeners make this definition (this is '*the* so and so'), they also recognize they're not the only person who knows this. They feel 'safety in numbers' and understand that they are subsumed into, or made part of, a 'crowd' of listeners, just as the song can be subsumed, or put into, a particular agreed and 'pre-existing category' of cultural value. The song thus becomes a 'socially established highlight', and the listener takes a 'vicarious part' in a community of listeners responding the same way. We might imagine one community could be a set of people who recognize a Shakespearean allusion. This community has power, as a kind of 'institution' recognizing and accrediting the song as worth valuing. There is an element of social but also personal entitlement here, which Adorno says is the next stage: ' "Oh, I know it; this belongs to me." ' What seems like a mass response actually appears individual too.

Characteristically, and somewhat predictably, Adorno doesn't think the effects of this are liberating or empowering. The effects are, in fact, to turn an 'experience' into an 'object'. People recognize not only the song, but that they own it, or endure a delusional desire to do so. When they do this, they buy into a commercial format that relies on many other people giving something worth, and on these people being manipulated by pluggers and adverts. In such terms, they are deceiving themselves, and this is the final part of the 'recognition process':

> The listener feels flattered because he, too, owns what everyone owns. By owning an appreciated and marketed hit, one gets the illusion of value. . . . The musical owner who feels 'I like this particular hit (because I know it)' achieves a delusion of grandeur comparable to a child's daydream about owning the railroad. . . . [S]ong hits pose only questions of recognition which anyone can answer. Yet listeners enjoy giving the answers because they thus become identified with the powers that be. (1941a, 454–57)

We don't need to subscribe totally to Adorno's view to see the value of his points. When people discuss hearing a Shakespearean allusion in a song, they respond in various ways, some of which conform to Adorno's scheme, some of which don't. Some respondents don't notice Shakespearean allusions, and even if they do seem not to care: how, then, can their enjoyment depend on recognition, as Adorno suggests? Some respondents thought the idea that Shakespeare and popular music might be related was a bit daft, and were not interested in respecting the cultural or material value of Shakespeare in their idols' work. Quite the opposite, in fact: to some respondents, Shakespeare is one of those institutional 'powers that be' identified by Adorno; but, contradicting Adorno, such respondents are well aware of this.

Obviously, this survey of fan responses does not offer an ethnographically representative sample. Obviously, too, fans of other artists who employ Shakespearean allusion and citation might have offered other responses. Yet this survey does perhaps present one kind of method, or some material, we might bear in mind for future investigations of Shakespeare's relations with popular music and those who consume it. Furthermore, this survey would suggest that academic debates about how and why Shakespeare is related to popular music (and culture) need to accommodate the variety of patterns of consumption fans display, patterns that do not always confirm assumptions – including my own, and Adorno's – about appropriation and reception.

But then – equally obviously – in intellect and temperament I am no Adorno. I am, though, a fan of popular music and of Shakespeare. This book is itself a fan's attempt to rethink both in light (or sound) of each other: 'Fans produce meanings and interpretations' (Jenkins, 1992, 214). *My* 'interpretations' suggest that Shakespeare and popular music *do* connect, and this connection produces new 'meanings' for them (and me). That is part of the point of this book. And by making this point, this book also tries to unsettle the distinctions many studies of fans reproduce. These distinctions characterize fans as emotive slaves subject to a popular culture industry, with researchers cast as objective, rational aficionados of what is seen as high culture.[3] Writing a book about a recognizably prestige subject like Shakespeare involves a degree of unemotive, objective, rational behaviour. But perhaps the interpretations this book exhibits are an excessive display of fanatic devotion to seemingly non-prestige materials, like popular music. As a fan, and as a researcher, I make no apologies for this.

NOTES

1 See, for example, Radway, 1991; Lewis, 1992; Hills, 2002; and Gray et al., 2007.
2 See Baym, 2000.
3 For an insightful skewering of this distinction in such research, see Jenson, 1992.

CODA: THE REST IS?

This book began with the aims of trying to bring together Shakespeare and popular music, and of exploring the fascinating things that happen to both when they meet. Has it achieved those aims? Though some listeners and some critics would resist this conclusion, in the course of this book Shakespeare has emerged as a figure integral to the idioms, mediums and politics of popular music – how we think about, hear, enjoy, criticize, make and share songs. Just as popular music deals in and with fantasies and realities, so Shakespeare inhabits the dreams and nightmares of artists and fans. Popular musics – and consumers – adapt, rewrite and recreate Shakespeare, sometimes combatively, sometimes lovingly, and he is made to relate through innumerable allusions, citations and appropriations. Shakespeare's authority can often complement and license musicians' experiments with new media, or in new genres: he is used in crossover hits and breakthrough smashes. But popular music doesn't reference Shakespeare simply because of some sense of inferiority or a lack of confidence in its own artistic authority, and it doesn't just show that such inferiorities and lacks can be compensated only by the Shakespearean seal of approval. On the contrary, many uses of Shakespeare reveal popular music's self-confidence. Artists may express aspiration when they quote or copy his words and images, but they are not necessarily aspiring to his status as an *elite* cultural authority, as much as his long-standing *popular* success. In some cases, this self-confidence communicates itself in brash statements through which pop signals its power to both sustain and surpass Shakespeare's impact. Madonna is willing to gamble that Romeo and Juliet never felt the way she feels (as she puts it on 'Cherish'), though she maintains their primacy as signifiers of passion to say so. In other cases, though popular music, critics and fans may seem to insist on a separation from Shakespeare, incompatibility is never total. A very early incarnation of the British band Pulp conceived a song titled 'Shakespeare Rock', featuring a girl whose tendency to quote *Hamlet* severely compromised her desirability (cited in Sturdy, 2003, 8). This tongue-in-cheek song realized how unlikely and unsatisfying any union of Shakespeare and popular music might be. Yet the song itself had to quote Shakespeare to make this point, and so though its title (and chorus) is ironic, it also records a connection that the lyrics can only repeat.

If all this means that Shakespeare helps popular music assume different forms, then popular music makes Shakespeare mean different things too, putting a new spin on his words in new contexts. Sampling and remixing Shakespeare changes him, but also develops existing potentials in his work. Popular music amplifies ambiguities and contradictions in this work, and between it and the dominant discourses of Shakespeare's period and our own. At the same time, popular music's use of Shakespeare realizes contradictions within such music, and within its relations to the contexts in which it is made and consumed.

Musicians and critics compare the modes and conditions of a mass medium like pop to the modes and conditions of work like Shakespeare's. Perceived continuities in relations between Shakespeare and popular music come in terms of cultural chronology (Shakespeare as a precursor to or residual inspiration for later popular cultural forms, including music), in terms of the means of cultural production (Shakespeare and popular musicians share artistic creativity, common contexts and joint constraints on artistic creation), and in terms of the means of reception and consumption (Shakespeare and popular music can both be understood in relation to debates about culture and politics). Perceived discontinuities between Shakespeare and popular music take similar forms and new ones as popular musicians, and those elevating or deriding popular music alike, construct 'Shakespeare as pop's Other' (Lanier, 2007, 99).

These processes are ongoing. A recent and acclaimed account of contemporary *classical* music by Alex Ross seemed to insist on precisely such continuities and discontinuities, by featuring a significantly Shakespearean allusion in its title: *The Rest is Noise: Listening to the Twentieth Century*. Ross's appropriation of Hamlet's last words suggests a desire to offer *his* last word on modern music, terminating debate about what is or is not music, and what, by implication, is or is not mere noise. So, though inclusive and wide ranging, Ross is fairly authoritative about who or what properly constitutes post-Romantic music: the Second Viennese School, Modernism, Mahler, Strauss, Stravinksy, Sibelius, Britten and so on. On one level, Ross simply repeats the discrimination employed by many other writers that 'music' is by definition inherently *classical* music, even in its obtuse modern forms. And Ross also implicitly reinforces the notion that popular music requires that modifier, *popular*, to distinguish it from other 'music' that is superior or more profound. More than this, by consigning anything other than high-cultural classical music to the status of the 'rest', a 'noise', Ross turns popular music *into* noise, inarticulate and anti-musical. But why reference Shakespeare to make these discriminations? Recollecting the first epigraph with which *Shakespeare and Popular Music* began, perhaps Shakespeare still has a role to play in policing what is or is not music, and in separating noise, popular or otherwise, from it. The recognisable Shakespearean resonance adds authority to Ross's stance as a cultural gatekeeper.

Given this authority, and the long-standing discriminations it sustains, have I been right to hear harmonies between Shakespeare and popular music when it still sometimes seems as if none exist? Yes. Ross himself shows that the distinctions and discriminations surrounding and constructing Shakespeare, popular and classical music, and noise, are not certain. Ross repeatedly conveys how avant-garde 'classical' musicians have collaborated with and influenced no less avant-garde 'popular' musicians up to the present. And he admits that many people discern modern 'classical composition' to be 'noise', sometimes 'because it *is* noise, or near to it, by design', suggesting the 'interchangeability' of noise and music (Ross, 2008, xii, 483). These *in*distinctions are recorded in what Ross does to the Shakespearean phrase, and the phrase itself. For the dying Hamlet, 'The rest is silence' (5.2.310), *not* 'noise'. Yet even this 'silence' is followed *by* significant noise: Hamlet's own 'O, O, O, O!' (5.2.311), and Horatio's sonorous suggestion that 'flights of angels' will 'sing' Hamlet to his 'rest', punctuated by the sound of Fortinbras' 'drum' (5.2.313–14). As Hamlet's 'silence' resounds musically, so Ross turns 'silence' into 'noise'. And as this link with *Hamlet* implies, there are preludes to how Ross orchestrates connections between silence, noise, music and Shakespeare. This is because at certain points in societies and their histories, it is been hard to hear the difference between noise and music:

> Noise itself constantly dissipates, as what is judged noise at one point is music or meaning at another. . . . Noise is not an objective fact. It occurs in relation to perception – both direct (sensory) and according to presumptions made by an individual. These are going to vary according to historical, geographical and cultural location. (Hegarty, 2009, ix, 3)

Noise is 'constantly failing – failing to stay noise, as it becomes familiar, or acceptable practice' (Hegarty, 2009, ix). Music is simply 'the organization of noise', and noise signifies something, not least when it is Shakespearean, musical or popular (Attali, 2003, 4).

In the early modern period, noise could *mean* music. The *Psalms* of King James' *Authorized Version* of the Bible resound with the 'loud' (33:3) and 'joyful noise' (66:1) of voices, trumpets, harps and cornets in praise of the divine (Carroll and Prickett, 1998). John Milton records the 'stringed noise' that rings out 'On the Morning of Christ's Nativity' (1626, 105). And in *2 Henry IV*, Shakespeare would capture an echo of popular tavern life for the stage, with the reference to 'Sneak's noise' (2.4.11): 'Mr Sneak was the gentleman who gave his name to the particular band of instrumentalists who favoured the "Boar's Head"' (Naylor, 1931, 103). Of course, noise in Shakespeare's time wasn't always musical, as the dying Henry IV implies in the same play:

Let there be no noise made, my gentle friends,
Unless some dull and favourable hand
Will whisper music to my weary spirit. (4.3.133–35)

But even when a distinction between noise and music is made audible in the worlds of Shakespeare's plays, it isn't certain that music is *preferable* to noise, or more evocative. As one character memorably observes in *The Merchant of Venice*, overly ordered, harmonious music is sometimes incapable of expressing uneasy, complex realities, or of evoking and provoking our more unsettling, complicated impulses:

JESSICA   I am never merry when I hear sweet music. (5.1.69)

Some modern reimaginings of the plays have realised this discontent, and what makes it, *with* noise. In Taymor's *Titus*, a film mindful of recent conflicts in the Balkans, the rapist brothers Chiron and Demetrius cavort to the grinding thud of atonal, feedback-laden, industrially ultraheavy metallic sounds, sounds signifying 'destruction, dirt, pollution' and 'aggression' (Attali, 2003, 27). This accords with their psychotic states, and a world in which those states are nurtured:

The subliminal message of most music is that the universe is essentially benign, that if there is sadness or tragedy, this is resolved at the level of some higher harmony. Noise troubles this worldview.

This is why noise groups invariably deal with subject matter that is anti-humanist – extremes of abjection, obsession, trauma, atrocity, possession. (Reynolds, 1990, 57)

It might be strange to end a book on Shakespeare and popular music by thinking about noise, a sonic and social extreme, what sounds like the end of expression, communication and meaning. Yet if this seems an un-musical coda, and one that breaks but does not confirm connections between Shakespeare and music, it needn't and doesn't. *This* kind of noise, and what it means acoustically and politically, is just one more manifestation of the discontinuities (and continuities) evoked by Shakespeare's relations with popular music.

When it comes to those relations, early modern and modern, the rest *isn't* silence (and there's definitely no long fade out), but concatenations of globalized, sampled, remixed, transmitted, downloaded, digital, multimedia, post-phonographic, cacophonous, polyvocal, polyphonic, plunderphonic, multi-instrumental 'noises, / Sounds, and sweet airs, that give delight', where no one has the last word. This is something to celebrate, not lament, as Caliban counsels: 'Be not afeard' (*The Tempest*, 3.2.138–39). And the beat goes on . . .

WORKS CITED

Echoing the aims of this book, this list of works cited does not divide primary from critical material, or musical sources from literary texts.

Adorno, Theodor. (2002) *Essays on Music*, ed. Richard Leppert, transl. Susan H. Gillespie. Berkeley, Los Angeles, London: University of California Press.

—. (1951) *Minima Moralia: Reflections from Damaged Life*, transl. E. F. N. Jephcott. London: Verso, 2000.

—. (1936) 'On Jazz', in Adorno, *Essays on Music*. 470–95.

—. (1941a) 'On Popular Music', in Adorno, *Essays on Music*. 437–69.

—. (1938) 'On the Fetish-Character in Music and the Regression of Listening', in Adorno, *Essays on Music*. 288–317.

—. (1932) 'On the Social Situation of Music', in Adorno, *Essays on Music*. 391–436.

—. (1997) *Prisms*, transl. Samuel and Shierry Weber. Cambridge, MA: MIT Press.

—. (1927/1965) 'The Curves of the Needle', in Adorno, *Essays on Music*. 271–76.

—. (1941b) 'The Radio Symphony', in Adorno, *Essays on Music*. 251–70.

—. (1955/1967) 'Toward an Understanding of Schoenberg' (1955/1967), in Adorno, *Essays on Music*. 627–43.

—. (1945) 'What National Socialism Has Done to the Arts', in Adorno, *Essays on Music*. 373–90.

Akala. (2007) 'Comedy Tragedy History', *Freedom Lasso*. Illa State.

—. (2009) 'High Culture in Hoxton: The Hip Hop Shakespeare', *The Guardian*. Available at <http://www.guardian.co.uk/music/video/2009/apr/15/hip-hop-shakespeare-akala>, accessed 15 April 2009.

—. (13 October 2008) Interview with the author.

—. (2006) 'Shakespeare', *It's Not a Rumour*. Illa State.

Ang, Ien. (1985) '*Dallas* and the Ideology of Mass Culture', *Cultural Theory and Popular Culture: A Reader*, ed. John Storey. New York and London: Harvester Wheatsheaf, 1994. 274–83.

Arctic Monkeys. (2005) 'I Bet That You Look Good on the Dancefloor'. Domino.

Ash. (2004) 'Starcrossed', *Meltdown*. Infectious.

Attali, Jacques. (2003) *Noise: The Political Economy of Music*, transl. Brian Massumi. Minneapolis and London: University of Minnesota Press.

Bacharach, Burt. (2005) 'Go Ask Shakespeare', *At This Time*. Sony BMG.

Bamber, Linda. (1982) *Comic Women, Tragic Men: A Study of Gender and Genre in Shakespeare.* Stanford: Stanford University Press.

Baym, Nancy. (2000) *Tune In, Log On: Soaps, Fandom and Online Community.* Thousand Oaks, CA, and London: Sage.

Beatles, the. (1964) 'Around the Beatles', on *Fun with the Fab Four 4.* Good Times Home Video, 1986.

—. (1967) 'I Am the Walrus', *Magical Mystery Tour.* Parlophone.

—. (1967) *Sgt. Pepper's Lonely Hearts Club Band.* Parlophone.

Benjamin, Walter. (1936) 'The Work of Art in the Age of Mechanical Reproduction', in Benjamin, *Illuminations,* ed. Hannah Arendt. London: Pimlico, 1999. 211–44.

Bersani, Leo and Ulysse Dutoit. (1999) *Caravaggio.* London: British Film Institute.

Bicknell, Jeannette. (2009) *Why Music Moves Us.* Houndmills: Palgrave Macmillan.

Birthday Party, the. (1982) 'Hamlet (Pow Pow Pow)', *Junk Yard.* 4AD.

Biz Markie. (2003) 'Tear Shit Up', *Weekend Warrior.* Groove Attack.

Boden, John. (13 March 2009) Interview with the author.

Born, Georgina and David Hesmondhalgh (eds). (2000) *Western Music and Its Others: Difference, Representation, and Appropriation in Music.* Berkeley, Los Angeles, London: University of California Press.

Bowie, David. (1973) 'Cracked Actor', *Aladdin Sane.* RCA.

—. (1976) 'Station to Station', *Station to Station.* RCA.

Bozza, Anthony. (2004) *Whatever You Say I Am: The Life and Times of Eminem.* London: Corgi.

Bretzius, Stephen. (1997) *Shakespeare in Theory: The Postmodern Academy and the Early Modern Theater.* Ann Arbor: University of Michigan Press.

Brignone, Guido (dir.). (1937) *Vivere!.* Appia Cinematografica.

Bristol, Michael D. (1996) *Big-Time Shakespeare.* London: Routledge.

—. (1990) *Shakespeare's America, America's Shakespeare.* London and New York: Routledge.

Brotherhood, the. (1996) 'One', *Elementalz.* Virgin.

Buck, Gene, Herman Ruby and David Stamper. (1912) 'Shakespearean Rag'. Joseph. W. Sterne and Company.

Buhler, Stephen M. (2005) 'Form and Character in Duke Ellington's and Billy Strayhorn's *Such Sweet Thunder*', *Borrowers and Lenders: The Journal of Shakespeare and Appropriation,* 1:1, 1–8. Available at <http://www.borrowers.uga.edu/cocoon/borrowers/about>, accessed 19 December 2007.

—. (2007) 'Musical Shakespeares: Attending to Ophelia, Juliet and Desdemona', *The Cambridge Companion to Shakespeare and Popular Culture,* ed. Robert Shaughnessy. pp. 150–74.

—. (2002) 'Reviving Juliet, Repackaging Romeo: Transformations of Character in Pop and Post-Pop Music', *Shakespeare After Mass Media,* ed. Richard Burt. pp. 243–64.

Burnett, Mark Thornton. (2007) *Filming Shakespeare in the Global Marketplace.* Houndmills: Palgrave Macmillan.

Burnett, Robert Meyer (dir.). (1998) *Free Enterprise.* Mindfire Entertainment.

Burt, Richard. (2003a) 'Shakespeare and Asia in Postdiasporic Cinemas: Spin-offs and Citations of the Plays from Bollywood to Hollywood', *Shakespeare the Movie II: Popularizing the Plays on Film, TV, Video and DVD,* eds Richard Burt and Lynda E. Boose. London and New York: Routledge. 265–303.

—. (2003b) 'Shakespeare, "Glo-cal-ization," Race , and the Small Screens of Post-Popular Culture', *Shakespeare the Movie II,* eds Burt and Boose. 14–36.

—. (2002) 'Slammin' Shakespeare in Acc(id)ents Yet Unknown: Liveness, Cinem(edi)a and Racial Dis-integration', *Shakespeare Quarterly,* 53:2, 201–26.

—. (1998) *Unspeakable ShaXXXspeares: Queer Theory and American Kiddie Culture.* New York: St. Martin's Press.

Burt, Richard (ed.). (2002) *Shakespeare After Mass Media.* New York: Palgrave.

Buxton, David. (1983) 'Rock Music, the Star System, and the Rise of Consumerism', *On Record: Rock, Pop, and the Written Word,* eds Simon Frith and Andrew Goodwin. pp. 427–40.

Byrds, the. (1967) *Younger Than Yesterday.* Columbia.

Cardigans, the. (1996) 'Love Fool', on *William Shakespeare's Romeo + Juliet: Music from the Motion Picture,* various artists. Capital Records.

Carroll, Robert and Stephen Prickett (eds.). (1998) *The Bible: Authorized King James Version.* Oxford: Oxford University Press.

Carter, Angela. (1967) 'Notes for a Theory of Sixties Style', *The Faber Book of Pop,* eds Hanif Kureishi and Jon Savage. London: Faber and Faber, 1995. 316–20.

Carthy, Martin with Dave Swarbrick. (1992) 'Perfumes of Arabia', *Skin and Bone.* Topic.

Cathy. (2008) Online contribution to Bruce Springsteen fan site, <Greasylake. org>, accessed 18 April 2008.

Chambers, E. K. (1923) *The Elizabethan Stage.* Oxford: Clarendon. 4 vols.

Chambers, Iain. (1985) *Urban Rhythms: Pop Music and Popular Culture.* Houndmills: Macmillan.

Chaudhuri, Sukanta. (2007) 'Shakespeare in India', *Shakespeare's Local Habitations,* eds Krystyna Kujawińska Courtney and R. S. White. pp. 81–97.

Chedgzoy, Kate. (1995) *Shakespeare's Queer Children: Sexual Politics and Contemporary Culture.* Manchester and New York: Manchester University Press.

Christgau, Robert. (1970) 'Look at That Stupid Girl', *The Faber Book of Pop,* eds Kureishi and Savage, 1995. 365–9.

Clark, Sandra. (2001) 'Shakespeare and Other Adaptations', *A Companion to Restoration Drama,* ed. Susan J. Owen. Oxford: Blackwell. 274–90.

Clayton, Thomas. (1986) 'Theatrical Shakespearegresses at the Guthrie and Elsewhere: Notes on "Legitimate Production"', *New Literary History*, 17:3, 511–38.

Cohn, Nik. (1969) *Pop: From the Beginning*. London: Weidenfeld and Nicolson, 1969.

Corcoran, Neil (ed.). (2002) *'Do You, Mr Jones': Bob Dylan with the Poets and Professors*. London: Chatto and Windus.

Corrigan, Alan. (2005) 'Jazz, Shakespeare, and Hybridity: A Script Excerpt from *Swingin' The Dream*', *Borrowers and Lenders*, 1:1, 1–14. Available at <http://www.borrowers.uga.edu/cocoon/borrowers/about>, accessed 19 December 2007.

Costello, Elvis. (1989) 'Miss Macbeth', *Spike*. Warner Bros.

—. (1977) 'Mystery Dance', *My Aim Is True*. Stiff.

—. (1989) 'Tramp the Dirt Down', *Spike*. Warner Bros.

—. (1981) *Trust*. F-Beat, 2003.

—, with the Brodsky Quartet. (1993) 'Damnation's Cellar', *The Juliet Letters*. Warner Bros.

—, with the Brodsky Quartet. (1993) 'Romeo's Seance', *The Juliet Letters*. Warner Bros.

—, with the London Symphony Orchestra and Michael Tilson Thomas. (2004) *Il Sogno*: ballet after Shakespeare's *A Midsummer Night's Dream*. Deutsche Grammophon.

Cowen, Ron. (2009) 'Earliest Known Sound Recordings Revealed'. Available at <http://www.sciencenews.org/view/generic/id/44267/title/Earliest_known_ sound_recordings_revealed>, accessed 13 August 2009.

Crooke, Helkiah. (1615) *Microcosmographia*, in *The English Renaissance: An Anthology of Sources and Documents*, ed. Kate Aughterson. London: Routledge, 2002. 383–7.

Curtis, Richard. (1981) 'The Skinhead Hamlet', *The Faber Book of Parodies*, ed. Simon Brett. London: Faber, 1984. 316–20.

Cybercat. (2008) Online contribution to Bruce Springsteen fan site, <Greasy-lake.org>, accessed 18 April 2008.

Danson, Lawrence. (2000) *Shakespeare's Dramatic Genres*. Oxford: Oxford University Press.

Davis, Laura Lee. (2005) 'Will the Real Elvis Stand Up?', *The Times*. Available at <timesonline.co.uk>, accessed 15 April 2009.

Davis, Miles. (1970) *Bitches Brew*. Columbia Records.

Dawidoff, Nicholas. (1997) *In the Country of Country*. London: Faber and Faber.

Dearden, Basil (dir.). (1962) *All Night Long*. Rank.

Dire Straits. (1980) 'Romeo and Juliet', *Making Movies*. Vertigo.

Dollimore, Jonathan. (1 August 2009) Correspondence with the author.

—. (2001) *Sex, Literature and Censorship*. Cambridge: Polity Press.

— and Alan Sinfield. (1985) 'Foreword to the First Edition: Cultural Materialism', *Political Shakespeare: Essays in Cultural Materialism*, eds Dollimore and Sinfield. Manchester: Manchester University Press, 1994. vii–viii.

Donaldson, Peter S. (2002) ' "In fair Verona": Media, Spectacle, and Performance in *William Shakespeare's Romeo + Juliet*', *Shakespeare After Mass Media*, ed. Richard Burt. New York: Palgrave. 59–82.

Donne, John. (1996) *The Complete English Poems*, ed. A. J. Smith. London: Penguin.

Donovan. (1967) *a gift from a flower to a garden*. Pye.

Duffin, Ross. (2004) *Shakespeare's Songbook*. New York: Norton.

Duke Ellington and his Orchestra. (1957) *Such Sweet Thunder*. Columbia Records.

Du Noyer, Paul. (2009) *In the City: A Celebration of London Music*. London: Random House/Virgin.

Duxbury, Janell R. (1988) 'Shakespeare Meets the Backbeat: Literary Allusion in Rock Music', *Popular Music and Society*, 12, 19–23.

Dyer, Richard. (1979) 'In Defense of Disco', *On Record*, eds Frith and Goodwin, 2007. 410–18.

Dylan, Bob. (1963) 'A Hard Rain's A-Gonna Fall', *The Freewheelin' Bob Dylan*. Columbia Records.

—. (1969) 'Country Pie', *Nashville Skyline*. Columbia Records.

—. (1965) 'Desolation Row', *Highway 61 Revisited*. Columbia Records.

—. (2001) 'Floater (Too Much to Ask)', *Love & Theft*. Columbia Records.

—. (1997) 'Not Dark Yet', *Time Out Of Mind*. Columbia Records.

—. (1974) 'On a Night Like This', *Planet Waves*. Columbia Records.

—. (1991) 'Seven Curses', *Bootleg Series I–III*. Columbia Records.

—. (1965) 'Subterranean Homesick Blues', *Bringing it All Back Home*. Columbia Records.

—. (1974) 'You Angel You', *Planet Waves*. Columbia Records.

Eisenberg, Evan. (1987) *The Recording Angel: Explorations in Phonography*. New York: McGraw-Hill.

Eliot, T. S. (1921) 'The Metaphysical Poets', *Selected Prose*, ed. Frank Kermode. London: Faber and Faber, 1975. 59–67.

Ellis, Jim. (1999) 'Queer Period: Derek Jarman's Renaissance', *Out Takes: Essays on Queer Theory and Film*, ed. Ellis Hanson. Durham and London: Duke University Press. 288–315.

Epstein, Brian. (1964) *A Cellarful of Noise*. London: Souvenir Press.

Everett, William A. and Paul R. Laird (eds). (2002) *The Cambridge Companion to the Musical*. Cambridge: Cambridge University Press.

Faith, Adam. (1962) 'As You Like It'. Parlophone.

—. (1961) 'Who Am I'. Parlophone.

Ferry, Bryan. (2002) 'Sonnet 18: "Shall I compare thee" ', *When Love Speaks*, various artists. EMI Classics.

Fingers Inc. (1988) 'Can You Feel It'. Trax.

Finney, Gretchen L. (1947) 'Ecstasy and Music in Seventeenth-Century England', *Journal of the History of Ideas*, 8:2, 153–86.

Folkerth, Wes. (2002a) 'Roll Over Shakespeare: Bardolatry Meets Beatlemania in the Spring of 1964', *Journal of American and Comparative Cultures*, 23:4, 75–80.

——. (2006) 'Shakespeare in Popular Music', *Shakespeares After Shakespeare: An Encyclopedia of the Bard in Mass Media and Popular Culture*, ed. Richard Burt. Westport, CT, and London: Greenwood Press. 2 vols. I: 366–407.

——. (2002b) *The Sound of Shakespeare*. London and New York: Routledge.

Freed, Arthur. (1952) 'Make 'Em Laugh' (performed by Donald O'Connor), *Singin' in the Rain: Original Motion Picture Soundtrack*. Turner Entertainment, 2002.

Freud, Sigmund. (1920) 'Beyond the Pleasure Principle', *The Penguin Freud Library, Vol. 11: On Metapsychology: The Theory of Psychoanalysis*, ed. Angela Richards. Harmondsworth: Penguin, 1991. 269–338.

——. (1925) 'Negation', *The Penguin Freud Library, Vol. 11: On Metapsychology*, ed. Richards. 435–442.

——. (1905) *The Penguin Freud Library, Vol. 6: Jokes and Their Relation to the Unconscious*, ed. Angela Richards, transl. James Strachey. Harmondsworth: Penguin, 1991.

——. (1900) *The Penguin Freud Library, Vol. 4: The Interpretation of Dreams*, ed. Angela Richards, transl. James Strachey. Harmondsworth: Penguin, 1991.

——. (1919) 'The 'Uncanny', *The Penguin Freud Library, Vol. 14: Art and Literature*, ed. Albert Dickson. Harmondsworth: Penguin, 1990. 335–76.

Frith, Simon. (1989) 'Introduction', *World Music, Politics and Social Change*, ed. Frith. Manchester and New York: Manchester University Press. 1–6.

——. (1988) *Music for Pleasure: Essays in the Sociology of Pop*. Cambridge: Polity Press.

——. (1998) *Performing Rites: Evaluating Popular Music*. Oxford, New York: Oxford University Press.

——. (2004a) 'Pop Music', *The Cambridge Companion to Pop and Rock*, eds Simon Frith, Will Straw and John Street. Cambridge: Cambridge University Press. 93–108.

——. (1983) *Sound Effects: Youth, Leisure, and the Politics of Rock*. London: Constable.

——. (2000) 'The Discourse of World Music', *Western Music and Its Others: Difference, Representation, and Appropriation in Music*, eds Georgina Born and David Hesmondhalgh. pp. 305–22.

——. (2004b) 'The Popular Music Industry', *The Cambridge Companion to Pop and Rock*, eds Frith et al. Cambridge: Cambridge University Press. 26–52.

—, Will Straw and John Street (eds). (2004) *The Cambridge Companion to Pop and Rock*. Cambridge: Cambridge University Press.

— and Andrew Goodwin. (eds). (2007) *On Record: Rock, Pop, and the Written Word*. London and New York: Routledge.

Galey, Alan and Ray Siemens. (2008) 'Introduction: Reinventing Shakespeare in the Digital Humanities', *Shakespeare: Special Issue: Reinventing Digital Shakespeare*, 4:3, 201–7.

Gammond, Peter (ed.). (1991) *The Oxford Companion to Popular Music*. Oxford and New York: Oxford University Press.

Garratt, Sheryl. (1984) 'Teenage Dreams', *On Record*, eds Frith and Goodwin, 2007. 399–409.

Garrioch, David. (2003) 'Sounds of the City: The Soundscapes of Early Modern Towns', *Urban History*, 30:1, 5–25.

Gates Jr., Henry Louis. (1988) *The Signifying Monkey: A Theory of African-American Literary Criticism*. Oxford and New York: Oxford University Press.

Gillespie, Stuart. (2006) 'Shakespeare and Popular Song', *Shakespeare and Elizabethan Popular Culture*, eds Stuart Gillespie and Neil Rhodes. London: Arden. 174–92.

— and Neil Rhodes. (2006) 'Shakespeare and Elizabethan Popular Culture', *Shakespeare and Elizabethan Popular Culture*, eds Gillespie and Rhodes. 1–17.

Gooch, Bryan N. S. and David Thatcher (eds). (1991) *A Shakespeare Music Catalogue*. 5 vols. Oxford: Clarendon Press.

Goodwin, Andrew. (1988) 'Sample and Hold: Pop Music in the Age of Digital Reproduction', *On Record*, eds Frith and Goodwin, 2007. 258–73.

Gordon, Robert and Morgan Neville (dirs). (2007) *Shakespeare was a Big George Jones Fan: Cowboy Jack Clement's Home Movies*. Tremolo Productions DVD.

Gouldstone, David. (1989) *Elvis Costello: God's Comic*. New York: St. Martin's Press.

Gracyk, T. A. (1992) 'Adorno, Jazz and the Aesthetics of Popular Music', *Musical Quarterly*, 76: 4, 526–42.

Grady, Hugh and Terence Hawkes (eds). (2007) *Presentist Shakespeares*. London and New York: Routledge.

Grateful Dead, the. (1980) 'Althea', *Go to Heaven*. Arista.

Gray, Jonathan, Cornel Sandvoss and C. Lee Harrington (eds). (2007) *Fandom: Identities and Communities in a Mediated World*. New York: New York University Press.

Greenhalgh, Susanne. (2007) 'Shakespeare Overheard: Performances, Adaptations, and Citations on Radio', *The Cambridge Companion to Shakespeare and Popular Culture*, ed. Shaughnessy. 175–98.

Greer, Germaine. (1969) 'Mozic and the Revolution', *The Faber Book of Pop*, eds Kureishi and Savage, 1995. 339–43.

Grossberg, Lawrence. (1986) 'Is There Rock After Punk?', *On Record*, eds Frith and Goodwin, 2007. 111–23.

Guilbault, Jocelyne. (2004) 'World Music', *The Cambridge Companion to Pop and Rock*, eds Frith et al. 176–92.

Hammill, Peter. (1981) 'Ophelia', *Sitting Targets*. Virgin.

Harris, John. (2003) *The Last Party: Britpop, Blair and the Demise of English Rock*. London and New York: Fourth Estate.

Hartnoll, Phyllis (ed.). (1966) *Shakespeare in Music*. London: Macmillan.

Hawkes, David. (1996) ' "The Shadow of This Time": The Renaissance Cinema of Derek Jarman', *By Angels Driven: The Films of Derek Jarman*, ed. Chris Lippard. Trowbridge: Flicks Books. 103–16.

Hawkes, Terence. (2002) *Shakespeare in the Present*. London and New York: Routledge.

—. (1986) *That Shakespeherian Rag: Essays on a Critical Process*. London and New York: Methuen.

—. (2005) 'The Duke's Man: Ellington, Shakespeare, and Jazz Adaptation', *Borrowers and Lenders*, 1:1, 1–5. Available at <http://www.borrowers.uga.edu/cocoon/borrowers/about>, accessed 19 December 2007.

Hebdige, Dick. (1996) *Subculture: The Meaning of Style*. London: Routledge.

Hegarty, Paul. (2009) *Noise/Music: A History*. New York, London: Continuum.

Henderson, Diana E. (2007) 'From Popular Entertainment to Literature', *The Cambridge Companion to Shakespeare and Popular Culture*, ed. Shaughnessy. 6–25.

Hennion, Antoine. (1983) 'The Production of Success: An Antimusicology of the Pop Song', *On Record*, eds Frith and Goodwin, 2007. 185–206.

Hesmondhalgh, David. (2000) 'International Times: Fusions, Exoticism, and Antiracism in Electronic Dance Music', *Western Music and Its Others*, eds Born and Hesmondhalgh. 280–304.

Hess, Nigel. (2009) 'The Music of *Romeo and Juliet*', Globe Theatre *Programme Notes*.

Hewick, Kevin. (17–18 September 2009) Correspondence with the author.

—. (1982) 'Ophelia's Drinking Song'. Factory Communications.

Hibbert, Ryan. (2005) 'What is Indie Rock?', *Popular Music and Society*, 28:1, 55–77.

Hills, Matthew. (2002) *Fan Cultures*. New York: Routledge.

Hodgdon, Barbara (1991) 'Kiss Me Deadly, or, the Des/Demonized Spectacle', *Othello: New Perspectives*, eds Virginia Mason Vaughan and Kent Cartwright. London and Toronto: Associated University Press. 214–55.

Howard, Jean E. and Phyllis Rackin. (1997) *Engendering a Nation: A Feminist Account of Shakespeare's English Histories*. London: Routledge.

Howard, Tony. (2007) 'Shakespeare's Cinematic Offshoots', *The Cambridge Companion to Shakespeare on Film*, ed. Russell Jackson. pp. 303–23.

Indigo Girls, the. (1992) *Rites of Passage*. Epic Records.

—. (1994) 'Touch Me Fall', *Swamp Ophelia*. Epic Records.

Inglis, Ian. (2000) 'Introduction: A Thousand Voices', *The Beatles, Popular Music and Society: A Thousand Voices*, ed. Inglis. Houndmills: Macmillan. xv–xxii.

—. (2003) 'Introduction: Popular Music and Film', *Popular Music and Film*, ed. Inglis. London and New York: Wallflower. 1–7.

Jackson, Russell (ed.). (2007) *The Cambridge Companion to Shakespeare on Film*. Cambridge: CUP.

Jaret, Charles. (1993) 'Characteristics of Successful and Unsuccessful Country Music Songs', *All That Glitters: Country Music in America*, ed. George H. Lewis. Bowling Green, OH: Bowling Green State Popular University Press. 174–85.

Jarman, Derek. (1984) *Dancing Ledge*. London: Quartet Books.

— (dir.). (1978) *Jubilee*. Megalovision.

—. (1996) *Kicking the Pricks*. London: Vintage.

—. (1992) *Modern Nature: The Journals of Derek Jarman*. London: Vintage.

— (dir.). (1976) *Sebastiane*. Distac.

— (dir.). (1985) *The Angelic Conversation*. British Film Institute and Channel Four.

— (dir.). (1987) *The Last of England*. Anglo International Films.

— (dir.). (1979) *The Tempest*. Boyd's Company.

Jay-Z feat. Eminem. (2001) 'Renegade', *The Blueprint*. Roc-A-Fella.

— feat. Nas. (2007) 'Success', *American Gangster*. Roc-A-Fella.

Jenkins, Henry. (2003) 'Interactive Audiences?', *Critical Readings: Media and Audiences*, eds Nightingale and Ross. pp. 279–95.

—. (1992) '"Strangers No More, We Sing": Filking and the Social Construction of the Science Fiction Community', *The Adoring Audience: Fan Culture and Popular Media*, ed. Lisa A. Lewis. New York: Routledge. 208–36.

Jennings, Waylon. (1975) 'Let's All Help the Cowboys (Sing the Blues)', *Dreaming My Dreams*. RCA Victor.

Jenson, Joli. (1992). 'Fandom as Pathology: The Consequences of Characterization', *The Adoring Audience*, ed. Lewis. 9–29.

Johnson, Samuel. (1765) 'Preface to Shakespeare', *Samuel Johnson: Selected Writings*, ed. R. T. Davies. London: Faber and Faber, 1965. 261–91.

Jonson, Ben. (1640) *Explorata: Or Discoveries*, in *The Complete Poems*, ed. George Parfitt. Harmondsworth: Penguin, 1996. 375–458.

—. (1618) 'To the Memory of My Beloved, the Author Mr William Shakespeare: And What He Hath Left Us', *The Complete Poems*, ed. Parfitt, 1996. 263–65.

Jookyle. (2008) Online contribution to Bob Dylan fan site, <Expectingrain.com>, accessed 18 April 2008.

Joughin, John J. (ed.). (1997) *Shakespeare and National Culture*. Manchester: Manchester University Press.

Kaiser Chiefs. (2005a) *Enjoyment* DVD. B-Unique.

—. (2005b) 'I Predict a Riot', *Employment*. B-Unique.

—. (2005c) 'The Modern Way', *Employment*. B-Unique.

Karpeles, Maud. (1967) *Cecil Sharp: His Life and Work*. London: Routledge and Kegan Paul.

Keb' Mo'. (2002) 'Sonnet 35: "No More Be Grieved"', *When Love Speaks*, various artists. EMI Classics.

Keightley, Keir. (2004) 'Reconsidering Rock', *The Cambridge Companion to Pop and Rock*, eds Frith et al. 109–142.

Kelis feat. Nas. (2003) 'In Public', *Tasty*. EMI/Virgin.

Kipp. (2008) Online contribution to Bruce Springsteen fansite: Greasylake.org., accessed 18 April 2008.

Ko, Yu Jin. (2006) 'Honolulu Theatre for Youth's Rap *Othello*', *Borrowers and Lenders*, 2:1, 1–9. Available at <http://www.borrowers.uga.edu/cocoon/borrowers/about>, accessed 19 December 2007.

Kujawińska Courtney, Krystyna and R.S. White (eds). (2007) *Shakespeare's Local Habitations*. Łódź: Łódź University Press.

Kureishi, Hanif and Jon Savage (eds). (1995) *The Faber Book of Pop*. London: Faber and Faber.

Kyd, Marcus and David Polk. (15 February 2009) Correspondence with the author.

Ladysmith Black Mambazo. (1987) *Shaka Zulu*. Warner Bros.

—. (2002) 'Sonnet 8: 'Music to Hear, Why Hear'st Thou Music Sadly?', *When Love Speaks*, various artists. EMI Classics.

—. (1990) *Two Worlds One Heart*. Warner Bros.

Laine, Cleo and John Dankworth. (1978) 'The Compleat Works', *Wordsongs*. RCA/Mercury.

Lanier, Douglas. (2005) 'Minstrelsy, Jazz, Rap: Shakespeare, African-American Music, and Cultural Legitimation', *Borrowers and Lenders*, 1:1, 1–29. Available at <http://www.borrowers.uga.edu/cocoon/borrowers/about>, accessed 19 December 2007.

—. (2006) *Shakespeare and Modern Popular Culture*. Oxford: Oxford University Press.

—. (2007) 'Shakespeare ™ : Myth and Biographical Fiction', *The Cambridge Companion to Shakespeare and Popular Culture*, ed. Shaughnessy. 93–113.

Larkin, Colin (ed.). (1993) *The Guinness Who's Who of Country Music*. Enfield: Guinness.

Lee, Peggy. (1958) 'Fever'. Capitol Records.

Leitch, Donovan. (2005) *The Autobiography of Donovan: The Hurdy Gurdy Man*. New York: St Martin's Press.

Lennon, John. (1965) *The Penguin John Lennon*. Harmondsworth: Penguin.

Leppert, Richard. (2002). 'Commentary', in Adorno, *Essays on Music*. 327–72.

—. (1995) *The Sight of Sound: Music, Representation and the History of the Body*. Berkeley, Los Angeles, London: University of California Press.

Lester, Richard (dir.). (1964) *A Hard Day's Night*. Proscenium Films.

Levine, Lawrence W. (1988) *Highbrow/Lowbrow: The Emergence of Cultural Hierarchy in America*. London, Cambridge, MA: Harvard University Press.

Lewis, Lisa A. (ed.). (1992) *The Adoring Audience: Fan Culture and Popular Media*. New York: Routledge.

Lindley, David. (2006) *Shakespeare and Music*. London: Arden.

Lindsay, Cam. (2008) 'Conversations: Titus Andronicus'. Available at <http://www.exclaim.ca/articles/multiarticlesub.aspx?csid1=122&csid2=946&fid1=31628>, accessed April 2009.

Lipsitz, George. (1990) *Time Passages: Collective Memory and American Popular Culture*. Minneapolis, Oxford: University of Minnesota Press.

Loncraine, Richard (dir.). (1995) *Richard III*. Bayly.

Luhrmann, Baz (dir.). (1996) *William Shakespeare's Romeo + Juliet*. Twentieth Century Fox.

Lydon, John with Keith and Kent Zimmerman. (1994) *Rotten: No Irish, No Blacks, No Dogs. The Authorised Autobiography Johnny Rotten of the Sex Pistols*. London: Hodder and Stoughton.

MacDonald, Ian. (1995) *Revolution in the Head: The Beatles' Records and the Sixties*. London: Pimlico.

—. (2003) *The People's Music*. London: Pimlico.

Madonna. (1989) 'Cherish'. Sire Warner Records.

Mamablue. (2008) Online contribution to Indigo Girls fan site, <IndigoVortex.com>, accessed 18 April 2008.

Mandel, Johnny and Mike Altman. (1970) 'Song from M*A*S*H (Suicide is Painless)'. Columbia Records.

Mann, William. (1963) 'What Songs the Beatles Sang', *In the Sixties*, ed. Ray Connolly. London: Pavilion, 1995. 59–60.

Marshall, Cynthia. (2000) '"Who Wrote the Book of Love?" Teaching *Romeo and Juliet* with Early Rock Music', *Approaches to Teaching Shakespeare's Romeo and Juliet*, ed. Maurice Hunt. New York: Modern Language Association of America. 98–107.

Marcus, Greil. (1993) *In the Fascist Bathroom: Writings on Punk, 1977–1992*. London: Viking.

—. (2001) *Lipstick Traces: A Secret History of the Twentieth Century*. London: Faber and Faber.

—. (2000) *Mystery Train: Images of America in Rock 'n' Roll Music*. London: Faber and Faber.

—. (1992) 'Notes on the Life & Death and Incandescent Banality of Rock 'n' Roll', *The Faber Book of Pop*, eds Kureishi and Savage, 1995. 739–752.

Marwick, Arthur. (1996) *British Society Since 1945*. Penguin: Harmondsworth.

Marx, Karl and Friedrich Engels. (1848) *The Communist Manifesto*, ed. Gareth Stedman Jones. Harmondsworth: Penguin, 2002.

Mazelle, Kym. (1996) 'Young Hearts Run Free', *William Shakespeare's Romeo + Juliet: Music from the Motion Picture*, various artists. Capitol Records.

McClary, Susan and Robert Walser. (1988) 'Start Making Sense! Musicology Wrestles with Rock', *On Record*, eds Frith and Goodwin, 2007. 277–92.

MC Honky. (2003) *I am the Messiah*. mm:ss.

McKinney, Devin. (2003) *Magic Circles: The Beatles in Dream and History*. Cambridge, MA, London: Harvard University Press.

McLaren, Malcolm. (1990) 'II Be or Not II Be', *Round the Outside! Round the Outside!*. Virgin.

Mekons, the. (1982) *it falleth like the gentle rain from heaven – The Mekons Story, 1977–1982*. CNT.

—. (1979) *The Quality of Mercy Is Not Strnen*. Virgin.

Merchant, Natalie. (1998) 'Ophelia', *Ophelia*. Elektra Records.

Middleton, Richard. (2000) 'Musical Belongings: Western Music and Its Low-Other', *Western Music and Its Others*, eds Born and Hesmondhalgh. 59–85.

—. (1983) ' "Play It Again Sam": Some Notes on the Productivity of Repetition in Popular Music', *Popular Music 3: Producers and Markets*. Cambridge: Cambridge University Press. 235–70.

—. (1990) *Studying Popular Music*. Milton Keynes and Philadelphia: Open University Press.

—. (2006) *Voicing the Popular: On the Subjects of Popular Music*. Abingdon: Routledge.

Miles, Barry. (1998) *Paul McCartney: Many Years from Now*. London: Vintage.

Milton, John. (1629) 'On the Morning of Christ's Nativity', *The Poems of John Milton*, eds John Carey and Alastair Fowler. London: Longman, 1968. 97–112.

Misadventure. (2008) Online contribution to Bruce Springsteen fan site, <Greasylake.org>, accessed 18 April 2008.

Mitchell, Joni. (1971) 'A Case of You', *Blue*. Reprise.

Modern Lovers, the. (1972) 'Roadrunner'. Beserkley.

Morrison, David E. (2003) 'Good and Bad Practice in Focus Group Research', *Critical Readings: Media and Audiences*, eds Nightingale and Ross. 111–30.

Mowitt, John. (1987) 'The Sound of Music in the Era of Its Electronic Reproducibility', *Music and Society: The Politics of Composition, Performance and Reception*, eds Richard Leppert and Susan McClary. Cambridge: Cambridge University Press. 173–97.

Mullaney, Steven. (2007) *The Place of the Stage: License, Play, and Power in Renaissance England*. Ann Arbor: University of Michigan Press.

Naylor, Edward W. (1931) *Shakespeare and Music: With Illustrations from the Music of the 16*th *and 17*th *Centuries*. London and Toronto: J. M. Dent.

Nas. (1994) 'N. Y. State of Mind', *Illmatic*. Columbia Records.

New Age Steppers. (1983) 'Stormy Weather', *Foundation Steppers*. On-U.

Nightingale, Virginia and Karen Ross. (2003) 'Introduction', *Critical Readings: Media and Audiences*, eds Nightingale and Ross. pp. 1–9.

Nightingale, Virginia and Karen Ross (eds). (2003) *Critical Readings: Media and Audiences*. Maidenhead: Open UP.

Nordenstam, Stina. (1996) 'Little Star', *William Shakespeare's Romeo + Juliet: Music from the Motion Picture*, various artists. Capital Records.

NorthSideJimmy. (2008) Online contribution to Bruce Springsteen fan site, <Greasylake.org>, accessed 18 April 2008.

Olivier, Laurence (dir.). (1944) *Henry V*. Two Cities Films.

— (dir.). (1955) *Richard III*. L. O. P.

O'Neill, Chris. (2008) *A Bard Day's Night*. Unreleased musical.

—. (24 September 2008) Interview with the author.

One True Voice. (2003) 'Shakespeare's (Way With) Words'. Jive/Zomba Records.

O'Pray, Michael. (1996) *Derek Jarman: Dreams of England*. London: British Film Institute.

Orkin, Martin. (2005) *Local Shakespeares: Proximation and Power*. London and New York: Routledge.

Outkast. (1996) 'ATLiens', *ATLiens*. La Face.

Parker, Maceo. (2005) 'To Be or Not To Be', *School's In*. BHM.

Parton, Dolly. (1993) 'Romeo', *Slow Dancing with the Moon*. Sony BMG.

Patterson, Annabel. (1989) *Shakespeare and the Popular Voice*. Oxford: Blackwell.

Paul, Charlie (dir.). (2004) 'I Predict a Riot'. Itch Films.

Perry, Mark. (2008) Online contribution to Elvis Costello fan site, <elviscostellofans. com>, accessed 18 April 2008.

Pink Floyd. (1967) 'Astronomy Domine', *The Piper at the Gates of Dawn*. EMI.

Plato. (1970) *The Laws*, transl. Trevor J. Saunders. Harmondsworth: Penguin.

Pope, Alexander. (1978) *Poetical Works*, ed. Herbert Davies. Oxford: Oxford University Press.

Pratt, Ray. (1990) *Rhythm and Resistance: Explorations in the Political Uses of Popular Music*. New York, Westport, CT, London: Praeger.

Presley, Elvis. (1960) 'Are You Lonesome Tonight?' (present-day title). RCA.

Radiohead. (1996) 'Talk Show Host', *William Shakespeare's Romeo + Juliet: Music from the Motion Picture*, various artists. Capitol Records.

Radway, Janice. (1991) *Reading the Romance: Women, Patriarchy and Popular Culture*. Chapel Hill: University of North Carolina.

Reed, Lou. (1989) 'Romeo had Juliette', *New York*. Sire Warner Records.

Reflections, the. (1964) '(Just Like) Romeo and Juliet'. Golden World.

Reynolds, Simon. (1990) *Blissed Out: The Raptures of Rock*. London: Serpent's Tail.

—. (1998) *Energy Flash: A Journey Through Rave Music and Dance Culture*. London: Picador.

—. (2006) *Rip It Up and Start Again: Post-punk 1978–84*. London: Faber and Faber.

Ricks, Christopher. (2003) *Dylan's Visions of Sin*. London: Penguin.

Rietveld, Hillegonda C. (1998) *This is Our House: House Music, Cultural Spaces and Technologies*. Aldershot: Ashgate.

Ritchie, Fiona. (2005) '*The Big Life*, by Paul Sirett (Review)', *Borrowers and Lenders*, 1:1, 1–6. Available at <http://www.borrowers.uga.edu/cocoon/borrowers/about>, accessed 19 December 2007.

Robinson, Deanna Campbell, Elizabeth B. Buck and Marlene Cuthbert. (1991) *Music at the Margins: Popular Music and Global Cultural Diversity*. London: Sage.

Rose, Tricia. (1994) *Black Noise: Rap Music and Black Culture in Contemporary America*. Hanover, London : Wesleyan University Press.

Ross, Alex. (2008) *The Rest is Noise: Listening to the Twentieth Century*. London: Fourth Estate.

Ross, Karen and Virginia Nightingale. (2003) *Media and Audiences: New Perspectives*. Maidenhead: Open University Press.

Rozalla. (1991) 'Everybody's Free (To Feel Good)' *William Shakespeare's Romeo + Juliet: Music from the Motion Picture*, various artists. Capital Records.

Russell, Dave. (1987) *Popular Music in England 1840–1914: A Social History*. Manchester: Manchester University Press.

Rutter, Carol Chillingham. (2007) 'Looking at Shakespeare's Women on Film', *The Cambridge Companion to Shakespeare on Film*, ed. Jackson, 2007. 245–66.

Sallyangie, the. (1969) 'Midsummer Night's Happening', *Children of the Sun*. Warner Bros.

Sanders, Julie. (2007) *Shakespeare and Music: Afterlives and Borrowings*. Cambridge: Polity.

Sarne, Michael (dir.). (1993) *The Punk and the Princess: Romeo and Juliet with Attitude*. M2 Films.

Savage, Jon. (1992) *England's Dreaming: Sex Pistols and Punk Rock*. London: Faber and Faber.

—. (2009) *The England's Dreaming Tapes*. London: Faber and Faber.

Sawyer, Robert. (2005) 'Country Matters: Shakespeare and Music in the American South', *Borrowers and Lenders*, 1:1, 1–19. Available at <http://www.borrowers.uga.edu/cocoon/borrowers/about>, accessed 19 December 2007.

Schonherr, U. (1991) 'Adorno and Jazz: Reflections on a Failed Encounter', *Telos*, 87, 85–97.

Seeger, Pete. (1966) *Dangerous Songs!?*. Columbia Records.

Sellers, Peter. (1965) 'A Hard Days Night'. Parlophone.

Sex Pistols, the. (1977) 'Holidays in the Sun'. Virgin.

Shakespeare, William. (2005) *The Complete Works*, eds John Jowett, William Montgomery, Gary Taylor and Stanley Wells. Oxford: Clarendon Press.

Shake Spears, the. (1965) 'Do the Shake Spear', on *Sixties Archive Vol. 1: The Sound of the Sixties*, various artists, EVA Records, 1991.

Shapiro, Peter. (2009) 'Turntablism', *The WIRE Primers: A Guide to Modern Music*, ed. Rob Young. London: Verso. 103–109.

Shaughnessy, Robert (ed.). (2007) *The Cambridge Companion to Shakespeare and Popular Culture*. Cambridge: CUP.

Silverman, Stanley. (1993) *Duke Ellington's Incidental Music for Shakespeare's Play Timon of Athens*. Varese Sarabande Records.

Sinfield, Alan. (1994) 'Introduction: Reproductions, Interventions', *Political Shakespeare: Essays in Cultural Materialism*, eds Dollimore and Sinfield. 154–7.

—. (1989) *Literature, Politics and Culture in Postwar Britain*. Oxford: Basil Blackwell.

—. (2006) *Shakespeare, Authority, Sexuality: Unfinished Business in Cultural Materialism*. London and New York: Routledge.

Simon, Paul. (1986) *Graceland*. Warner Bros.

Sixty9chevy. (2008) Online contribution to Bruce Springsteen fan site, <Greasylake.org>, accessed 18 April 2008.

Skrebels, Paul. (2008) 'All Night Long: Jazzing Around with *Othello*', *Literature/Film Quarterly*, 36:2, 147–56.

Slits, the. (1979) *Cut*. Island.

Smith, Bruce R. (2006) 'Shakespeare's Residuals: The Circulation of Ballads in Cultural Memory', *Shakespeare and Elizabethan Popular Culture*, eds Gillespie and Rhodes. 193–217.

—. (1999) *The Acoustic World of Early Modern England: Attending to the O-Factor*. Chicago and London: University of Chicago Press.

Sousa, Geraldo U. de (1999) *Shakespeare's Cross-Cultural Encounters*. Houndmills: Macmillan.

Springsteen, Bruce. (1973) 'Incident on 57th Street', *The Wild, The Innocent and the E-Street Shuffle*. Columbia Records.

—. (1980) 'Point Blank', *The River*. Columbia Records.

Staton, Candi. (1976) 'Young Hearts Run Free'. Warner Bros.

Stephenoxford. (2008) Online contribution to Bob Dylan fan site, <Expectingrain. com>, accessed 18 April 2008.

Stone Roses, the. (1988) 'Elephant Stone' backed with 'Full Fathom Five'. Silvertone.

Storey, John. (2005) 'Popular', *New Keywords: A Revised Vocabulary of Culture and Society*, eds Tony Bennett, Lawrence Grossberg and Meaghan Morris. Oxford: Blackwell. 262–4.

Stranglers, the. (1977) 'No More Heroes'. United Artists.

Sturdy, Mark. (2003). *Truth and Beauty: The Story of Pulp*. London: Omnibus.

Stylewar (dir.). (2005). 'I Predict a Riot'. Stink.

Sylk-E. Fyne. (1998) 'Romeo and Juliet', *Raw Sylk*. RCA.

Tatspaugh, Patricia. (2007) 'The Tragedies of Love on Film', *The Cambridge Companion to Shakespeare on Film*, ed. Jackson. 141–64.

Taylor, Gary. (2004) 'Prince Charmless', *The Guardian*. Available at <http://www.guardian.co.uk/stage/2004/jul/26/rsc.theatre>, accessed 15 April 2009.

Taylor, Timothy D. (1997) *Global Pop: World Music, World Markets*. London and New York: Routledge.

Taymor, Julie (dir.). (1999) *Titus*. Twentieth Century Fox.

Teague, Fran. (2005) 'Swingin' Shakespeare from Harlem to Broadway', *Borrowers and Lenders*, 1:1, 1–9. Available at <http://www.borrowers.uga.edu/cocoon/borrowers/about>, accessed 19 December 2007.

Temple, Julien (dir.). (2000) *The Filth and the Fury*. FilmFour.

— (dir.). (1980) *The Great Rock 'n' Roll Swindle*. Boyd's Company.

Tennenhouse, Leonard. (1986) *Power on Display: The Politics of Shakespeare's Genres*. New York: Methuen.

Théberge, Paul. (2004) '"Plugged In": Technology and Popular Music', *The Cambridge Companion to Pop and Rock*, eds Frith et al. 3–25.

Thickboy. (2008) Online contribution to Bob Dylan fan site, <Expecting rain. com>, accessed 18 April 2008.

Thompson, Hunter S. (1967) 'The 'Hashbury' is the Capital of the Hippies', *The Faber Book of Pop*, eds Kureishi and Savage, 1995. 290–302.

Thompson, Richard. (31 August 2009) Correspondence with the author.

—. (2003) 'Outside of the Inside', *The Old Kit Bag*. Cooking Vinyl.

—. (2006) 'The Story of Hamlet', *RT: The Life and Music of Richard Thompson*. Free Reed.

Thorpe, Richard (dir.). (1954) *The Student Prince*. MGM.

Timelords, the. (1988) 'The Manual (How to Have a Number One the Easy Way)', *The Faber Book of Pop*, eds Kureishi and Savage, 1995. 673–7.

Titus Andronicus. (2008) *The Airing of Grievances*. Merok Records.

Tomcraft. (2003) 'Loneliness'. Data.

Townsend, Peter. (2000) *Jazz in American Culture*. Edinburgh: Edinburgh University Press.

UK Decay. (1981) 'Last in the House of Flames', *For Madmen Only*. Fresh.

Van Kampen, Claire. (2001) *Sleep No More: Incidental Jazz Music Composed by Claire Van Kampen with the Shakespeare's Globe Musicians*. International Shakespeare Globe Centre CD.

Van Sant, Gus (dir.). (1991) *My Own Private Idaho*. New Line Cinema.

Various artists. (2002) *When Love Speaks*. EMI Classics.

Various artists. (1996) *William Shakespeare's Romeo + Juliet: Music from the Motion Picture*. Capital Records.

Various artists. (1997) *William Shakespeare's Romeo + Juliet: Music from the Motion Picture*. Capital Records.

Wainwright, Rufus. (2005) 'Memphis Skyline', *Want Two*. Polydor.

—. (2002) 'Sonnet 29: "When, in Disgrace"', *When Love Speaks*. EMI Classics.

Waits, Tom. (1978) 'Romeo is Bleeding', *Blue Valentine*. Asylum Records.

Wall, Chris. (4 May 2009) Correspondence with the author.

—. (1994) 'Cowboy Nation', *Cowboy Nation*. Cold Spring Records.

Wallis, Roger and Krister Malm. (1984) 'Patterns of Change', *On Record*, eds Frith and Goodwin, 2007. 160–80.

Walters, Barry. (1988) 'Stayin' Alive', *The Faber Book of Pop*, eds Kureishi and Savage, 1995. 644–53.

Westinghouse, Otis. (2008) Online contribution to Elvis Costello fan site, <elviscostellofans.com>, accessed 18 April 2008.

Whitcomb, Ian. (1972) *After the Ball: Pop Music From Rag to Rock*. Baltimore: Penguin.

White, R. S. (2007) 'Introduction', *Shakespeare's Local Habitations*, eds Kujawińska Courtney and White. 5–10.

Wilcken, Hugo. (2005) *Low: 33 1/3*. London, New York: Continuum.

Wilcox, Toyah. (1991) *Ophelia's Shadow*. EG.

Williams, Deniece. (1984) 'Let's Hear it for the Boy'. Columbia Records.

Williams, Raymond. (1977) *Marxism and Literature*. Oxford: OUP.

— (ed.). (1968) *May Day Manifesto*. Harmondsworth: Penguin.

—. (2005) 'Notes on Marxism in Britain Since 1945', in Williams, *Culture and Materialism: Selected Essays*. London, New York: Verso. 233–51.

Wilson, Christopher. (1922) *Shakespeare and Music*. London: The Stage.

Wipers, the. (1981) 'Romeo'. TRAP.

Witkin, Robert W. (2000) *Adorno on Music*. London and New York: Routledge.

Wymer, Rowland. (2005) *Derek Jarman*. Manchester and New York: Manchester University Press.

Zeffirelli, Franco (dir.). (1968) *Romeo and Juliet*. Paramount Pictures.

Zombies, the. (1968) *Odessey and Oracle*. CBS.

Index